REVELATION AND THEOLOGY

Monograph Supplements to the
Scottish Journal of Theology

General Editors:
T. F. TORRANCE and J. K. S. REID

REVELATION
AND
THEOLOGY

An analysis of
the Barth–Harnack
correspondence of 1923

H. MARTIN RUMSCHEIDT

Assistant Professor of Historical Theology
University of Windsor, Canada

CAMBRIDGE
AT THE UNIVERSITY PRESS 1972

Published by the Syndics of the Cambridge University Press
Bentley House, 200 Euston Road, London NW1 2DB
American Branch: 32 East 57th Street, New York, N.Y. 10022

Library of Congress Catalogue Card Number: 78-166947

ISBN: 0 521 08365 6

Printed in Great Britain
by R. & R. Clark Ltd, Edinburgh

CONTENTS

To
Joseph C. McLelland
my *Doktorvater*

PREFACE

The present members of the theological guild are the heirs and guardians of an immensely rich theological activity. This began just about the end of the First World War. That particular period of theological history may be described as a time of tension between the Word of God and the word of man. It was a period of dialectical theology. The men who were engaged in that activity felt compelled to restate our theological knowledge, for they found it impossible to think and to say the same words and ideas about God and man which they had learned from their teachers.

With hindsight we can now call that a time of reconstruction. The impetus and the echo of the questions which those theologians asked are still very much with us, so much so in fact that we, their children and grandchildren, continue to give a great variety of answers to those same questions. Today we are still engaged in evaluating what was said then, what it implies for us and how we may perhaps continue the direction of theological thought indicated then.

But we shall not make much progress in theological activity if we have not answered for ourselves whether or not that which was done by previous generations was genuine theology. We must determine whether we can build on what they have given us or whether they were merely an episode 'between the times'.

This monograph, based on the records of a public discussion between one of the teachers (Harnack) and one of the disillusioned pupils (Barth), seeks to answer the question about the meaning for contemporary theology of that period of dialect. The answer reached is essentially in concert with those who believe that theology was and will continue to be reconstructed by our going with Barth on the way he went and by our going on beyond him in the direction indicated by him. The way of this man, who constantly invited theology and Church to 'break camp, to retrace their steps and to make their confession' (this, incidentally, is the title of an address on which Barth was working the night he died), began after all with the kind of questioning which is apparent in this discussion with Harnack. The basis, the ultimate aim and the meaning of this way of breaking camp, retracing steps and making one's confession is, if not given conclusively, then certainly well indicated in this exchange of letters. A document of the beginning of the Church's new reformation – that is what we seem to find in this confrontation.

A number of guardian angels have hovered over this study ever since its inception, which goes back to the writer's happy student-days at the University of Basel in 1961 and 1962. It was the time of Barth's last semester there. He himself is the most illustrious of those 'angels', in fact he suggested that this correspondence would be a very fruitful place to study his early thought. Others among this theological 'host' are Professor Max Geiger, also of Basel, Professor Walter Kreck of Bonn, the late Professor Otto Weber of Göttingen, Professor Karl Löwith of Heidelberg and Professor Joseph McLelland of Montreal. It is a very happy thing to give thanks to them in this manner.

Three people, however, need an especial word of acknowledgment. The Reverend Dr Eberhard Busch, assistant to Karl Barth during the last five years of Barth's life, with whom the writer shared the hospitality of Professor Oscar Cullmann's Alumneum in Basel, helped me to discover what is the real issue between Harnack and Barth in this correspondence. Dr Dietrich Braun of Berlin illumined the background of the meaning of Harnack's accusation, that Barth was a modern Marcion. The Reverend Professor Thomas F. Torrance of Edinburgh encouraged the writer to work out the implications of the correspondence for present-day theologians. He also graciously took pity on my incurable 'Teutonic' English and suggested numerous stylistic changes.

To them all I owe an irrepayable debt of gratitude. It only remains to hope that this study reflects and perhaps even furthers their endeavour to be faithful witnesses to Christ in the pilgrim theology of the *ecclesia semper reformanda*.

I would be most unkind to the congregations of the Enterprise Pastoral Charge in Enterprise, Ontario, and of Deer Park United Church in Toronto, if I deleted an expression of gratitude to them here. They were very patient with their 'studying' minister and allowed him much time for this work.

University of Windsor, *Oculi* 1971 H. M. R.

ACKNOWLEDGMENTS

The author would like to acknowledge with gratitude permission from the following publishers to quote from the works listed below:

Collins Sons and Co. Ltd, London: Bonhoeffer, *Act and Being*
Dover Publications Inc., New York: Harnack, *History of Dogma*
EVZ Verlag, Zürich: Howe, 'Parallelen zwischen der Theologie Karl Barths und der heutigen Physik', in *Antwort* (Festschrift für Karl Barth, 1956)
   Willems, *Karl Barth*
   Wolf, 'Kerygma und Dogma?' in *Antwort* (Festschrift für Karl Barth, 1956)
de Gruyter und Co., Berlin: Harnack, *Reden und Aufsätze*
   Harnack, *Aus Wissenschaft und Leben*
   Harnack, *Ausgewählte Reden und Aufsätze*
   Zahn-Harnack, *Adolf von Harnack*
Hinrichs Verlag, Leipzig: Harnack, *Das Christentum und die Geschichte*
   Harnack, *Marcion*
Kaiser, Munich: Storch, *Exegesen und Meditationen zu Karl Barths kirchlicher Dogmatik*
   Vielhauer, 'Franz Overbeck und die neutestamentliche Wissenschaft', in *Aufsätze zum Neuen Testament*
Klostermann, Frankfurt: Heidegger, *Holzwege*
Klotz Verlag, Stuttgart: Harnack, *Die Entstehung der christlichen Theologie und des kirchlichen Dogmas*
John Knox Press, Richmond, Va.: J. M. Robinson (ed.), *The Beginnings of Dialectic Theology*
Mohr, Tübingen: Senft, *Wahrhaftigkeit und Wahrheit*
Schwabe and Co., Basel: Overbeck, *Christentum und Kultur*
Siebenstern Taschenbuch Verlag, Munich and Hamburg: Harnack, *Das Wesen des Christentums*
   Busch (ed.), *Barth–Thurneysen, ein Briefwechsel*
Zwingli Verlag, Zürich: Thurneysen, *Christoph Blumhardt*

A special expression of gratitude is due to the Commission responsible for the literary estate (*Kommission für den literarischen Nachlass*) of Professor Karl Barth for their permission to quote from the following works by Barth: *Der Römerbrief* (1st ed.); *Der Römerbrief* (2nd ed.); *Suchet Gott, so werdet ihr leben*; *Das Wort Gottes und die Theologie*; *Theologie und Kirche*; and *Theologische Fragen und Antworten*.

The author wishes to thank also Professor Glick and Professor Frei for their permission to quote from their dissertations, 'Harnack as Historian and Theologian' (University of Chicago, 1957) and 'The Doctrine of Revelation in the Thought of Karl Barth, 1909–1922' (Yale University, 1956), respectively.

INTRODUCTION

BARTH AND HARNACK – AN ENCOUNTER OF DIFFERENT WORLDS

In the early months of 1923 the journal *Christliche Welt* published an exchange of letters between Adolf von Harnack and Karl Barth. It consists of five letters, three by the former, two by the latter. This correspondence is the basic document of this study.

The journal, founded and edited for many years by Martin Rade, reflected the theological orientation of Albrecht Ritschl in so far as it intended to 'reconcile culture and the gospel as it had been made known to and become loved by the people of Germany through Dr Martin Luther'.[1] Harnack had a great influence on the programme of this journal, indeed he was at one time one of its editors. In view of its intention the journal cannot be labelled 'liberal' offhand. The many contributors, among whom were Barth and Gogarten, as well as the variety of items published, indicate that it was meant to be a journal for 'the man in the pew' and not the mouthpiece of one tradition or theological school.

Nonetheless, the theological re-orientation which began with the men whose thought was called 'dialectical theology' caused a break between this group of men and those who were responsible for the continuation of the journal's intention. The break caused the journal to become what it had never wanted to be: identified with and expressive of the 'liberal' wing of theology.

The public discussion between Harnack and Barth in this 'liberal' paper lasted a little longer than four months.[2] It was a confrontation which we may call an encounter of different worlds. How those worlds differed should become evident in the following chapter. Now we must try to explain what caused them to differ.

In order to do this we must go back to the year 1906, when Barth was enrolled as a student in the faculty of theology of the University of Berlin. At that time the faculty was what might easily be labelled 'an all-star' faculty. There was Karl Holl, the Church-historian, Julius Kaftan, the dogmatician, Herrmann Gunkel, the Old Testament scholar, Otto Pfleiderer, the New Testament scholar, and Adolf von Harnack, the historian of dogma and at that time surely the most famous among them. He was an aristocrat among them and the other great minds of his time and among historians he is someone whose work still commands attention.

To this scholar Barth was attracted. He requested and obtained permission to participate as a regular member in Harnack's seminars. He was the youngest student ever to participate in those *colloquia*, an indication that Harnack himself must have been impressed by the student. 'With great devotion and single-mindedness Barth attended Harnack's lectures and seminars.'[3] Barth himself once confessed to Father Willems, a Dutch Dominican, 'that he followed Harnack's lectures with growing enthusiasm. Harnack's attempt to bring religion and culture into harmony scientifically impressed him so much that he wholly neglected the rich cultural opportunities Berlin afforded ... He was chained to Harnack ... in a kind of stupor so that even the Berlin Philharmonic could not lure him from his studies.'[4]

But in addition to his intellectual brilliance, Harnack was a man endowed with a very high moral sense; he stood up for the absolute value of the human person.

In 1908 Barth went to Marburg in order to study under Wilhelm Herrmann. And here we must begin to trace the development that led Barth away from Harnack, for it was Herrmann and not Harnack who became Barth's most revered and influential teacher.

From him, whom Barth later called 'the most pious of liberal theologians of his day',[5] Barth learned the concept or doctrine of the *autopistia* of faith. Its basic factors are the absolute transcendence of God and the impossibility of proving his existence scientifically. Faith is in no need of an ancillary science for its legitimisation. In Barth's theology this teaching became of fundamental importance for, as he is reported to have said, it is 'the rat-poison against all intellectualising subtleties in theology'.[6] It is probably this doctrine which Barth has in mind when he remarked that 'Herrmann is the one from whom I have learned something most basic, something which, once I followed it out to its consequences, caused me to say everything else in a wholly different way, even to interpret that most basic matter quite differently from him'.[7]

It appears, therefore, that at Herrmann's feet Barth learned something which led him to a change of direction, something which caused him to stop and to reconsider his theological thinking. In other words, here is the beginning of Barth's differences with his previous teacher Harnack. Here begins the course which led Barth from being an enthusiastic pupil of Harnack's to that position which the latter called 'a despiser of scientific theology'.

Herrmann opposed what he called the intellectual interpretation of religion. What he has in mind is the cognition of God through the traditional proofs of his existence or through any other means of scientific cognition of objects. In an address to a student conference at Aarau in 1908 he said: 'A God who has been proven to exist is of the world and a God of the world is an idol.'[8] Fifteen years later Barth wrote these words to Harnack: 'One must not have any delusions about the fact that faith is an unprecedented event, that here one must speak of the Holy Spirit, if all the objections Herrmann rammed into us against "mere credence" in historical facts apart from this basis of cognition are not to hold good.'[9] The reference is to Herrmann's view that the God of faith is not a demonstrable reality or even a demonstrable possibility because God is God and not an object or subject like those of the world.

If this polemic of Herrmann's is directed against the proofs of God's existence, it is equally directed against the cognition of God in historicism. For it, the historicity of a phenomenon affords the means of comprehending its essence and reality. Historical knowledge and critical reflection are the basic tools with which the philosopher or theologian grasps the object to be analysed.

Harnack makes frequent reference to these tools in his letters to Barth and, as we shall see later, with their application to the data of religion he believes that he has given theology a scientific, an objective method of speaking about God. On account of its scientific nature this method can command respect, speak persuasively and thus can convince the 'cultured despisers' of religion.

Herrmann's teaching about the *autopistia* of faith is a challenge to the historicism of Harnack. By making that particular concept his own, Barth begins to differ from Harnack's position.

Upon his graduation in 1909 Barth joined the staff of the journal *Christliche Welt*; he was its assistant editor at Marburg. Although he left for Geneva that same year to assume pastoral responsibilities in a German-speaking congregation there, he continued to contribute articles and reviews to the journal.

Then two years later Barth was called to the congregation of the Swiss Reformed Church at Safenwil in the Aargau. It may be said that his real work as preacher and theologian began here. Eduard Thurneysen writes that 'it all began with the fact that Karl Barth was minister in a rural community. He took this office seriously, he fulfilled it with the involvement and all-inclusiveness so characteristic of him . . . Every day of the week he studied the Bible so that he might carry out his commission to preach. He ploughed through it in his new way like a farmer who goes out early in the morning to his fields and ploughs furrow after furrow . . . Already then Barth stands before us as one who reads and interprets; the pages of the Holy Scriptures are before him . . . The Bible is the source today as it was at that time from which his theology draws. It has grown on the labour spent on the sermon and it serves the proclamation of the Church . . . It was exactly this concentration on the Scriptures and on proclamation which led him even in Safenwil to a very thorough discussion with the theology of the time . . . Out of this discussion grew the new perspective and the beginning associated with the name of Karl Barth.'[10]

Here we must pause in our consideration of Barth's movement away from Harnack. It was this occupation with the Bible which brought Barth into a pronounced disagreement with the type of biblical study carried out by Harnack.

In 1916 Barth delivered an address entitled *Die neue Welt in der Bibel*.[11] He said in it that the concern of the Bible is the message of God's holiness, righteousness and mercy. This message states that God does not need to be defended, for he speaks his Word sovereignly and with authority. Above all, God wishes to be found only in his Word; indeed the Scriptures say that only in it can God be found. God's Word is Jesus Christ. He is the centre of time, around whom the ages revolve. He brings the kingdom of God which comes upon us through him in the midst of time. The Bible speaks of that kingdom as the new world of God, not as the new world of man. And yet God does not bring his kingdom merely to save men's souls, while the kingdom of man is left to itself. The message of the Bible is rather that God loves the world of man, which is apparent even in his judging the world in the cross and the resurrection.

In his preoccupation with the Scriptures and its testimony, Barth became familiar with and captivated by the work of Johann Christoph Blumhardt and his son Christoph Blumhardt. They helped Barth to see through forms of pious security and satisfaction and all false ecclesiastical 'busy-ness', and to discuss the dangers of overestimating man-sponsored renewals of society, Church and world.

Twice during the period with which we are concerned, at Safenwil and the early years at Göttingen, Barth published articles in which he acknowledged his support for the Blumhardts. He stated in them why 'he felt at home'[12] with them. The first of these was a review of Christoph Blumhardt's book of meditations for home use; the second a comparison between Friedrich Naumann and the younger Blumhardt on the occasion of their deaths.[13]

What made him 'feel at home' in the work of these men? Barth answers: 'The unhappy word "religion", which contains also the inflexibility of the "real" world, this word, with which man, tired of life, turns to the distant unknown, was no longer used in Möttlingen and Boll. The "god" about whom these men inquired and to whom they witnessed was the *living* God. This was true in the double sense that they wanted to understand him as the Bible does, as the one who lives, from whom new deeds, powers and proofs are to be expected, and that they wanted to seek for and await his kingdom not only in the souls of individual men or in a distant heaven, but above all and first of all in life, precisely in the "real" life of men on earth. Once more the relation of God to the world appeared to them as a mighty, historical process, a movement, a victorious struggle which must end with the renewal of all things.'[14] Something new, something that was in accordance with the New Testament was being said, lived and confessed by these men. To put it in one word, it was 'hope – hope for a visible and tangible appearing of the lordship of God over the world (in contrast to the simple, and often so blasphemous, talking about God's omnipotence); hope for radical help and deliverance from the former state of the world (in opposition to that soothing and appeasing attitude, which must everywhere come to a halt before unalterable 'relationships'); hope for all, for mankind (in contrast to the selfish concern for one's own salvation and to all the attempts to raise up religious supermen and aristocrats); hope for the physical side of life as well as for the spiritual, in the sense that not only sin and sorrow, but also poverty, sickness and death shall one day be abolished (in contrast to the purely spiritual ideal of the so-called "religious-moral" life). To believe in "God" meant . . . to take this comprehensive hope seriously, more seriously than all other considerations.'[15]

Here lies the second point where we must pause in tracing Barth's 'estrangement' from Harnack. As he worked on his sermons and studied, interpreted, as he tried to fulfill his commission to preach the gospel, he came under the influence of the two Blumhardts.

What caught Barth's attention in these men was their zeal in the attempt to understand what was really being said in the books of the Bible. They did not try to systematise, 'set up theses or produce historical and psychological deductions. They neither philosophised nor politicised. No "problems" are dug up and no lines drawn.'[16] When asked about the meaning of their utterances they would say: 'I mean it as it is written there', pointing to the Bible.[17] And this wrestling with the message of the Scriptures made Barth feel at home with them.

Thurneysen's characterisation of the younger Blumhardt is equally true for the older man. 'He wanted to draw attention to God . . . He was a man who lived in a sphere in which people long and look for the kingdom that is to come and rule in solitary majesty over all spheres . . . He was a man of astounding and unheard of faithfulness and objectivity in the matters of God.'[18] This is what influenced Barth so deeply and set him apart so much from Harnack.

Faithfulness and objectivity towards anything is to accept it as it actually confronts man, that is, respect its dignity and

uniqueness. These two factors in theology will allow a proper
interpretation of God's revelation which is what the Bible
speaks of.

The message the Blumhardts found in the Scriptures was
this: God is a free and sovereign God. Man is powerless without
him. In order to find God man cannot rely on his own attempts
to bring God to man. Nonetheless, God does not wish to remain
separated from him, indeed he had himself come to man in his
Son. Yet in so doing he remains wholly God and as such he
redeems us from our powerlessness.[19]

This message was not new. Indeed the Church had always
taught that God is person, that he does not desire solitude but
rather community with man and that in Jesus Christ he had
found man. But for the Blumhardts this traditional message
had become simply a matter of pious feeling, of religious contemplation. They therefore proclaimed it as something that
had to become an actual event again, since our feelings and
contemplations are not themselves the event of God's com-
muning with us. Our feelings and contemplations do not take
us to God but only to the boundaries of ourselves.

God must enter the world in order to establish that *real* or
actual relationship between himself and us. Man is of the world
so that God must come to the world, become temporal, become
flesh, become history.[20] That is who Jesus Christ is, God come
to the world, God become temporal, flesh, history.

The incarnation shows how vast God's mercy is to man and
also how far man is away from God. Man's existence is in sin,
death and transitoriness, not on 'some pinnacle of culture and
religion' in the words of Barth's letter to Harnack.[21] For
Blumhardt God's entry into that existence establishes the relation between God and man, as nothing else does.[22] Over against
idealistic and spiritualistic interpretations of God's community
with man he maintained the view that 'it is the objective aspect
of God which makes *history* and causes man to *experience* it until
the day (of God) comes'.[23]

God remains God, however, even when incarnate. Thus he
who experiences a history of God experiences something wholly
different from himself and sovereign over him. God is not an
object among others, he is the one who questions and judges all
objects. He is the ground of all objects, as Tillich would say,

he is the end of time appearing in the midst of time, in Cull-mann's phrase.

The Blumhardts never tired of emphasising this. God enters time as its crisis, and this becoming temporal makes for a history which leads to the day of Christ, to the *eschaton*.[24] Con-trary to Rothe and the Hegelian wing of theology, Blumhardt maintained that the *eschaton* was not a new age of man but rather the very end of all ages. It was *God's* new age with man, but not the age of a new humanity brought about by man. God brings in the kingdom of God. So he speaks about it in terms of hope and Christ's resurrection. 'It must come to the point where we do not merely hold on to an old confession of faith but in new experience call out one to another "he is risen in-deed!" and "he lives among us!".' Or just before that sentence, 'Precisely what is the centre, the actual centre of gravity in the kingdom of God? The resurrection! The revelation of God in the resurrection! ... Jesus lives and lives, as it is written, as the risen one ... Only the power of the resurrection, in which we shall see him coming on the clouds of his Father's glory, will achieve things. Only the one who rose and who will come again takes the world into his hands from above and shakes it so that in the end it can do nothing but surrender and give him praise.'[25]

When Blumhardt speaks of the cross and resurrection he witnesses above all to the living God *in our midst*, to him who is to come *at the end of time*, to him whose kingdom, which is to come, *has already come*. It is a witness to the living God who is radically different from the world and who is beyond the world, who yet became flesh and therefore is in the world.

It is in this insistence on God's otherness and in the double emphasis – God *on earth* and on earth *God* – that there is to be sought the element that influenced Barth and that was so distasteful to Harnack, namely eschatology.

But even the insistence on God's otherness and the emphasis that God is God even when on earth are an empty ideology unless God himself makes them become real. Only he can bring about a real encounter between himself and man. Through his Son that event becomes reality on earth. Here the Blumhardts spoke of the Holy Spirit, for it is through him that this reality obtains actuality.[26] 'Revelation occurs through the Spirit ... Even St Peter could not recognise Jesus as God's Son and as the

Christ without revelation from the Father through the Spirit.'[27]

Thurneysen calls this aspect of the Blumhardts' preaching the nucleus of their thought. 'What does it mean that both Blumhardts put all their thinking under the proviso of the Holy Spirit? It is the test as to whether they took the "God himself" and the "God only" really seriously even to the last. It means that they did not think: *we* believe in God, believe and hope that he will come and do great things to us and *because we* believe that, it shall come to pass; no, this proviso, which alone allows full understanding of God, enters here and says: God comes not because *you* hope and believe, he comes and helps (when in fact he does come and help) only because he *wants* to do that. Even our faith and hope are worth nothing, are flesh, are senseless grasping and calling out into emptiness if it does not please God to redeem us. But has not God promised redemption? Can our faith not base itself on this word of promise? That may well be, but only as a word of *promise* is it *his* word. That means that it helps us only because *God* has committed himself to it in his free decision. When God comes and we experience his help, when he really appears among us and is recognised for what he is then a miracle has happened, the miracle of his mercy for which we can *only wait*.'[28]

Man is in need of a new outpouring of the Holy Spirit, or as the younger Blumhardt put it, a continuous revelation, an ever new, ever recurring revelation. 'Under the weight of preaching without preceding revelation, even that which revelation has already given can be smothered completely. Thus we cannot avoid saying that, when there is no revelation, the sermon is no longer the gospel but a spiritual art of talking in the service of human systems.'[29] But, and this is the point of these remarks, man does not *have* or *possess* the Holy Spirit, does not *have* or *possess* revelation, although that was what the accepted theology of the day maintained. Man must rather wait for the Holy Spirit, wait for revelation in reliance on and in hope for God's word and faithfulness which through the Spirit will ever renew his promise.[30]

In these views Blumhardt opposed the concepts and the consequences of the word 'religion', which in view of its great philosophical significance had assumed an immensely important position in theology. Against it Blumhardt put what he called

the kingdom of God. We noticed that for him the *eschaton* was
the very end of all ages. Similarly, the kingdom of the *eschaton*,
of God, is the power of God, the government of God, the
revelation of the life of God. 'The whole kingdom is a heavenly,
an eternal kingdom. It is contrary to our earthly nature. The
boundary is precise, it cannot be altered or mixed in with other
things . . . It does not please everyone that God's kingdom does
not come with external gestures. There are many who would
rather have it with violence, externally, so that they might
shout "Look here, look there, we have it, we can do it, . . . look
how much blessing we bring to mankind." . . Beloved, let your
flesh die, your spiritual flesh, let it die! God will surely not be
embarrassed if you do not blow the trumpet, if you give up
your campaigning. He has trumpets, too, he won't need yours.
He has voices, too, he won't need yours. And when *you* are
quiet, he will sound *his trumpet*, raise *his voice* and then he will
create his kingdom and not we poor humans.'[31]

The kingdom is God's, yes, but it is also a kingdom, not
merely a realm of inwardness, a sphere where God rules souls.
The emphasis is on God's sovereignty over the whole creation
now, just as it is in the futuristic aspect of that kingdom which
has already begun to come upon us. In another sermon
Blumhardt said: 'The aim of all intercession is . . . connected
with the coming of the Son of man. The presence of the Saviour
is therefore not yet salvation . . . The last thing in the coming
of salvation is the return of the Saviour. Thus far everything is
just the beginning, the foundation. The actual fulfilment is
tied to his coming, to his appearance, to his becoming revealed
in the world, it is tied to the fact that God comes with him . . .
and then we are saved.'[32]

What are the characteristic features in the thought of the
Blumhardts that influenced Barth? These men were witnesses
for God in so far as they wanted above all to call man's attention to God. Exactly for this reason they saw themselves compelled to attack the Christianity of their day. The tools, so to
speak, of their witness to God were faithfulness to the message
of the Bible and objectivity towards the 'object' of their proclamation: God as revealed in Christ and testified to us in the
biblical witness. Thus, we see them involved in an eschatological dialectic which speaks of God in the flesh, of God

present in the world and in history, of God who is to come, who is radically different from the world, who nevertheless entered into the world in an earthly form. It is a dialectic which states that God is understood and even found only through himself; his revelation in fact creates the ears and eyes with which he is heard and seen.

There is in this dialectic an objectivity which allows no pre-understanding to impose itself on the event of God's confrontation with man. But since the reality of God is taken seriously, there is also a very serious questioning for the real powers of God's kingdom. Precisely because God lives man must arise from his slumber of inwardness and pious otherworldliness, for the presence of God in the world demands a change in man and the world. But these men knew that sermons, protests and moral instructions do not bring about that kind of change. They did not therefore dismiss the ability of man to become converted; no, they had confidence in the real reality and the natural nature of man and in the emergence into visibility of what is still hidden in man. They trusted in God. And thus they also believed that the world was renewable.

Yet this confidence made every form of religious subjectivism, of otherworldly inwardness impossible. That sleep had to come to an end. The world's salvation is God's return to it, his actual coming into it again. In this expectation of God's return there arises an eschatology and an eschatological dialectic which allows man to speak of God in such a way that his uniqueness and dignity are honoured. Barth admits that this influenced him profoundly.

One may see this influence in the sermons published in the little volume entitled *Suchet Gott, so werdet ihr leben*. It would be false to assume that Barth discovered eschatology and dialectic in the Blumhardts. Rather he saw in them kindred spirits, who in their confrontation with the Scriptures preached that the kingdom was coming and that we can only wait for it. Yet this did not prevent them from upholding an ethics in which we are urged to hasten towards the kingdom. *Wait and hasten* were keywords in Möttlingen and Boll. Barth's address, *The Christian's Place in Society*, delivered at Tambach in September 1919, leaves no doubt that for him ethics may not become lost in eschatology. The latter leads to the former. Barth rather guides us through the middle between mythical views of the end and the resigned denial of hope, we are guided past the idea which brought about the renunciation of hope and the consequent shift from God to man as the one who brings in or creates the kingdom to come.

We see Barth here as a man deeply concerned about the preaching of the gospel. His real, his primary aim was to allow the depth of the Scriptures to become visible again, the springs of the Bible to flow freely once more, and the message of the biblical writers to become concrete again in man's life and existence. We may say indeed that Barth wanted the Scriptures to become 'political', involved in the events of community, nation and world. Hence his interpretation of God's judgment as a judgment which puts things in the right, in the phrase borrowed from the Blumhardts.[33]

The minister from Safenwil therefore actually worked with his congregation through Ephesians and 2 Corinthians as well as through Romans, the fruit of which was published as a commentary on that epistle. The book was meant to do one thing: to call for an intensification of the study of the Scriptures for the sake of the Church's preaching. It was an attempt 'to stand materially involved on the side of Paul and not nonchalantly *vis-à-vis* him'.[34] It was because of this book that Barth was offered the newly created chair of reformed dogmatics at Göttingen.

The content of that work need not concern us here. We shall see later, however, why the exegetical method advocated in it and in the next edition was to bring upon Barth the charge of his old teacher, Harnack, that he deserved to be called 'a despiser of scientific theology'.

It is difficult to know whether Harnack and Barth had met or been in contact with each other since Barth's days in Berlin and Marburg. They did meet in 1920, however, at the student conference at Aarau, where both had been asked to deliver an address, and a second time at the home of Eberhard Vischer in Basel.

At Aarau Harnack spoke on *Was hat die Historie an fester Erkenntnis zur Deutung des Weltgeschehens zu bieten?*[35] In comparison with Barth's lecture which was entitled *Biblische Fragen, Einsichten und Ausblicke*,[36] Harnack's address was not the one that was remembered.

Harnack approached Aarau with a certain degree of hesitancy. His daughter and biographer, Agnes von Zahn-Harnack, writes that for a good number of years Harnack had been quite worried about the way in which theology was proceeding. 'He feared that the generation of younger theologians was moving in a dangerous direction. He was concerned over the decline in the respect for historical research. What he found was rather a romantic leaning towards the primitive, a tendency to draw all knowledge from the depth of one's soul. All this merely supplanted a methodical analysis of the sources. But this tendency seemed to be controllable, partially due to Harnack's own work . . . On the whole a shift in emphasis was noticeable in the world of theological endeavour, yet one was still able at least to understand one another's language, one could assume that all strove for the same end.'[37]

Then Harnack went to Aarau. When it was over he confessed to Eberhard Vischer that 'the effect of Barth's lecture was just staggering. Not one word, not one sentence could I have said or thought. I saw the sincerity of Barth's speech, but its theology frightened me . . . The severity of the charges made in that address is still very vivid in my mind. Instead of losing any of its force, it appears to me more and more hazardous, yes, in a way even scandalous. This impression is in no way softened by the consideration that this sort of religion is incapable of being translated into real life, so that it must soar above life as a meteor rushing toward its disintegration. So I ask myself again and again how he as a minister, who is charged with the cure of souls, can judge in such a fashion.'[38]

Did Harnack not know Barth's *Römerbrief* before he went to Aarau? There is no indication in his own writings or in his biography that would allow an answer in either the affirmative or the negative. It is beyond question that he knew Jülicher's famous review of that work. But it did not appear until July 1920, three months after Aarau. The reason for such a long delay in its review is due to the fact that even though the book had been published in 1919 by Bäschlin in Bern it became known to a wider circle of readers in Germany only after the Kaiser Press in München took it over and sold the copies which Bäschlin still had on hand in 1920. We would conclude therefore that Harnack became fully aware of Barth's decisive departure from his own theological position only during the conference at Aarau. His remark to Vischer supports this conclusion.

We must try to imagine Harnack's feelings during Barth's lecture, as his devoted and now somewhat famous pupil was saying things such as these in his presence: 'We are inside and not outside . . . the knowledge of God and of the last things, of which the Bible speaks, is the premise of all our life and thought . . . But this is apparently contradicted by our dark, enigmatical, inexplicable sense of being outside and of lacking a premise.'[39] What Barth gave with one hand he took away with the other, since the first part of that statement reflects the religious certainty of the Christian and the second part throws him into confusion and uncertainty. The former described the assured possession of the believer, a possession that is undergirded by the results of scientific theology; the latter crushes it and leaves the believer in the position of the gnostic or of someone who does not yet know what he believes.

Then Barth says: 'Our quest for God cannot be due to the influence of theology and the Church, for *theology* and *Church* from the beginning of the world have done more in this respect to narcotise than to stimulate.'[40] But who raises the question of God if not the community of believers, the Church and its scientific relative, theology? Where else but in theology can this question be raised and expected to be answered with precision and with the proper tools? Barth is in fact cutting off the branch on which he as a theologian sits and speaks. That statement is a contradiction in terms. 'Religion and thought concerning God have never meant the same thing.'[41] This is also a contradiction because religion is by definition the sense for God. The listener must have wondered what kind of logic was operative in Barth.

'When we admit our knowledge of God, we apparently admit something else besides. When we hold to our partly inside position, we are apparently at the same time establishing a position partly outside. We set up for ourselves a duality, a dualism. We admit our knowledge of God only as an antithesis to other knowledge.'[42] Is this some kind of Hegelian dialectics, a metaphysics of which theology had just recently and justifiedly rid itself? Harnack had striven endlessly to synthesise the knowledge of the world, of the *universitas litterarum* and the knowledge of God. What is this duality, this dualism? Is it not the gnosticism the Church had anathematised? Is Barth not aware of this? Did he not say himself that 'when the human soul becomes actually conscious of its autonomy and freedom, the gravity of the question about unity, the question about God, is not lessened but increased'?[43] The Enlightenment had made plain the freedom and autonomy of the soul and ever since then the 'way of grasping the object, who is God, epistemologically has attained to greater clarity and maturity'.[44] How can anyone deny this maturity by reverting to a pre-Enlightenment position?

'When we ask the Bible what it has to offer, it answers by putting to us the fact of *election*. What we call religion and culture may be available to everybody, but the belief, simple and comprehensive, which is offered in the Bible, is not available to everybody: not at any time nor in any respect can any one who will reach out and take it.'[45] This removes from the believer's grasp the confidence and reliability of his having overcome the world and the material forces. Rather 'every link between faith and what is human is severed'.[46] Then the reference to the doctrine of election recalls orthodox dogmaticism which relegated faith to an intellectual assent to authoritatively defined propositions. Had not the Reformation spent endless energy on overcoming the similar authoritarianism of scholasticism? Why is that heritage disregarded then?

And then there is Barth's characterisation of the content of the Bible. '. . . always there is the same seeing of the invisible, the same hearing of the inaudible, the same incomprehensible but no less undeniable epidemic of standing still and looking up . . . We think of John the Baptist in Grünewald's painting of the crucifixion, with his strangely pointing hand. It is this hand which is in evidence in the Bible.'[47] But how is this to be reconciled with the undeniable conclusions of biblical research which has established that 'the Bible is the literary monument of an ancient racial religion and of a Hellenistic cultus religion of the Near East', which Barth himself admits?[48] Why grant validity on the one hand to the tested results of literary and historical criticism and then on the other take them away by saying that only when these results are granted and put behind us do we come to the actual content of the Bible? By what avenue do we come to know that content then?

And finally this statement: 'In the biblical experience there is a final element to which nothing in psychology corresponds, which cannot be reproduced in feeling, which cannot be demonstrated in experience . . . Biblical religious history has the distinction of being in its essence, in its inmost character, neither religion nor history – not religion but reality, not history but truth.'[49] Can this be anything more than rhetorical language? How can reality be contrasted with the data of psychology and history? Even a special history, even *Heilsgeschichte* must be historical datum or else we are using language equivocally and not helpfully.

One could continue and show how question after question would arise for Harnack in response to Barth's remarks. Suffice it to say that the lecture left him with a sense of bewilderment. He saw clearly that Barth was not only breaking with the theological position in which Harnack stood but that he was also challenging it.

Two elements may be distinguished in that sense of bewilderment. On the one hand there was the realisation of what this kind of thinking means for the established theological position. On the other there was a feeling of not really understanding what that thinking wants to express.

Harnack spoke about that feeling several times. On 16 January 1923 he wrote to Barth about reading a 'half incomprehensible outburst by Gogarten',[50] on 8 March in the same year he states that Barth's 'concept of revelation is completely incomprehensible to me; much else stays under the cover of a heavy fog. Other things remain totally obscure for me.'[51] On 20 January 1929 he wrote to Martin Rade his concern over this 'speculation for which I have no antenna'.[52]

The element referred to first may be seen in the kind of reaction made by Harnack and other colleagues of his to that 'new' thinking. 'I am filled with anxiety for the future of scientific theology' Harnack wrote to Barth.[53] He had it because he feared that the solid ground on which theology stood on account of the possession of final knowledge, assured by the critical-historical method, would be shaken. He feared for the good conscience theology had finally achieved in its successful struggle to establish harmony between faith and the world, between the teaching of Jesus and the wisdom of Goethe and Kant, between the kingdom of God and the policies of Kaiser Wilhelm II.[54] So he said that 'these views may not claim general validity, exclusive validity. They represent a stage which can and must be overcome . . . There are melancholy and easy-going Christians (not thoughtless or careless Christians). The former are always those who give us dogmatics; at the same time they hold a gun into the latters' faces and interpret their God-given temper as nothing but an enduring state of sinnerhood . . . Yet I can understand that most melancholy Christians are unable to judge differently and that therefore they must condemn.'[55]

According to Harnack, Barth is one of those melancholy Christians, for this theological ancestry alone would show that. There is the melancholy Dane, Kierkegaard, the Russian mystic, Dostoyevsky, the pessimist from Basel, Overbeck, and the man so concerned about the *eschaton*, Blumhardt. And how roundly Barth condemns. In a 'holy egoism' (a phrase used by Jülicher) he walks past the fruits of earlier research and what men before him had thought of as holy. He questions not only individual conclusions but the whole presupposition and foundation of the thought of his teachers. He says No! where Neo-Protestant theology emphasised the uniqueness and difference of the Christian religion over and against all other matters of human and spiritual concern. No! also to the barriers which were raised by this emphasis, claiming that they make what is unique to God into something unique to man. No! where Protestant thinkers of the nineteenth and early twentieth centuries said there was a significance of Christianity for human and spiritual matters, where they stressed its influence on culture, society and science. Barth went so far as to say that certain boundaries had been disregarded causing God's revelation to become regarded as a transfiguration of the world, as something inherent in the world. And how Barth protested against the union of Church and culture, asking whether in the midst of it Neo-Protestantism was still speaking of *God*.

Yet, Harnack acknowledged the No's, acknowledged the questions and called them 'a ferment' which prevents 'our easy-going temper from changing into carelessness, our childlike attitude from changing into spiritual foolishness and our openness to the world from changing into worldliness'.[56] At the same time he could not help wondering why in this theological ferment 'Ritschl is the most despised of all today, although he has much to offer . . . But the sons of today are more hostile to their fathers than to their grandfathers.'[57]

Ritschl and those fathers, of whom Harnack was one, had given precise and scientific answers to the question of how the Church and theology are to speak the Word of Christ. That answer might not be the final one, but it was good enough for Barth to agree that the faith of the Church and theology comes about 'through the preaching of the Word of Christ'.[58] Then, why challenge the fathers, why turn against them and their conclusions with the critical question: 'How *can* we preach the Word of Christ?' As if the theology of the last century had not shown that that Word is the simple gospel which can and must be preached. But the hostility goes deeper than that. Stating the obvious, namely that the preacher's and the theologian's concern is not their feelings or their heuristic knowledge, Barth introduces an epistemology of the Word which is gnostic in character.[59] This speculative, metaphysical element with its use of dualism, non-historical reality and the 'wholly other' is a clear breach with the work of 'the fathers'.

Thus the new thinking was not merely a ferment. If it were that only, then it would pass once its aims had been achieved. But why the attack, why the rejection and condemnation, why the speculation? When one leaves the ground of actual history, the confidence of faith becomes illusory, science is exchanged for suitable fantasies and the real Jesus Christ and his Word are made into imaginary figures. The result can only be an occultism which the Church must reject. What was the meaning of it then? Harnack therefore formulated his anxiety and the questions arising out of it into that series of fifteen questions which in January 1923 he put forth before the melancholic, gnostic and dogmatic despisers of scientific theology.

For the sake of discussion we have distinguished two elements in Harnack's sense of bewilderment. But it is apparent that the realisation of the meaning of the new thinking for the established theological position and the feeling of not really understanding what this thinking wants to express cannot be separated in actual fact. Both become manifest in the questions Harnack asks.

What of Barth's published work did Harnack actually know? It is not possible to determine this accurately. Using Miss von Kirschbaum's *Bibliographia Barthiana* in the *Festschrift Antwort* one may select those works with which Harnack might have been familiar.

Barth had contributed eleven times to *Christliche Welt* prior to the correspondence with Harnack in it. Seven of these contributions were reviews, one a sermon. Only three were independent studies from which one might deduce a personal point of view, a theological position. Two of them were published in 1922 just prior to the correspondence. Barth's participation as a writer in *Zeitschrift für Theologie und Kirche* amounts to three articles, all of which appeared before 1915. None of them could have done more than confirm Harnack in his general suspicion referred to above. Then there are some fifty-one publications in various local, congregational and ecclesiastical newspapers and journals, very few, if any, of which would have come to Harnack's attention even if the war had not been on. Two articles were written for the first edition of *Die Religion in Geschichte und Gegenwart*, vol. 5. As they are about Swiss thinkers, they would not allow much deduction as to their author's theological position. Whether Harnack knew and read the *Schweizerische Theologische Zeitschrift* or the *Reformierte Kirchenzeitung* is not certain. Since the two items in them are an article and a sermon they would not really be decisive for a knowledge of Barth. Harnack may have read the two essays *Der Christ in der Gesellschaft* and *Zur inneren Lage des Christentums*, which like *Biblische Fragen, Einsichten und Ausblicke*, delivered in Harnack's presence, were published by Kaiser of München, and would be of interest to Harnack after the experience in Aarau. But this does not mean that he in fact read them. He probably was aware of *Zwischen den Zeiten* in which Barth prior to the correspondence had published only *Not und Verheissung der christlichen Verkündigung*. Of the seventy-six titles listed by Miss von Kirschbaum before the Harnack–Barth discussion there remain the three books published up to that time: the first collection of sermons by Thurneysen and Barth and the two editions of the *Römerbrief*.

It would appear that Harnack might have been familiar with the following works of Barth's published before their discussion: the two editions of the *Römerbrief*, *Der Christ in der Gesellschaft*, *Zur inneren Lage des Christentums* (an article now reprinted as *Unerledigte Anfragen an die heutige Theologie* in the second anthology of essays by Barth: *Die Theologie und die Kirche*), *Biblische Fragen*, *Einsichten und Ausblicke*, *Immer noch unerledigte Anfragen*, *Das Wort Gottes als Aufgabe der Theologie* and *Not und Verheissung der christlichen Verkündigung*.[60] These works constitute the major publications of Barth's up to that time and give sufficient insight into his position then.

Nonetheless that position was puzzling and shocking to Harnack. Why should a man of world renown say that neither his nor anyone else's theology really matters and then in the very next breath add that if his opponent's way of teaching the gospel were to prevail the gospel would cease to be taught?[61]

Even though Harnack may have been emotionally involved in this confrontation and even though he may have felt that he did not have an antenna for the message of Barth, he had definite reasons nevertheless why he was opposed to the 'new look' in theology.

Two things specifically estranged Harnack from his one-time pupil. There is first of all the apparent disdain for critical-historical analysis, for the scientific evaluation of the source material. Secondly, there is what he called the tendency to draw one's understanding of the material from one's soul which for Harnack meant the free creation of the truth for oneself.

He once characterised Barth's position like this: 'We live in a time, which dominated by certain vital questions, is in danger of devaluating the critical question of truth. Strictly methodical work in relation to those questions is dispensed with and even rejected under the label of historicism. It is true that history does not speak the last word anywhere, but in the science of religion, especially of the Christian religion, it certainly has the first word.'[62] Harnack was a scientific historian and in his methodology an historicist. For him the patient tracing of the existence of some object or truth in the course of history was the key to the understanding of it. This involves the critical appraisal of the object or truth in its environment so that one clears away what is accidental to it at any particular time.

Thus, one comes to know the object or truth gradually. The critical rejection of methodical, historical analysis amounted to the desire to know an object or truth fully 'in a twinkling of an eye'. But that has been exactly the desire and method of gnosticism. 'The most unbearable feature of gnostic theology was its view of man. As long as man is one of the *pneumatikoi* (the "spirituals") he is in essence related to, yes, even a part of God. Both these views replaced the Christian understanding of God. They put into its place a foreign understanding which leads to epistemological absurdities, which is what we see happening again today. Again we hear of knowledge that cannot be known and of experiences which cannot be had.'[63]

The gnostic *pneumatikos*, claiming to be a bearer of revelation, believed he had full knowledge of God in a sudden revelation. He therefore did not need discussion with others of his own or preceding times in order to find that knowledge. According to his opponents he harboured an arbitrariness and a dualistic one-sidedness in which he rejected logic and became irrational. Only what emerged from his soul was regarded as true, but this only meant that he created truth freely on his own. He was a man filled with 'holy egoism'.

For Harnack science was a sphere of methodical, unprejudiced, stately and well-thought-through approach to the cognition of some object or truth. Any passionate involvement in the object or truth in question was foreign to him. No doubt it might act as a ferment in an otherwise too slow process. But in that case the approach would not be scientific and if it claimed to be scientific but rejected or denied history, thereby showing that it had no reverence for what is great in history, then it could not really appreciate the achievements of the gospel in its two millennia of history. This would not only be irreverence toward greatness, with a total lack of interest in the historical development of the gospel, it would also be real 'ignorance of what is going on. It would only pour water into its own wine and depart from the field of scientific theology.'[64]

But can such an approach be called science? How could it? It is not interested in establishing proofs; in time it creates its own theology, theory, dogma, morality and even its science in order to achieve its goal which is to edify and to win souls. The existentialist-pietist emphasis on sheer faith, the attitude that if something seems doubtful, try believing harder, is not scientific. How much Harnack abhors the tendency toward the primitive is apparent in his remark to Barth: 'This point of view, known to the point of nausea from recent, second-rate Church history, opens the gates to every suitable fantasy and theological dictatorship which dissolves the historical element in our religion and seeks to torment the conscience of others with one's own knowledge derived from actual observations of facts or events.'[65]

The rejection of critical-historical study, irreverence toward the great moments and personalities of the past and the claim of full, instantaneous knowledge, are the objections Harnack raises in the name of science to Barth's position, to the method of the *Römerbrief*. But in addition he finds three other points in Barth to which he is opposed.

In his lifelong attempt to relate religion to culture and science Harnack had insisted that science and human cognition had to be seen in their relation to the divine. He shared Goethe's view that it would not be worth living as long as seventy years if all man's wisdom were to be no more than foolishness before God.[66] It was incomprehensible for him how anyone could say that human cognition, experience, self-knowledge, that psychology and historical reflection are possible in questions *not* concerned with God and put down to them the loss of reverence on which rests man's righteousness before God. But this is just what Barth seemed to maintain. The result of such an outlook was the separation of reason and science from the divine,[67] which Harnack could interpret only as a victory of the irrational and demonic over man.

Secondly, Harnack did not regard culture and morality as non-divine. Doubtless culture is not religion, nor is morality identical with religion. But a culture and a morality deeply indebted to and influenced by religion are – if not divine – then certainly transparent to the divine. Barth, however, believed that the divine had as much and as little to do with either the civilised and the religious as with the barbaric and the non-religious.[68]

And thirdly, Harnack was deeply suspicious of everything metaphysical or speculative. For him the teaching of Christ was simple, unequivocal, even characterised by a childlike straightforwardness. The apparently speculative philosophy of dialectical theology seemed to him a falsification of the gospel. He was unhappy about terminologies drawn from sources other than the gospel, and then used in its explication.[69] The easy comprehensibility of Christ's teachings was for him the supreme proof of their divinity. Agnes von Zahn-Harnack tells about a principle to which her father adhered to his life's end, a principle honoured by him especially in the field of religion: Do not express what is commonplace in uncommon terms, rather express what is not common in common words.[70]

Harnack believed that these three points, in which he felt himself separated from Barth, are essential in the establishment of a religiously, morally and scientifically unified community. As far as he was concerned the thinking of the author of the *Römerbrief* tore apart what he, Harnack, had endeavoured to unite, namely religion and culture, morality and science, the divine and the human. It made difficult and obscure what to Harnack looked simple and lucid. Such thinking could not bring men together, either in the Church or in the *universitas litterarum*, much less in both of these spheres together. How could anyone, in the name of theology, in the name of religion, think and judge as a minister in that fashion?

Harnack faced the point of view of Barth with bewildered and shocked lack of understanding. In this frame of mind and desirous to find understanding and communication he wrote the fifteen questions. But this desire 'to reach clarity *vis-à-vis* a theologian-friend'[71] was not to be fulfilled. For, nearly six years after the public discussion, he wrote to Rade: 'It is encouraging to see the seriousness of intention in our contemporary theology and its desire to address itself to the main issues of theology. But how weak it is as a science, how narrow and sectarian its horizon, how expressionistic its logic and how shortsighted its view of history ... What seems to be lost completely is the link between theology and the *universitas litterarum* and culture. There are rather new links between this evangelical theology and Catholicism and Romanticism. But let us hope that we have here no more than the cocoon-stage of something that some day will turn out to be a genuinely evangelical butterfly.'[72]

The verdict about this encounter of Harnack and Barth of

1923 is that it was and remained an encounter of different theological worlds. The participants, although fully aware of this, nevertheless continued their cordial personal relationship right to the end of Harnack's life.[73]

PART ONE

Text and analysis of the Barth–Harnack correspondence of 1923

THE TEXT

HARNACK TO BARTH

(1) Is the religion of the Bible, or are its revelations, so completely a unity that in relation to faith, worship and life one may simply speak of 'the Bible'? If this is not so, may one leave the determination of the content of the gospel solely to the individual's heuristic knowledge (*Erfahrung*), to his subjective experience (*Erlebnis*), or does one not rather need here historical knowledge and critical reflection?

(2) Is the religion of the Bible, or are its revelations, so completely a unity and so clear that historical knowledge and critical reflection are not needed for a correct understanding of their meaning? Or are they the converse, namely so incomprehensible and indescribable that one must simply wait until they radiate out in man's heart because no faculty of man's soul or mind can grasp them? Are not both these assumptions false? Do we not need, for an understanding of the Bible, next to an inner openness, historical knowledge and critical reflection?

(3) Is the experience of God (*Gotteserlebnis*) different from the awakening of faith or identical with it? If it is different, what distinguishes it from uncontrollable fanaticism? If it is identical, how can it come about otherwise than through the preaching of the gospel? And how can there be such preaching without historical knowledge and critical reflection?

(4) If the experience of God (*Gotteserleben*) is contrary to or disparate from all other experience (*Erleben*), how is the necessity of a radical withdrawal from the world to be avoided or how is one to escape the sophism that one has to remain in the world since even the withdrawal from it is based on a decision of the will and thus something worldly?

(5) If God and the world (life in God and life in the world) are complete opposites, what is one to make of the close union,

29

indeed the equivalence of the love of God and the love of one's fellow, which comprise the core of the gospel? How is this equivalence possible without the highest valuation of morality?

(6) If God and the world (life in God and life in the world) are complete opposites, how does education in godliness, that is in goodness, become possible? But how is education possible without historical knowledge and the highest valuation of morality?

(7) If God is simply unlike anything said about him on the basis of the development of culture, on the basis of the knowledge gathered by culture, and on the basis of ethics, how can this culture and in the long run one's own existence be protected against atheism?

(8) If Goethe's pantheism, Kant's conception of God or related points of view are merely opposites of real statements about God, how can it be avoided that these statements are given over to barbarism?

(9) But if the converse is true, namely that here as in all physical and spiritual developments opposites are at one and the same time steps and steps are opposites, how can this basic knowledge be grasped and furthered without historical knowledge and critical reflection?

(10) If the knowledge that God is love is the highest and final knowledge of him and if love, joy and peace are his sphere, how may one remain forever between door and hinge, how may one give autonomous standing to what are transition points in Christian experience (*Erfahrung*) and thus perpetuate their dread?

(11) 'Whatever is true, honourable, just, gracious, if there is any excellence, anything worthy of praise, think on these things' – if this liberating admonition still stands, how can one erect barriers between the experience of God (*Gotteserlebnis*) and the good, the true and the beautiful, instead of relating them with the experience of God by means of historical knowledge and critical reflection?

(12) If all sin is nothing other than the lack of reverence and love, how can this lack be checked other than by the preaching of God's holy majesty and love? How dare one introduce all kinds of paradoxes and whims here?

(13) If it is certain that whatever is subconscious, sensory,

numinous, spell-binding (*Fascinos*), etc., remains sub-human as long as reason has not taken hold of, comprehended, purified and protected it in its unique essence, how can one rebuke this reason, yes even wish to eradicate it? And what has one to offer once this Herostratean deed is done?* Is not even gnostic occultism rising up now out of the rubble?

(14) If the person of Jesus Christ stands at the centre of the gospel, how else can the basis for reliable and communal knowledge of this person be gained but through critical-historical study so that an imagined Christ is not put in place of the real one? What else besides scientific theology is able to undertake this study?

(15) Granted that there are inertness, short-sightedness and numerous ills, yet is there any other theology than that which has strong ties, and is in blood-relationship, with science in general? Should there be one, what persuasiveness and value belong to it?

Berlin–Grünewald   Adolf von Harnack

BARTH TO HARNACK

FIFTEEN ANSWERS TO PROFESSOR ADOLF VON HARNACK

In reference to the title (of your questions): someone objecting to that form of Protestant theology which has become determinative since Pietism and the Enlightenment, especially during the last fifty years of German history, is not necessarily a 'despiser of scientific theology'. The point of the objection is that *this* particular theology might have moved further away from its theme than is good. (The Reformation was the last instance where it was stated clearly.)

(1) *The one revelation of God* might be considered the theme of theology and this beyond the 'religion' and the 'revelations' of the Bible. 'Historical knowledge' could tell us that the communication of the 'content of the gospel' can be accomplished,

---

* Herostrates, an Ephesian, so desired notoriety that he set fire to the temple of Artemis in Ephesus on the night when Alexander the Great was born. (Translator's note.)

according to the assertion of the gospel, only through an act of this 'content' itself. But 'critical reflection' could lead to the conclusion that this assertion is founded in the essence of the matter (the relation of God and man) and is therefore to be seriously respected. The 'scientific character' of theology would then be its adherence to the recollection that its object *was once subject* and must become that again and again, which has nothing to do whatever with one's 'heuristic knowledge' (*Erfahrung*) and experience' (*Erlebnis*) in themselves.

(2) 'Inner openness, heuristic knowledge, experience, heart' and the like on the one hand and 'historical knowledge and critical reflection' on the other are possibilities which can be equally helpful, irrelevant or obstructive to the 'understanding' (*Verstehen*) of the Bible. It is understood through neither this nor that 'function of the soul or mind' but by virtue of *that* Spirit which is identical with the content of the Bible and that by *faith*.

(3) The so-called 'experience of God' (*Gotteserlebnis*) is therefore as different as heaven and earth from the faith awakened by God and is *practically* indistinguishable from 'uncontrolled fanaticism'. But why *could* it not be a more distinct or more confused symptom of and a testimony to the awakening of faith? Faith does come about *practically* through preaching, but preaching comes about through 'the Word of the Christ' (no matter in what state the preacher's historical knowledge and critical reflection are). The task of theology is at one with the task of preaching. It consists in the reception and transmission of the Word of the Christ. Why should 'historical knowledge and critical reflection' not be of preparatory service in this?

(4) The faith awakened by God will never be able to avoid completely the necessity of a more or less radical protest against this world as surely as it is a hope for the promised but invisible gift. A theology, should it lose the understanding of the basic distance which faith posits between itself and this *world*, would in the same measure have to lose sight of the knowledge of God the *Creator*. For the 'utter contrast' of God and the world, the *cross*, is the only way in which we as *human beings* can consider the original and final *unity* of Creator and creature. Sophistry is not the realisation that even our protest against the world

cannot justify us before God. It is rather the common attempt
to bypass the cross by means of a shallow doctrine of creation.

(5) The coordination of the love of God and the love of man
which the gospel makes is precisely the most forceful reference
to the fact that the relation between our 'life in the world' and
our 'life in God' is one of 'utter contrast' which is overcome
only through the miracle of the eternal God himself. Or is
there a stranger, more incomprehensible factor in this world,
one more in need of God's revelation, than one's 'fellow-man'?
'Highest valuation of morality' – gladly, but do we *love* our
neighbour? Are we capable of it? And if we do *not* love *him*,
what about our love of *God*? What shows more plainly than
this 'core' (not of the gospel, but of the law) that God does not
give life unless he takes it first?

(6) 'No one can come to me unless the Father who sent me
draws him and I will raise him up at the last day.'

(7) Statements about God derived from 'the development
of culture, from the knowledge gathered by culture and from
ethics' may as expressions of special 'experiences of God'
(*Gotteserlebnisse*) (e.g. the experiences of the War) have their
significance and value in comparison with the experiences of
primitive peoples who do not yet know such great treasures.
(Consider, for example, the significance and value of the statements of the War-theologians of all countries.) *These* statements
can definitely not be considered as the 'preaching of the
gospel' (3). Whether they *protect* culture and the individual
'against atheism' or whether they *sow* atheism, since they come
out of polytheism, would remain an *open* question in each
individual case.

(8) 'Real statements about God' are made in any way only
where one is aware of being confronted by *revelation* and therefore of being placed under judgment instead of believing oneself to be on a pinnacle of culture and religion. Under this
judgment stand together with all other statements about this
subject also those of Goethe and Kant. Schleiermacher's alarm
about 'barbarism' is to be rejected as non-essential and irrelevant because the gospel has as much and as little to do with
'barbarism' as with culture.

(9) It may be that *in the sphere* of human statements about
God 'opposites are at one and the same time steps and steps are

opposites, as in all physical and spiritual development', yet it is still true that between *God's* truth (which may be expressed in human terms also) and *our* truth there is only contrast, only an *either–or*. (It is more urgent, for *theology* in any case, to 'grasp' and to 'develop' *this* knowledge!) Humility, yearning and supplication, will always be the first and also the last thing *for us*. The way from the old to the new world is *not* a stairway, *not* a development in any sense whatsoever; it is a being born anew.

(10) If the knowledge that 'God is love' is the *highest* and *final knowledge about God*, how can one consistently pretend to be in possession of it? Is not the 'transition point' just as long in duration as time? Is not *our* faith also always unfaith? Or should we believe in our *faith*? Does not faith live by being faith in God's *promise*? Are we saved in a way other than in *hope*?

(11) 'The peace of God which is higher than our understanding,' Phil. 4: 7. The 'barrier' of this 'higher' is a basic and insurmountable one. If he does 'keep our hearts and minds in Christ Jesus' and thus makes *possible* the admonition of Phil. 4: 8 ('Whatever is true . . .'), then *as such* he is *higher* than our understanding. There is a relation between him and what *we* call good, true and beautiful, but this relation is precisely the 'barrier', the divine *crisis*, on the basis of which alone one may first speak seriously about the good, the true and the beautiful.

(12) If sin should perhaps be more than a 'lack of reverence and love', namely man's *fall* from *God* and his being lost in a godlikeness the end of which is *death*, then the preaching of God's holy majesty and love is a task which does not seem to spare our human thinking and speaking from wandering on *curious* ways. A *spectator*-theology may then speak of 'all kinds of paradoxes and whims'. He who is in a position to solve this – but *this* same – task more easily must show how it is done. Historical knowledge tells us that Paul and Luther were *not* in that position.

(13) *Which* theological tradition is it that, having begun with the apotheosis of 'feeling', has apparently landed happily in the swamp of the psychology of the unconscious? *Who* thought that a special 'religious' source of knowledge could be

opened up apart from critical reason? And *ad vocem* 'gnostic occultism': which theology is at every moment notoriously close to the danger of losing its ablest devotees to Dr Steiner?

(14) The reliability and communality of the knowledge of the person of Jesus Christ as the centre of the *gospel* can be none other than that of the God-awakened *faith*. Critical-historical study signifies the deserved and necessary end of *those* 'foundations' of this knowledge which are no foundations at all since they have not been laid by God himself. Whoever does not yet know (and this applies to all of us) that we *no* longer know Christ according to the flesh, should let the critical study of the Bible tell him so. The more radically he is frightened the better it is for him and for the matter involved. This might turn out to be the service which 'historical knowledge' can render to the actual task of theology.

(15) If theology were to regain the courage to face up to concrete objectivity (*Sachlichkeit*), the courage to bear witness to the *Word* of revelation, of judgment and of *God's* love, the outcome might well be that 'science in general' would have to seek 'strong ties and a blood-relationship' with theology instead of the other way around; for it would be better perhaps also for jurists, physicians and philosophers if they knew what theologians ought to know. Or should the present fortuitous *opinio communis* of others really be the instance through which we have to let our work be judged as to its 'persuasiveness and value'?

Göttingen   Karl Barth

HARNACK TO BARTH

OPEN LETTER TO PROFESSOR KARL BARTH

I thank you for replying to my 'fifteen questions'. They were addressed to you *also*, yes, especially to you.

Your answers have made a few things clearer to me, but for that very reason the opposition between us has become all the clearer. I shall try to show this in what follows. Other things have remained totally obscure for me or perhaps they have become so, especially your answer to my first question. Despite

much hard effort, it is wholly incomprehensible to me. Since
very much depends on this basic question, one of the main
issues, namely your concept of revelation, stays under the cover
of a heavy fog.

Concerning the title of my questions and question 15: you
see in contemporary scientific theology an unstable and transitory product which has been in the making since Pietism and
the Enlightenment and that it has the value of an *opinio
communis* only. I see in it the only possible way of grasping the
object epistemologically. This way is old and new at the same
time, new because it has attained to greater clarity and maturity only since the eighteenth century and old because it began
when man started thinking. You say that 'the task of theology
is at one with the task of preaching'; I reply that the task of
theology is at one with the task of science in general. The task
of preaching is the pure presentation of the Christian's task as
a witness to Christ. You transform the theological professor-
ship into the pulpit-ministry (and desire to hand over to secular
disciplines what is known as 'theology'). On the basis of the
whole course of Church-history I predict that this undertaking
will not lead to edification but to dissolution. Or is what you
have to say meant to act only as a 'ferment'? No one could
make this his intention and surely it is not part of your plan.
Nevertheless, I acknowledge the ferment: the courage to be
objective, the courage to be a witness.

Concerning questions 2 and 3: I cannot see what in your
opinion is to remain when one is obliged to do away with 'inner
openness, heuristic knowledge, experience, heart, historical
knowledge and critical reflection' in connection with the understanding of the religion of the Bible. It is true, you say the
'religion of the Bible is understood by virtue of that Spirit
which is identical with the content of the Bible and that by
faith', but since you add 'the so-called experience of God is thus
as different as heaven and earth from the awakening of faith
by God and is practically indistinguishable from uncontrolled
fanaticism', your 'thus' is as incomprehensible to me as the
justification of your illustration or your determination of the
relation between the experience of God and faith. I am unable
to speak about things incomprehensible. To my joy you sub-
scribe to the thesis 'faith comes from the preaching of the Word

of the Christ', but just as your 'the Christ' in place of 'Jesus Christ' looks unfortunate to me in view of Church-historical considerations, my suspicions are heightened because of the context in which you use the Pauline 'we know Christ no longer according to the flesh'. So, we do not know the historical Jesus Christ of the gospels any more? How am I to understand that? By the theory of the exclusive inner word? Or by which of the many other subjectivistic theories?

Concerning question 4: it grieves me that you gave it a very devious answer only; 'the faith awakened by God will never be able to avoid completely (!) the necessity of a more or less (!) radical protest against this world as surely as it is a hope for the promised but invisible gift'. Are you by any chance not quite sure about this point? It would have been better then to postpone the answer. But since it looks half-baked it lacks either understanding or the courage to witness.

Concerning question 5: you answer my question about the love of God and the love of one's neighbour in terms of a problematical conceptuality of 'the neighbour' and 'love of the neighbour' which is especially characteristic of your theology, yes, but not of the gospel which knows no problems here at all. In your presentation I see a very great separation from the simple gospel.

Concerning question 6 (about the possibility of education in godliness): you simply answer with John 6: 44. If that is all you have to say here, then you condemn all Christian pedagogy and sever, like Marcion, every link between faith and the human. In my view you have the example of Jesus against you.

Concerning questions 7 and 9: you assert that in each individual case it is an open question whether the cognition of God, evolved in the history of man, excepting revelation, protects against or sows atheism. This is only half an answer to my question as to whether God is *not at all* whatever is said about him on the basis of the development of culture, on the basis of the knowledge gathered by culture and on the basis of ethics. Or may I assume that you reject such an assertion with me? Hardly! For your sentence 'the gospel has as much and as little to do with barbarism as with culture' can be understood only as a radical denial of every valuable understanding of God within the history of man's thought and ethics. Your point of view becomes completely plain when you say that 'between God's truth and our truth there is only contrast, only an either–or. The way from the old to the new world is not a stairway, not a development in any sense whatsoever, but rather a being born anew.' Does this not exclude the belief that one's being a Christian happened precisely in that way, while at the same time one admits that God let it happen on a stairway on which eternal values had already been given? Remember Augustine's account of his becoming a Christian!

Concerning questions 10 and 11: your answers to them are in my view those which move away the furthest from the Christianity of the gospel on account of the problematics into which you draw the Christian faith. You said that the transition point from godlessness to God lasts for every Christian as long as time; *our* faith, you said, is also always unfaith; we are saved only in hope; there is a relation between what we call good, true and beautiful and the peace of God only insofar as a barrier is also a relation, etc. By answering my questions like this, in terms of what Christianity still lacks and of what we all know, you shatter what we already possess, for you make the Christian's confidence . . . in which he is allowed to live, an illusion, and his joy, which is to fill his life, you turn into frivolity. You will dispute this, but what you put in their place is the description of a state of mind which in the best of cases only a handful may know as the peace of God, a state of mind which is in no way a necessary precondition for all Christian humility.

From this vantage point your answer to question 12 becomes understandable. The simple gospel out of which Jesus told his understandable and comforting parables for the salvation of souls does not suit you; Christian preaching rather can 'not spare man's thinking and speaking from wandering on curious paths'. How many will ever be able to understand you, seeing that you are wholly submerged in highly sublime psychology and metaphysics? Then you turn surprisingly to Paul and Luther. But even here I have no doubt that today too every Christian will find it easier to live according to their teaching and example than to yours. But are Paul and Luther examples to be emulated? Can we slip on their armour? Must we smaller ones torment ourselves in order to experience what they did? It is – and now let me be problematical for once – our strength and at the same time our destiny to have experienced Paul and Luther. Against this destiny will work only the comforting word which precisely they call out to us: I believe in the forgiveness of sins.

You did not answer question 13 but merely left it with the remark that prevalent theology or one of its developments has led into the swamp of the psychology of the unconscious and into occultism. Since that question was not directed to you but to another address, I can remain silent here although I must say that occultism is by divine decree the punishment for every form of contempt of reason and science and that every period of time has only one science.

For question 14 I also miss a succinct answer. Does the awakening of faith, insofar as it includes the knowledge of the person of Jesus Christ as the centre of the gospel, take place without regard for his historical person? If this is to be answered negatively, can faith dispense with historical knowledge of that person? If this is to be answered affirmatively, can the critical-historical study of this person with regard to faith be something irrelevant or is it not rather absolutely necessary? What you say here in relation to biblical science may be formulated like this: the most radical biblical science is always right and thank heaven for that, because now we may be rid of it. This point of view, known to the point of nausea from recent, second-rate Church-history, opens the gate to every suitable fantasy and to every theological dictatorship which dissolves the historical ingredient of our religion and seeks to torment the conscience of others with one's own heuristic knowledge.

I do sincerely regret that the answers to my questions only point out the magnitude of the gap that divides us. But then neither my nor your theology matters. What does matter is that the gospel is correctly taught. Should however your way of doing this come to prevail it will not be taught any more; it will rather be given over into the hands of devotional preachers who freely create their own understanding of the Bible and who set up their own dominion.

Yours respectfully
von Harnack

BARTH TO HARNACK

AN ANSWER TO PROFESSOR ADOLF VON HARNACK'S
OPEN LETTER

Esteemed Dr von Harnack,

It is not necessary to state explicitly that your extensive discussion of my answers to your questions is an honour for which
I am grateful to you. Nevertheless I enter with hesitation upon
the task of giving more information to you about my theological
thoughts. The editor thought it something which in view of
your letter was the natural thing to do. But you yourself have
stated that my answers have shown you only the gap that
divides us. Is it not pointless and annoying to pose further
riddles to you now and more than likely to most of the readers
of *Christliche Welt*? My position is unpleasant in yet another way:
the first time you posed real questions to which I, as one of
those to whom they were addressed, had to answer as well or
as badly as I could. In your letter, however, you confront me
as someone – and I have absolutely no intention of challenging
your right in this, you, who are one of my revered teachers of
former times – who has accomplished his tasks, has obtained
knowledge and who, because of the experience and the reflections of a rich life, has no time and no ear not only for answers
different from those he would himself give but also for questions
other than his own. Is there any further answer to be given to
questions? Is the discussion not over? But since you wanted
to tell me that it was not my answers you had in mind when
you raised your original questions – something I never doubted
– I think that I owe it to you and to our listeners to confess that
I do consider my answers open to debate, but that still for
the time being and until I am shown a better way I reserve all
else to myself. Nonetheless, your objections cannot deter me
from continuing to ask along the line of those answers. Allow
me, therefore, to touch again on every point and to draw some
of them together. For a real understanding of my continued
opposition I would refer to my publications as well as to those
of my friends Gogarten and Thurneysen, something you would
do also were you in a similar situation. (For the other group
of those to whom you addressed yourself I assume no respon-

sibility.) More to the general public as to you I would like to
say that in the end no effective repudiation of our views will be
possible without a serious study of our point of view.

You see in what you call 'scientific theology' 'the only possible way of grasping the object epistemologically' and you call
it 'new because it has attained to greater clarity and maturity
only since the eighteenth century, old since it began when man
started to think'. I hope that I am not reading anything into
your position when I assume, based on that explicit reference
to the eighteenth century, that the Reformers Luther and
Calvin (together with that unfortunate tribe of 'revival preachers') would fail to qualify as 'scientific theologians', whereas
Zwingli and Melanchthon might not. I would also assume that
for you the idea of considering the Apostle Paul (in addition to
whatever else he was) as one of those theologians is quite out
of the question. Be that as it may, I believe I know 'thinking
men' in earlier and later centuries who as theologians pursued
wholly different ways from those which since the eighteenth
century have been regarded as normal, men whose scientific
quality (should 'scientific quality' mean objectivity) it would
in my opinion be hazardous to doubt. The appeal to Paul's or
Luther's theology is for you nothing but a presumptuous
attempt at imitation. On this side of the 'gap' the process looks
relatively simple. We have been irresistibly impressed by the
material superiority of those and other older theologians, however little they may fit into the present scheme of the guild. We,
therefore, cannot feel ourselves relieved, by the protest of the
spirit of modern times (which perhaps has to learn to understand itself first!) nor by the faith in the forgiveness of sins (!)
which you invoked, of our duty to consider the fundamental
point of departure of those theologians more seriously in regard
to its total justification than was done especially in recent
theology in spite of all the research into Paul and the enthusiasm
for Luther. There can be no question of any repristination here
whatsoever. It is my private view that the exercise of repristi-
nating a classical theological train of thought, which in the
days of medieval and Protestant scholasticism was known as
'theology', is probably more instructive than the chaotic business of today's faculties for which the idea of a determinative
object has become strange and monstrous in face of the deter-

minate character of the *method*. But I also think I know that
this *same* kind of thing can and should not return and that we
must think *in* our time *for* our time. Actually the point is not
to keep the historical-critical method of biblical and historical
research developed in the last centuries away from the work of
theology, but rather to fit that method, and its refinement of
the way questions are asked, into that work in a meaningful
way. I think I said this in my answers 2, 3, and 14 and may
thus be permitted to express astonishment that you still accuse
me of regarding critical biblical science as something 'devious',
of wishing to be 'rid of it', and must therefore be threatened with
the punishment of occultism which is decreed by 'divine order'
for despisers of reason and science. What I must defend myself
against is not historical criticism but rather the foregone conclusiveness with which – and this is characteristic also of your
present statements – the task of theology is *emptied*, that is to
say, the way in which a so-called 'simple gospel', discovered by
historical criticism *beyond* the 'Scriptures' and *apart from* the
'Spirit', is given the place which the Reformers accorded to the
'Word' (the correlation of 'Scripture' and 'Spirit'). Such a
gospel can be called 'God's Word' only metaphorically because
it is at best a human impression of it. The sentence so repug-
nant to you and others, to the effect that the task of theology is
at one with the task of preaching is for me an *inevitable* statement
of the *programme* (in the carrying out of which, of course, many
things must still be considered). In this I assume it is conceded
that the preacher must by right proclaim 'the Word' and not
perhaps his own heuristic knowledge, experiences, maxims and
reflections. You have said that the truth of preaching and of
faith come about 'through the Word of the Christ'. (The
definite article before 'Christ' is of no consequence to me at all.)
If the transmission of this 'Word' is the preacher's task then
it is also that of the theologian (who finds himself at least in
virtual personal union with the former). The tactical and
practical differences in accomplishing this are obvious as is the
understanding that some of the things which belong to the
lectern are to be left out in the pulpit and vice versa. The
theme, however, which the theologian must pursue in history
and which he must strive to express in a manner appropriate to
his situation, cannot be a *second* truth *next to* that which he is

obliged to present as a preacher. *That* was self-evident in the beginnings of Protestant theology (I think especially of Zürich and Geneva). I cannot see how the subsequent abstract separation of 'scholarly' and 'edifying' thought and speech can be derived from the essence of the matter. However, if it be right to assume the unity of the theologian's and the preacher's task, what is completely ruled out as a theme for one as well as for the other, along with everything that is merely human impression and not God's Word, is a 'simple gospel' which as alleged 'revelation' remains in the Bible, after the sufficient ground of cognition for all revelation, given in the correlation of 'Scripture' and 'Spirit', has been radically eliminated.

But at this point arises your categorical declaration that my *'concept of revelation'* is *'totally'* (the italics are yours!) 'incomprehensible' to you. You had asked in question 1 how one might come to find out what the content of the gospel is without historical knowledge and critical reflection. I answered in the first instance that the gospel itself tells us that this understanding occurs exclusively through an action (through deed and word) of this very 'content' (of God or Christ or the Spirit). Surely you will not demand individual citations for this thesis. In the second instance ,I said concerning critical reflection that it cannot be good to reverse the order and turn 'Thus says the Lord' into 'Thus hears man'. If there is a way to *this* 'content', then the content itself must be the way; the speaking voice must be the listening ear. All other ways do not lead to this goal, all other ears do not hear this voice. The fact that God is himself the goal as well as the way is something – and I gladly concede this – which to *me* as to *you* is *totally* incomprehensible, not only 'fog', but, to speak with Luther, darkness. If you were to tell me that one cannot believe in a way from God *to us*, to which there does not correspond apparently any way from us *to God* (for it is always most exclusively God's way *to us*), I could only reply that deep down in my heart I think exactly the same. But then, is it not already included, quite apart from what the Bible says about it on every page, in the concept of revelation (and really not only in *my* concept!) that one cannot 'believe' it? Would it not be better to renounce this highsounding word if revelation were only the designation of a very sublime or a very deep but still a possible human discovery?

Or should we theologians, if we do not wish to do this, not get up enough courage to let our theology begin with the perhaps essentially sceptical but nevertheless clear reminder of the 'totally incomprehensible', inaudible and unbelievable, the *really* scandalous testimony that God himself has said and done something, something *new* in fact, outside of the correlation of all human words and things, but which *as* this new thing he has injected *into* that correlation, a word and a thing next to others but *this* word and *this* thing? I am not talking now of the possibility of accepting this testimony. I only ask whether we should not for once *reckon* more soberly with the fact that what is called Christianity made its first and for us recognisable beginning with this testimony? This testimony, which historical criticism cannot analyse enough, and which will not cease being *this* testimony when thus analysed, I call in its totality 'the Scriptures'. The delineation of 'the Scriptures' over against other scriptures appears to me a secondary question. Should an extra-canonical writing contain in a notable fashion this very testimony, there can be no *a priori* impossibility of letting this testimony speak through it also, no, quite to the contrary. From this observation, however, to the canonisation of *Faust*, for example, there is a long way which a discerning Church just will *not* travel.

The Scriptures then witness to revelation. One does not have to believe it, nor *can* one do it. But one should not deny that it witnesses to revelation, *genuine* revelation that is, and not to a more or less concealed religious possibility of man but rather to the possibility of God, namely that *he* has acted under the form of a human possibility – and this as *reality*. According to this testimony, the Word became flesh, God himself became a human-historical *reality* and that this took place in the *person of Jesus Christ*. But from this it by no means follows for me that this event can also be an object of human-historical *cognition*; this is excluded because and insofar as *this* reality is involved. The existence of a Jesus of Nazareth, for example, which can of course be discovered historically, is not *this* reality. A historically discernible 'simple gospel', discernible because it is humanly plausible, a 'simple gospel' which causes no scandal, a 'simple gospel', that is, in your sense, a word or a deed of this Jesus which would be nothing other really than the realisation

of a human possibility – would not be *this* reality. I doubt
whether it is possible at any cogent point to separate one word
or one deed of Jesus from the background of this reality, even
considered only historically, that is, from the Scripture which
witnesses to revelation and so to the scandal it causes and then
proceed to interpret it as the 'simple gospel' in your sense. Why,
for example, I regard this as impossible in reference to the
command to love God and one's neighbour, I mentioned in
my fifth answer, for which you have chastised but not refuted
me. I can now only in passing enter protest against your description of the parables of Jesus (*die Gleichnisse Jesu*) as 'understandable and comforting' parables (*Parabeln*)* and I hope to
have in both cases at least some historians on my side. But even
if you could succeed in claiming some point or other in the
tradition for your position, it would merely mean that this
point is *not*, or *is* only in context with other points, the object of
the testimony or the kerygma which is surely in your judgment
also the sole issue for the New Testament writings. The object
of the *testimony* has been made known by the apostles and
evangelists to such an extent as *revelation*, as the action of God
himself, it has been thrust back so deeply into an impenetrable
hiddenness and *protected* so strongly from every desire for *direct*
perception, that not only all statements which obviously refer
to this 'centre of the gospel', found for example in that rather
threatening bundle in the second article of the Creed, but in
fact the 'Sermon on the Mount' as well, the parabolic and
polemical speeches of Jesus and the account of his passion, all
leave the circumspect reader with the conclusion that there can
be no question of speaking here of a direct historical *comprehensibility* of this 'historical' *reality* (revelation). All that is comprehensible is always that other which makes up the historical
context of the alleged revelation.

Beyond this 'other' that barrier goes up and the scandal, the
fable or the miracle threatens. The historical reality of Christ
(as revelation, as 'centre of the gospel') is not the 'historical
Jesus' whom an all too eager historical research had wanted to

---

* The word *Parabeln* carries a somewhat negative sound here. It does not
convey what the word actually used for the parables in the NT, *Gleichnis*, does.
Parabel is used in a sense of 'tale' as in: fishermen tell tales of their exploits.
(Translator's note.)

lay hold of in disregard of the very warnings made in the sources themselves (coming upon a banality which has been and shall be proclaimed in vain as a pearl of great price). Nor is it, as you said, an imagined Christ but rather the *risen one*, or let us say with more restraint in view of our little faith: the Christ who is *witnessed to* as the risen one. That is the 'evangelical, the historic Jesus Christ' and otherwise, that is, apart from the testimony to him, apart from the revelation which must here be believed, 'we know him no longer'. In this sense I think I can legitimately appeal to 2 Corinthians 5: 16. At this decisive point, that is, in answering the question: what makes Jesus the Christ? in terms of the reference to the *resurrection*, one is indeed left from man's point of view with what you called 'totally' incomprehensible. And I gladly confess that I would a hundred times rather take the side of the No, the refusal to believe which you proclaim on the basis of this fact, than the talents of a 'positive' theology which ends up making what is incomprehensible altogether self-evident and transparent once again, for that is an emptying and a denying of revelation which with its apparent witness to the revelation is worse than the angriest refusal to believe which at least has the advantage of being suited to the subject matter. My declaration of sympathy for the 'most radical' biblical science was meant in this sense. The theology of the Reformers did not need this negative discipline because it still had the courage not to avoid the scandal of revelation. It thus never raised the question of a historically discernible core of the gospel. *We* need it, however, because we have fallen into this impossible question through flight from the scandal. I see the theological function of historical criticism especially in the task of making clear to us *a posteriori* that there is *no road* this way, and that in the Bible we have to do with testimonies and *only* with *testimonies*. I notice that this is the function it has in fact fulfilled among us since David Friedrich Strauss, and done so excellently in its own way, even if it is not widely understood and above all unaware of what it was doing.

The *acceptance* of this unbelievable testimony of the Scriptures I call *faith*. Again I do not claim that this is a discovery of *my* theology. I do ask, however, what else faith could be – disregarding sentimentalities – but the obedience I give to a human word which testifies to the Word of God as a word

addressed to me, as if it were itself God's Word? Let no one
have any delusions here about the fact that this is an unprecedented event, that here one must speak of the *Holy Spirit* if all
the objections Herrmann rammed into our heads against a
'mere credence' in historical facts *apart* from this basis of cognition are not to hold good. Therefore I distinguish faith as
God's working on us (for only he can say to us, in such a way that
we will hear it, what *we* can*not* hear, 1 Corinthians 2: 9) from all
known and unknown human organs and functions, even our
so-called 'experiences of God'. Is that such an unheard-of
novelty? Must I, as one of the Reformed tradition, ask whether
Luther's explication of the third article in the *Small Catechism*
is valid or not? Do you really not see that through the rash
abandonment of *this* concept of faith in favour of the lentil-
pottage of a less paradoxical one, the doors have been opened to
the anthroposophic *tohuwabohu* of faith and occult 'capabilities' of
man, confronted with which official theology is simply at a loss?

It has to be thus: whatever may be said against the possibility of revelation can with equal strength be said also against
the possibility of faith. That leaves us with this as the *second*
excluded possibility: God who according to the witness of the
Scriptures has spoken 'the Word of Christ' speaks that Word
also to *me through* the witness of the Scriptures empowered
through the *testimonium Spiritus Sancti internum*, so that I *hear* it
and by hearing it *believe*. Is this the 'theory of the exclusive
inner word' or one of the many 'other subjectivistic theories'?
In your third question you yourself spoke of the *awakening* of
faith. I agree, but hold that what we are concerned with here,
as also in the 'understandable and comforting parable' of the
prodigal son, Luke 15: 32, is the awakening of someone dead,
that is, with *God's miracle* just as in revelation. Indeed, I have
no confidence in any objectivity other than the one described
in this way or in terms of the correlate concepts of 'Scripture'
and 'Spirit', least of all in the pontifications of a science which
would first have to demonstrate its absolute superiority over
the subjectivist activity of the 'preachers of awakening' by
means of results.

But then, honoured Sir, you have conjured up against me
the shadow of Marcion with the assertion that I 'sever the link
between faith and the human'. May I ask how you derive that

from my answers 2 and 3? Have I really made *tabula rasa* with
those human organs, functions and experiences? It is not my
intention to do this. I really think that man goes on living
whether he believes it or not, that he goes on as man, in time,
in the world of things, dependent from his point of view exclusively on his own human possibilities. I think I also know
that man's faith can at every moment be completely described
as 'inner openness', 'heuristic knowledge', 'experience', 'religion', 'historical knowledge', 'critical reflection', etc., just as
the testimony of revelation also *can*, yes, *must* be described as a
piece of unpleasantly dark human intellectual and cultural
history (unless God himself intervenes!). But I would do no
'severing' at all here or there (that would only be a completely
senseless undertaking!); I would rather say that the human is
the relative, the testimony, the parable and thus not the
absolute *itself* on some pinnacles or heights of development as
one would certainly conclude from your statements. The human
rather is the *reference* (understood or not understood) to the
absolute. In view of this the historically and psychologically
discernible, that which we know in ourselves and others as
'faith' would be a witness to and a symptom of that action and
miracle of God on us, of that faith, in other words, which,
created through the 'Word' and 'steeped in the Word' is, as
Luther said, our righteousness before God himself. The religions of the Bible, with which you began your first question,
would in the same way be witness to and symptom of the
historical reality of God's incarnation. But the ground for
knowing both justifying faith and revelation would be God's
action on us through his Word. Does my point of view really
not become clear to you?

⟨However, and here I think I come to the nerve of all your
objections, I am indeed *content* with the testimonial character
of all that which occurs here and there in time and as a result
of man. I explicitly *deny* the possibility of positing anything
relative as absolute, somehow and somewhere, be it in history
or in ourselves, or in Kierkegaardian terms, of going from
testimony to 'direct statement'.⟩ If I do not wholly misunderstand the Bible and the Reformation, the latter is and must
remain, in the most exclusive sense, God's concern. The fact
that eternity becomes time, that the absolute becomes relative,

that God becomes man (and *thus* – and only thus – in each case
the reverse also!), in other words, the fact that the matter
involved coincides with the sign pointing to it and *thus* the
coincidence of the sign with the matter to which it points, as
Luther, with final insight, remarked in his teaching on the
Lord's Supper, while touching on the natural-titanic presumptuousness of the *homo religiosus*, is true only as the 'Word and
work of God', as the act of the Trinity itself. This act can only
be *witnessed to* and *believed* because it is revealed. It is never a
historical-psychological reality which becomes directly cognisable for example in our religious experience, in the *dénou-
ments* of our consciences, in the relations between man and
man, even in the purest of them, in the thoughts of Goethe and
Kant about God or in whatever towers of human god-likeness
you may mention. When this reality becomes cognisable here
or there, then the miracle has occurred which we cannot *deny*,
with which, however, we cannot *reckon* as with any other
possibility or even with a general truth. We must worship it
when it is *present* (present as the miracle of God!). My rejoinder
to your reproof of 'severing' (which I cannot acknowledge as
justified), is that you empty faith by asserting a continuity
between the 'human' and faith just as you empty revelation by
saying that there is a continuity between history and revelation.
I do not sever; I do repudiate every continuity between hither
and yonder. I speak of a dialectical *relation* which points to an
identity which cannot be established nor, therefore, presumed
by us. *Parabolic* value only is, therefore, to be given to the
images of those stairways which 'Christian' *biography* of all ages
is in the habit of unfolding before us (an undertaking which
despite or rather in view of Augustine is just as promising as it is
ambiguous). *Parabolic* value only is to be given to the efforts
also and successes of 'Christian' *pedagogy*, which truly and for
good reason has never been able to be rid of heathenism. We
honour and do not dishonour this pedagogy when we put it
under the hope and judgment of John 6: 44. *Parabolic* value
is, however, also to be given to all 'Christian' protest against
the world which as a human undertaking (why do you insist
on concluding that I am irresponsible here? I shall repeat my
'devious' answer in its full form) is really a more or less 'radical'
protest only, a 'half-baked', a small protest, a demonstration,

a gesture which can never, never wish to anticipate and realise the end of this world and the coming of the kingdom. Parable, parable only can be all 'becoming' in view of the birth from death to life through which alone (but only on the way which God takes and is), we come from the truth of man to the truth of God.

Still in connection with the charge of Marcionism, you demand from me a full answer to the question 'whether God is simply unlike anything said about him on the basis of the development of culture, on the basis of the knowledge gathered by culture and on the basis of ethics'. Very well, then, but may I ask you really to listen to my whole answer. *NO*, God is 'absolutely not at all that', as surely as the Creator is not the creature or even the creation of the creature. But precisely in this *NO*, which can be uttered in its full severity only in the faith in revelation, the creature recognises itself as the work and the possession of the Creator. Precisely in this *NO* God is known as *God*, as the source and the goal of the *thoughts* of God which man, in the darkness of his culture and his decadence, is in the habit of forming. ‖For this *NO*, posited with finality by revelation, is not without the 'deep, secret *YES* under and above the *NO*' which we should 'grasp and hold to with a firm faith in God's Word' and 'confess that God is right in his judgment against us, for then we have won'. This is how it is with that *NO*: 'nothing but *YES* in it, but always deep and secretly and always seeming to be nothing but *NO*'. What lover of contradictoriness might have said that? Kierkegaard or Dostoyevsky? No, Martin Luther! (*E.A.* 11, 120). Is Luther to be suspected then of Marcionism too?‖According to Zwingli, yes, but I think that you and I understand him better than that. So, why should you not understand *me* a little better at the same time? Does the human really become insignificant when, in the faith in revelation, its *crisis* occurs which makes forever impossible every identification between here and the beyond, excepting always the one which it does not become us to express (about the end of all things forseen in 1 Corinthians 15: 28)? Does it really not become full of significance and promise, really serious and possible precisely through being moved out of the twilight of supposed fulfilment into the light of real *hope*? Is it really *not* enough for *us* to have and to behold in the transitory the parable of the intransitory, to live in it and to work for it, to be glad as men that we have at least the *parable* and to suffer as men under the fact that it is *only* the parable, *without*, however, anticipating the 'swallowing up of death in victory' in a spurious consciousness of eternity exactly *because* the great temporal *significat* applies to the greater eternal *est* and nothing else? Have I really made '*tabula rasa*'?

Yes, you say so, honoured Sir, and you must know *why*, although you cannot deduce it from my statements. I am afraid that you *must* really misunderstand me *precisely at this point*, even if we could agree about revelation and faith. Why is it that right here, where of all things the existential question of our relation to God and the world, where the confirmation in hope of faith in revelation is involved, you unambiguously exchange the role of the defender of *science* for that of the defender of the so-called 'Christian' possession? Why the lament about the 'sublimity' of my metaphysics and psychology, as if all of a sudden *popular intelligibility* were for you the standard of right theology? What is the meaning of measuring the distances which, more here and less there, separate me from the 'Christianity of the gospels', as if the topic of our discussion were all of a sudden the *Christian nature* of my theology? What is the meaning of the charge of 'commending' a 'state of mind', unpalatable to you, when the point of your scientific misgivings was that neither revelation nor faith was made understandable by me in the familiar, 'simple' fashion as a state of mind, when, in other words, *the state of mind* was introduced by you into our discussion? Why all those strong words about 'illusion', 'frivolity', 'lover of contradictoriness', etc., when you have certainly not demonstrated, from my perhaps unsatisfactory, but nevertheless circumspect answers, the right to such tumultuous conclusions and accusations? How am I to explain the transition from instruction to admonition and how am I to answer it? ʼYou can surely guess that I too have angry thoughts about the connection between the *scientific* character of your theology, which causes you to repudiate what I (and not only I) call revelation and faith, and your own *Christian position*, which comes out into the open in the idea that Paul's 'saved in hope' must be suspected as 'problematical'. ·I too would be in the position of registering strongest scruples and of uttering very sharp words where the misunderstanding between us seems so hopeless. Yet what else would I do then but seal this hopelessness on my part too, something that must not be done? It is better in every respect to break off here.

Yet let me repeat: I do not intend to entrench myself in those positions in which you, honoured Sir, and our voluntary-involuntary audience in this conversation have seen me, simply because I know how frighteningly relative *everything* is that one can *say* about the great subject which occupies you and me. I know that it will be necessary to speak of it in a way quite different from that of my present understanding. I would like to be able to listen attentively in the future to whatever *you* also will have to say. But at this time I cannot concede that you have driven me off the field with your questions and answers, although I will gladly endure it when it really happens.

Respectfully Yours
Karl Barth

HARNACK TO BARTH

A POSTSCRIPT TO MY OPEN LETTER TO
PROFESSOR KARL BARTH

Professor Barth has given a very detailed answer to my open letter. I thank him for his full presentation. To my disappointment I cannot continue the discussion now and in this journal, since the number and weight of the problems are too great to be dealt with briefly and in this place. But there are two things which I would not like to leave unsaid.

(1) Paul and Luther are for me not primarily subjects but objects of scientific theology as is Professor Barth and all those who express their Christianity as prophets or witnesses like preachers, whether they do it in biblical commentaries or in dogmatic writings etc. Scientific theology and witnessing are often enough mixed together in life, but neither can remain healthy when the demand to keep them separate is invalidated. Both are objective, not only the witnessing, as one may conclude from Professor Barth's statements, but the kind of objectivity is a very different one in each case. A scientific-theological

presentation *can* also inspire and edify, thanks to its object, but the scientific theologian whose *aim* it is to inspire and to edify brings a foreign flame to his altar. For as there is only *one* scientific method there is also only *one* scientific task: the pure cognition of its object. Whatever other fruit falls to science as a reward is an unexpected gift.

(2) Revelation is not a scientific concept; science can neither draw together under one generic concept nor explain in terms of 'revelation' the God-consciousness of the paradoxical preaching of founders of religion and prophets (and religious experiences in general). There is no future, however, in the attempt to grasp a 'Word' of this kind as something so purely 'objective' that human speaking, hearing, grasping, and understanding can be eliminated from its operation. I have the impression that Professor Barth tries something like that and calls in a dialectic in this attempt which leads to an invisible ridge between absolute religious scepticism and naive biblicism – the most tormening interpretation of Christian experience and Christian faith! But since for centuries it has again and again been presented, the only thing to change is its background, it may be justified individually and must, therefore, be treated with respect. But can it create a community and are the blows justified with which it beats down everything that presents itself as Christian experience? Will there be any room left on that glacial bridge for the children and friends of him who, interpreting the Christian faith in this and never any other way, has been able to find a foothold on it? Would it not be better for him to admit that he is playing *his* instrument only and that God has still other instruments, instead of erecting a rigid either–or?

In Barth's answers there becomes apparent in several places a certain sensitiveness which is intensified even to the assertion that my replies sounded like 'admonition'. I cannot be judge in my own case; hence I am glad to say that no other desire moved me in my letter than to reach clarity *vis-à-vis* a theologian friend.

Berlin   Adolf von Harnack

AN ANALYSIS OF THE TEXT

The dialogue begins

The initial questions of Harnack, the point of departure of the whole correspondence, were not at first an attempt 'to reach clarity *vis-à-vis* a theologian friend', as Harnack said at the end of his postscript (above, p. 53). They were rather the expression of a sense of concern for the future of scientific theology. That concern prompted him one day to sit down and on the spur of the moment, without any extensive analysis, to write his impressions of and reactions to the new thinking in academic theology.

What was that concern? What caused Harnack to be alarmed? He believed that in this new thinking theology would no longer retain its status at the university, its status of being a scientific discipline. On the one hand it appeared to avoid the genuinely scientific analysis of the source-materials of theology, leaving this to the 'secular' disciplines, and to uphold a treatment of those sources which is appropriate to the pulpit only. On the other hand it is 'profane because it trespasses on the secret of God and because it makes its understanding of him an export-article'.[1] This alarmed Harnack and he feared that on account of it theology would cease to edify, would rather lead to dissolution, and the gospel would no longer be taught correctly. Instead there would be a theological dictatorship, guided by second-rate men who would only torment others.

What began, however, as a general confrontation between Harnack and the new wave in theology developed, after Barth's first answers, into a dialogue between these two men. Specific points were raised, clarified and refuted. But in the final analysis, the confrontation, the dialogue came to an end without having achieved more than to have Barth 'continue to ask questions in the same direction' as before and to have Harnack unable 'to his disappointment to continue the discussion because the weight of the problems was too great'.

Yet between the first question and the final note of disappointment, between 11 January and 24 May 1923, there lies an encounter rich in challenges, declarations and clarifications. For in it one of the greatest historians of the Church and, from the vantage-point of the last third of the century, one of its greatest theologians meet and lay open to each other their own and their criticism of each other's position.

The fifteen questions can be reduced to a few points in which Harnack's position becomes apparent, along with what he believes to be that of the 'despisers'. But before we make this reduction every question will first be reiterated (in different words, however), so that those points may be more easily perceived.

(1) Is the Bible so plain in what it says that everyone can understand it clearly, simply on account of his experiences? Would it not rather require science to give him understanding?

(2) Can the Bible be understood without help? Or is it so obscure that inspiration alone can give the understanding? Are not rather both science and inner openness required for it?

(3) Is the experience of God identical with that of faith? If not, what is fanaticism in religion? If yes, does it not need the proclamation of the gospel, which requires science as a means of correct understanding?

(4) If the experience of God is different from any other kind of experience, how can one remain in the world and have that experience (for it is beyond question that many *in the world* have had this experience), or better, how can one remain honest, since the withdrawal from the world is a worldly decision (and thus not a real withdrawal, without which apparently that experience is not possible, but nevertheless an undeniable fact)?

(5) The gospel makes the love of God equivalent to the love of man. How then can God and the world be conceived of as opposites? How can one affirm that equivalence without the highest valuation of morality?

(6) (On account of the equivalence in the gospel of the love of God and the love of man) godliness is equivalent to goodness. How can one educate man in goodness without scientific knowledge of what goodness (i.e. godliness) is and without the highest valuation of morality?

C

(7) If God is not what the various aspects of (Christian) culture and morality say about him, how can that culture and morality be protected against their decline and fall into atheism?

(8) If similarly the treasures of that culture are not related to God, how can those treasures be saved from barbarism?

(9) In every development of culture, cultural treasures, or values, or of morality, opposites, i.e. things allegedly unrelated to other facts or factors, are really steps to a higher level. Is this conclusion not impossible to reach without the tools of science?

(10) God is love; love, joy and peace are his sphere. If this is so, how can one say that the Christian is never fully in that sphere and thus perpetuate what the Christian seeks to over-come: the frightening aspects of the ungodly sphere?

(11) If Paul's admonition to virtue, honour and dignity is valid, how can one separate the experience of God from what is good, true and beautiful, i.e. virtuous, honourable and digni-fied, instead of relating the two by means of scientific in-sights?

(12) If sin is a lack in reverence (for God) and love (of man), then it must be overcome. Yet what else but the proclamation of God's holy majesty (which we know through science) can overcome sin? Surely not paradoxes and whims (such as the doctrines of original sin, predestination and election).

(13) If reason is that power which grasps, comprehends, purifies and protects what are the primary data of our experi-ences, i.e. the subconscious, the sensory, the numinous, etc., how can one want to rid oneself of its powers? What else is this desire than to destroy like Herostrates what is excellent and praiseworthy and thus create what is occult?

(14) How is the real person of Christ, the centre of the gospel, to be known in such a way that he and not an imaginary Christ is proclaimed by the Church, if critical-historical study, of scientific theology is despised?

(15) Can there be any other theology than that which, even though it is not perfect, has close ties with science in general? Is theology even theology without such ties? If so, what value and persuasiveness does it have?

What then is the position Harnack *upholds* in these questions?

Historical knowledge and critical reflection are required for an understanding of the Bible and the revelations it contains. Yet something more is needed, an inner openness. Without them, especially without the former two, the awakening of faith as the experience of God is not possible. (Questions 1–3)

Life in God and life in the world are united in the life of religion. This is attested by the life of love for one's fellow-man which is equivalent to the love of God. This means that life in God is a life of high morality. (Questions 4–6)

Culture and morality show us through their development what God is. They are the deposits, so to speak, of the history of the Christian faith in the world. We need historical knowledge and a high moral disposition in order to recognise what God really is in the stairway-like development. (Questions 7–9)

Love, joy and peace are there where God is; they show us conclusively what God is. The true, good and beautiful, wherever they are experienced, show us or let us experience him when we recognise them as such through historical knowledge and critical reflection. (Questions 10 and 11)

The tools of historical knowledge and critical reflection are necessary for the proclamation of God's holy majesty with which one may overcome the sphere of ungodliness, evil and sin. Education in godliness, in the life in God and in high morality, is hindered and defeated when those tools and the criteria of high morality are abandoned. (Question 12)

Reason is necessary for the clear description of what is divine. It is also needed to protect the divine against profanation. Reason alone can show us the true person of Jesus Christ whom we experience. That is to say science alone grasps the historical Jesus, knowledge of whom is absolutely necessary for our religion. Only it can do this objectively and persuasively. (Questions 13–15)

What position does Harnack think the despisers of scientific theology hold? Again his questions can give us the answer.

Historical knowledge and critical reflection are unnecessary for an understanding of the Bible. A simple reference to it suffices because it is so completely a unity. Even if this unity is not perceived, the subjective experience of man is enough anyway because no other faculty of man can grasp that meaning. (Questions 1 and 2)

Harnack regards such a view as naive biblicism and religious fanaticism.

The experience of God is different from the awakening of faith, just as it is different from and even contrary to all other experiences of man. It follows from this that God and the world are complete opposites. (Questions 3–6)

Here Harnack sees a recurrence of a dualism which, as in ancient gnosticism, tears God and the world apart.

God is totally unlike anything said about him on the basis of cultural and ethical insights. So that Goethe's and Kant's wisdom are void of real statements about God. One cannot even regard what they say as opposites on the basis of which one might make deductions leading to the formulation of real statements. (Questions 7–9)

This was for Harnack an outright abrogation on the part of theology of its cultural task; theology has to mediate between the divine and the worldly. But that point of view, that kind of theology 'has lost its connection with the *universitas litterarum* and with culture', as Harnack wrote to Rade.[2]

The Christian may know what God's sphere is, what God is, but he himself is not in that sphere, but rather always 'between door and hinge', i.e. in a stage of transition, which has its own autonomy. (Question 10)

This is pure gnosticism, as far as Harnack is concerned. God's sphere is God's and man's sphere is man's and 'ne'er the twain shall meet'; both have their autonomy. This is the outcome of the dualism that has already been pointed out.

There is no relation between the good, true and beautiful and man's experience of God. Sin is therefore more than the absence of love, goodness and beauty. But what is said about sin is paradoxical and whimsical. (Questions 11 and 12)

The ugly head of a theology which the Church had condemned raises itself in this view-point: dualism and speculativeness. One might even say that it is not theology but ideology which appears here, for such notions as 'the fall, original sin and the like . . . do not stay within the reality of history'.[3]

Reason is belittled, yes repudiated. With it, of course, goes the historical-critical study of the gospels. Theology has in fact given up its relationship to science, its persuasiveness, its value. (Questions 13–15)

Harnack was indeed alarmed to see that the locus of theology was shifted from reason to the dark sphere of subjectivity, for it meant the end of theology as the objective science of the Christian religion, of God as revealed in Jesus Christ. The docetism of that position is a threat to the worship of the Church and has been rightly rejected by it as heresy.

Harnack therefore asks quite rightly: how valuable and how persuasive is a theology, when it is burdened with biblicism, fanaticism, dualism, docetism, gnostic speculations and paradoxes? Is it really theology, really science when it is subjective? How can it be persuasive when it puts itself above its duty to culture and the *universitas litterarum*?

Our sketch of the fifteen questions has shown in summary form the position Harnack upheld and that which he attacked, when he rejected and why he did so. But not until Barth had answered did his criticisms become specific or was his own position clearly stated. We shall therefore turn now, again in outline, to Barth's replies.

(1) The theme of theology is the one revelation of God of which the Bible speaks and to which it refers. This content, which is he who reveals himself as subject, must make itself known to us. What the gospel tells us is that the relation between God and man is the sphere where the content or datum of revelation is found, where it does in fact make itself known. But this sphere is not constituted simply by man's experiences or his heuristic knowledge.

(2) The understanding of the Bible and what it says may be furthered, hindered or not effected at all by man's experiences, the functions of his soul and mind, his knowledge and his reflections. The actual understanding of the Bible comes through him, of whom it speaks, i.e. through its content. Faith alone will understand it, not any function of the soul or mind.

(3) Man's experience of God and the faith awakened by him are thus two radically different things. But this does not mean that that experience cannot in its own way testify to the awakening of faith. Faith comes about, however, through the proclamation of the Word of Christ. Theology is committed to receive and transmit that Word – and so is preaching. In the preparation for the carrying out of that commitment reflection and one's knowledge may very well be helpful.

(4) Faith is the hope for a promised but invisible gift. It thus cannot avoid in some way or other going against the visible world. To forget the separation between the visible and the invisible is to blur the distinction between God and Creator, the source of being, and man the creature who derives from him. There is a unity, a oneness between these two worlds, evident in the cross, but in it the utter contrast between them is also very clearly seen. A theology which cannot stand before that cross, which seeks to bypass it in finding the relation between God and man cannot stand before God because it bypasses him as the Creator.

(5) By coordinating man's life in the world and his life in God, in other words, his life in the visible and the invisible worlds, the gospel points out the utter contrast between them which is overcome only by God himself. By overcoming it God showed us our neighbour. Even if we are highly moral, what if we do not love God? Can we then love our fellow-man? Or the converse, if we do not love our fellow-man, can we love God? Not until God overcomes that contrast, not until he takes life, i.e. in the cross, does he give life and thus open up the possibility of our loving him and our fellow-man with heart, soul and mind.

(6) Education in goodness, yes, gladly. But it will not lead to a life in God. Only God alone will draw us into that life, through death and resurrection.

(7) The various cultural concepts of God are interesting for comparative anthropology. They are not the 'concepts' of the gospel, they do not comprise what the gospel preaches. Whether the former concepts are helpful for culture in its opposition to the challenges of atheism is quite another matter.

(8) Real statements about God, on the other hand, derive from revelation, from one's awareness of being under judgment rather than on the heights of culture and religion. Under this judgment stand all cultural and ethical, all barbaric and atheistic expressions with which the gospel is equally little or equally much concerned.

(9) In the sphere of human expressions there may be graduated development which allows a classification of them into primitive or advanced. In theology, however, where God is spoken of, the rule is: either God's truth or ours. Even though

God's truth may be expressed in human speech, we can still not go beyond humility and supplication. If we are beyond them in the life of God then it is because we are born anew, because the miracle of God's overcoming the contrast, the barrier over which we cannot climb, has occurred.

(10) How can man pretend to have final knowledge of God when his existence in time, in the visible world, is in transition toward eternity, toward the invisible world, when faith is a hope for a promised, yet still invisible gift? Even *this* faith is always also unfaith because it is *man's* faith in something hoped for and thus not at all final and certain.

(11) The barrier between God and us is insurmountable. If, however, we are in Christ and live in God then we are enabled to follow Paul's admonition to virtue. Yet God remains beyond our understanding even then because the relation between him and what we call virtuous, etc. is the divine judgment of the world, the cross in which God has related himself and the world and shown us what is good, true and beautiful.

(12) Sin is also a lack of love but above all a fall away from God into a being lost in a 'godlikeness' which ends in death. The proclamation of God's love cannot avoid following curious avenues – see Paul and Luther for example. Outsiders will call that proclamation paradoxical, burdened with whims and only outsiders will do that.

(13) (This is a typically Barthian reply to an accusation, for all he does is this:) I *only* ask but I do *ask*!

(14) Only faith shows us Jesus Christ reliably as the centre of the gospel. Critical science and study are therefore the end of that knowledge which is not faith, that is which has not been awakened by God himself. We do not know Christ *kata sarka* (according to the flesh) any more, yet do we really know that? Historical knowledge might be of great help in our really coming to know that.

(15) Theology needs the courage to witness to revelation, judgment and God's love, in order to be an objective science with which other disciplines would then perhaps seek stronger relations. For they would then know what theologians ought to know. But the persuasiveness and value of theology are tested by something other than the opinions of those disciplines and vocations concerned with it.

Barth's answers in fact constitute the beginning of the dialogue. On the one hand the position of one of the 'despisers'
is more explicitly stated, so that one can estimate whether
Harnack's evaluation is a fair one, and on the other hand
Harnack's position is being attacked, so that in fact both
positions are challenged into a defence.

But we should establish first what Barth *upholds*.

Theology is concerned with the one revelation of God,
Jesus Christ, who is revealed only through himself. The subject and object of revelation is always God himself. That
means that the object of theology is solely the subject Jesus
Christ, whom we understand and whom we find only through the
Spirit, who again is God himself. This understanding is possible
through faith. But God awakens it through preaching, which
is nothing other than the Word of Christ. (Answers 1–3)

A God-awakened faith, as the hope for a promised but invisible gift, is also a protest against the visible world. This faith
perceives the unity of God and man in their utter contrast, in
the cross. The coordination of the love of God and of man
shows this contrast, insofar as the love of one's neighbour as
one's *neighbour* is not possible without God. The cross (i.e. to
die with Christ) is needed in order for man to perceive and then
to love his neighbour and thus to love God, which is to have
life. That means that the life in God is established in and
through Christ only. (Answers 4–6)

Culture and morality do not show what the gospel proclaims.
Knowledge of God is there only where God places us under the
NO of his judgment, the cross; there is no other alternative.
Thus our knowing God is a being born anew, not a gradual
scientific comprehension. (Answers 7–9)

Knowledge of God is faith which, however, is also always
unfaith because it lives through a promise, and not a fulfilment.
Thus God's love, his joy and peace are 'higher' than our understanding. What we know as good, true and beautiful is not
identical with the good, true and beautiful of God as such, for
only the divine crisis, the utter contrast of God and the world
in which their relatedness is seen, shows us the connection
between the earthly and divine goodness, truth and beauty.
(Answers 10 and 11)

Sin, man's desertion of God, is in need of the proclamation

of God's love and majesty, but this means the preaching of the
crisis, of God's *YES* in his *NO*. (Answer 12)

By lifting the numinous into the pure light of *ratio*, reason
does not achieve anything in terms of man's coming to know
God. Only faith sees Jesus Christ as the centre of the gospel.
This is not just the historical Jesus, Christ *kata sarka*, but the
Christ whom God alone can reveal to us in faith, but for that
reason theology can only bear witness to the Word of the Christ
given in faith. This testimony gives theology its objectivity,
persuasiveness and value. (Answers 13–15)

Barth's answers make it plain that he, too, has certain objections about his interlocutor's position.

Harnack's scientific method of biblical interpretation, that is
to say, his conception of how man comes to understand what
the Bible proclaims, is based on a historical positivism in which
theology and history are identified. But this fails to see that the
Bible is basically a document of testimonies. And here is the
reason why Harnack rejects the identification of the tasks of
theology and preaching. Barth defends his viewpoint because
the understanding of what the Bible proclaims, which is the
task of theology, occurs in an event of God's self-disclosure
which is precisely the event at which both the biblical witness
and the sermon aim.

This event takes place through Jesus Christ, but not simply
the man known by that name but Jesus as the crucified and
resurrected Christ. The cross as the *skandalon* of the biblical
witness must not be avoided, nor must the message of the resurrection be made innocuous. But this is just what Barth sees
occurring in Harnack's teaching. Here is instead a splendid
philosophical structure, founded on the belief in the stairway-
like progression of the divine into the world, here is an idealism
with an ontology of culture. But what has been lost is the
knowledge of the basic distance posited by faith between itself
and the world. The loss of that doctrine results in a weak
doctrine of creation, a cheapening of God's grace and of man's
justification by God.

But the message of the resurrection is equally 'perverted',
insofar as the question of the *historical* Jesus is regarded as
leading to a full understanding of the Christ of the *kerygma*;
the answer to that question leads in fact to 'an imagined instead

of to the real' Christ. The real context of the gospel is neglected
because the historically-psychologically determined view of
Jesus is Ebionite in nature.

When theology attempts to grasp its object by means of the
tools of critical-historical study instead of letting it come to man
through faith, and when furthermore it attempts to speak of
that object as if it were something comparable to the objects of
the other disciplines of science, and comprehensible as a general
truth, then theology may indeed have earned a place in the
ranks of science, of the *universitas litterarum*, but as such it is no
longer *theo*logy. It has lost sight of its object.

The lines of discussion have been drawn. Harnack no longer
faces merely a 'complex of impressions' but the precise formulations and the specific criticism of a particular opponent. The
dialogue, in other words, begins and Harnack can now go
about 'finding clarity *vis-à-vis* a theologian friend'.

HARNACK'S CRITIQUE OF BARTH

Harnack's Open Letter to Barth has the note of regret about it.
'The opposition between us has become more apparent . . .
Things remain totally obscure . . . wholly incomprehensible . . .
under the cover of a heavy fog' (above, p. 35). But even though
this is apparent to Harnack he proceeds to take up each one
of Barth's answers point by point and to state what he sees to
be their opposition. In each case there is a critique of Barth's
position.

'You regard contemporary theology as an unstable product,
which has no more than the value of an *opinio communis*. I
regard it as the only way of grasping the object, the divine,
epistemologically. For me it has attained to a degree of clarity
and maturity never reached before.'

'You regard theology and preaching as identical in their task.
I separate them; theology has the same task as science in general
– the search for truth. Preaching must inform the Christian of
his duties as a witness to Christ. Your point of view makes
academic theology into a preacher's platform and gives what
is divine to the profane, which will destroy theology. Or do
you wish merely to stir up lazy theologians and call them back
to their real work? If so, good, but does this have to be done
in a way such as yours?'

'You make a clean sweep of everything in connection with the understanding of the Bible. What have you left with which to seek that understanding? I am glad you speak of faith, but what do you mean by it when it is not the experience of God, when it is indistinguishable from uncontrolled fanaticism? You say preaching comes from the preaching of the Word of the Christ. Your use of 'the Christ' and your Paulinism – 'we know Christ no longer according to the flesh' – fill me with suspicion. Who is 'the Christ' in your opinion and how do we come to know him?' (The Open Letter on Barth's answers to questions 1–3, 15 and the original title)

Thus far the basic critique is this: Barth maintains a biblicism which leads the believer into gnosticism, because it avoids the systematic and critical analysis of the Bible. Harnack is only too well aware of the Paulinism of Marcion. That man also 'knew Christ no longer according to the flesh' and taught a docetic Christ as a result. Marcionite gnosticism, however, was also an uncontrolled fanaticism, which presented all kinds of speculative ideas. Harnack's keen perception of history led him to see in Barth's identification of the theologian's and the preacher's task an invitation to bypass the groundwork of theology, the analytical work in the Bible. He saw in it the abrogation of the responsibility of theology.

It is really not surprising, therefore, that he regarded this as a despising of scientific theology.

'Some of your answers show a lack of understanding or else a problematical terminology. Therefore, they are on the one hand useless as a witness to Christ and on the other inappropriate to the gospel which he preached. Indeed, you go so far in some instances as to oppose the very example of Jesus. This is because you involve yourself in a Marcionite and problematical conceptuality'. (The Open Letter on Barth's answers to questions 4–6)

Harnack was no 'despiser' of those whose witness to Christ was in the ministry of preaching. 'The task of preaching is the pure presentation of the Christian's task as a witness to Christ' (above, p. 36). Evidently, preaching is indispensable.

The evidence for this is Jesus himself. He preached the gospel simply; he preached the simple gospel. But Barth's preaching is not simple; it is paradoxical and full of penchants. Nor does

he proclaim the gospel; there is rather a speculative conceptuality which, unlike that of Jesus, who spoke of human things in
order to show the divine, cuts the human from the divine.

All this is tantamount to a loss of the gospel itself.

'You assert that whatever is said about God on the basis of
culture and ethics misses the truth of God as proclaimed in the
Bible. Indeed, for you there is only contrast between the truth
of God and ours. Instead of a gradual growth into that truth,
you propose – contrary to what many have confessed in relation to this matter – an instantaneous perception of that truth,
a new birth, as you put it. And you speak of it in this way
because for you the link between these truths is a barrier.

'But then you take back with the other hand what you just
gave. The new birth is a transition point from godlessness to God
which lasts in duration as long as the lifetime of the Christian,
because faith is also always unfaith; that is to say, it is not a
certainty but a hope.' (The Open Letter on Barth's answers
to questions 7–11)

Not only is there a dualism apparent in this, that Marcionite
speculation, but there is also a radical separation of the godly
and the worldly. This is a falsification of the gospel. By speaking of a contrast between God and man, between God's truth
and man's truth, between time and eternity, by denying every
progress of the mind toward the divine, every graduated ascent
to him and by repudiating every valuable insight into the divine
in the history of man's intellect and morality, Barth destroys
what the believer possesses, robs him of his certainties, shakes
his confidence and transforms his faith into an illusion and his
joy into frivolity. How many will understand why a minister
does that? How many will learn humility, the presupposition
of faith, from that? This sort of thing is no longer witnessing to
Christ. Barth has moved far away from the Christianity of the
gospels.

'You are so far removed from the gospels that you are unable
to see the simplicity of Jesus' message. His kind of preaching
does not suit you, instead there is a curious path in your
preaching, metaphysical and psychological obscurities which
very few will be able to grasp. Even Paul and Luther do better
than you with their message of the forgiveness of sins.

'That kind of metaphysics and psychology results from the

repudiation of scientific and reasoned analyses of the source materials. Only occultism, gnostic speculations, yes, sectarianism will come of it.[4]

'There is no doubt that you rid yourself of science and reason in regard to the search for a genuine picture of Christ. Historical knowledge, critical-historical study and critical reflection are essential in that search. But you repudiate that. History, even of recent decades, shows that such a point of view leads to fanaticism, fantasies and dreams and even to an intolerant exclusivism. Instead of religious openness there will be a narrow outlook, instead of love suspicion.' (The Open Letter on Barth's answers to questions 12–14)

Harnack sees the root of this anti-scientific, this speculative or metaphysical theology of Barth's in the historical scepticism Barth had inherited from Overbeck. 'I am in no way inclined to become involved in anything regarding Overbeck', he wrote to Barth on 16 January 1923.[5] What Overbeck denied was what Harnack had spent a lifetime in demonstrating: that historical events as such contain in themselves a reference to a final and all-embracing reality, the divine. He also repudiated the harmony Harnack sought to establish between Christianity and culture. So Overbeck writes that 'Christianity must now make clear how seriously its own affirmation is to be taken, that it is not of this world . . . It is impossible to live the Christian life in this world; whoever tries to give himself equally to the world and to Christianity, and believes that he can live in the former while belonging to the latter, must become lost.'[6] And then there were those attacks on Harnack in Overbeck's *Christentum und Kultur* which, even though they were made in a diary never meant for publication, were not what one might accept as scholarly criticism.

Harnack reacted, therefore, with special vigour to Barth's Overbeckian historical scepticism. He was on the look out for any turning away from the study of the historical Jesus, for that was the outward manifestation of this scepticism.

If historical-critical study of the Jesus of history does not give us the understanding of the real Jesus of the gospels, i.e. if we know the real Jesus no longer according to the flesh, how do we know him except through subjectivistic fantasies? History shows that there is no other alternative, and the Church, as history also shows, has rejected those fantasies as heresies.

Harnack perceives in Barth's endeavours a prophetical and fanatical threat to the freedom of the Church, which it owed to Luther and the Enlightenment.

He thus concludes his critique with the prediction that if Barth's theology comes to prevail, the gospel will no longer be taught; it will rather be given over into the hands of fanatics who preach the Bible edited to their fancies and who will set up their own dominion.

What a confrontation this is! One man accusing the other that in his theology the gospel is lost, the other man replying that he should not even be called a theologian!

Our task is now to analyse the two positions as they are outlined in the 1923 correspondence of these two men.

HARNACK

The key question Harnack asks is this: how can we obtain reliable understanding of Christ? As a superb historian and expert in the history of dogma he answers: not through subjective processes but through a critical analysis of man's testimonies to Christ. The religion of Christianity is Christocentric, nothing can alter that. The way to grasp the correct picture of Christ cannot be metaphysical, for this would introduce categories of judgment which are inapplicable to religion. Such categories are of value in one's quest for a correct picture of nature and the world, but not for man's relation to the supernatural, to the divine. If, therefore, this relation to the divine is based on a correct understanding of Jesus Christ, that understanding is to be gained by a critical study and historical evaluation of Jesus. Certainly, religion is not a matter of the mind only, but reason and reflection are indispensable in giving religion its focus. Given the inner disposition toward the divine, theology must give to the person thus disposed a true image of Christ, of his words and deeds and explain their significance. That is to say, theology must reproduce for each generation the gospel of Christ. In the contemporary world this must be done scientifically, which means, in terms of historical knowledge of the Bible, of the beginnings of the Christian religion and of the course it has taken in history. This method will permit the Church to relate the gospel to the society, the culture and the *Weltanschauung* in which it lives at any particular time and place.

As a theologian, therefore, Harnack is concerned with the need for a continuous reformation of the Church, and a constant redirecting of the Church back to the gospel of Jesus Christ.

If in this concern we may speak of one fundamental principle on which Harnack rests it is this: faith in God comes through the preaching of the gospel of Jesus Christ. Such faith includes as an indispensable factor the cognition of Jesus Christ as the very centre of the gospel. Without knowledge of Christ's person faith is directed towards false, imaginary ends. Faith needs historical understanding of 'the Christ of history', and so the critical-historical study of the historical Jesus is fundamental. In other words, history is the basis for man's religious knowledge. The historical method of analysis is therefore of immense significance for the creation of faith. Theology as the study of the gospel depends in its endeavours to grasp its object epistemologically on the method of critical-historical analysis.

Theology, the historical science of grasping the gospel

'The task of theology is at one with the task of science in general', Harnack said (above, p. 36). In the terminology of what we called Harnack's principle it means that theology is as a science a historical science. It is the science of critical-historical analysis of the various sources of the Christian religion. By maintaining a close contact, in fact, a blood-relationship with science in general, theology will be enabled to pursue its task in which its scientific nature is upheld as the pure cognition of its object.

'How do we come to know Jesus Christ and proclaim him correctly, so that the faith evoked in him is in fact directed to him and not a false God?' Harnack's answer is unequivocal: through the principles of historical analysis, through 'historical knowledge and critical reflection'.

In 1874, when Harnack defended his *Habilitationsschrift* in Leipzig, he maintained that no other method of exegesis will allow us to find out the real meaning of the Bible except the literary-historical method.[7] This statement reflects his opposition on the one hand to the dogmatic approach of Orthodoxy to the Bible and on the other to the mystical or subjectivistic approach of Pietism to it. When Harnack in his concern for the reformation of the Church wrote to Barth that scientific theology, which had attained a high degree of clarity and maturity only since the eighteenth century, was for him the only possible way of grasping the gospel epistemologically and thus of bringing about the reformation of the Church, he was referring to that particular theology which repudiates the method of orthodox and pietistic theology.

The Enlightenment, for that is what the eighteenth century means in this context, raised the question of how the accidental occurrences in a small corner of the Roman Empire in the first century A.D. could be of influence and of necessary standing for man nearly two millenia later. In Lessing's own words: how can the gap between an accidental truth of history and the necessary truth of reason be bridged? The answer is twofold according to Harnack. First of all one must really understand what that accidental truth of history is, but that is what historical knowledge and critical reflection actually do. Once this has been done one can go on to show that in the case of Christianity what was first taken to be an accidental truth is in fact the truth of reason. As Harnack was to put it later in his lectures on the essence of Christianity: the essence of Christianity, of that accidental truth, is in fact religion *per se* which corresponds to what history shows to be man's highest and purest form of relation to the divine. As such the essence of Christianity is the necessary truth of reason.

It is only since the Enlightenment, however, that this has become clear, supremely through Ritschl. He and his pupils, of whom Harnack is one, criticised Orthodoxy because they believed that it spoke of revelation and faith without really grasping that man's encounter with God's revelation in Christ is not in terms of abstractions such as the pre-existence of Christ, a duality of natures, a triune Person, but rather in terms of 'a person who appeared in time and space', as Harnack put it.[8] Orthodox theologians speak of comprehending God's being in himself. But do we know God in himself? Do we not rather encounter God *pro nobis*? Is it not God as he acts on us through his revelation in Christ? Thus Harnack writes: 'Theology is concerned with religion and within it with the greatest historical

event mankind has ever experienced: Jesus Christ and the effects
he caused. We abhor metaphysics, which gives metaphysical
significance to an historical fact; it draws a person who
appeared in time and space into cosmology and religious
philosophy.'[9] Such a method of approach to the religion and
revelations in the Bible cannot give us an understanding of the
real meaning of the gospel. The faith of Orthodoxy is misdirec-
ted to a divinity other than that of the gospel.

Harnack is similarly opposed to the a-historical understanding of the gospel found in Pietism. Here the gap between the
first and our present centuries does not need to be bridged since
it does not exist. A contemporaneity of Jesus and the individual
is established in the latter's subjective experience of Christ.
The meaning of the Bible, of its religion and revelations, is so
clear that 'one may simply speak of the Bible'. Even though
the events described in the gospel are regarded as having
occurred in that corner of the Roman Empire at that time,
historical knowledge and critical reflection are not required for
their understanding, since Jesus really comes alive only as he
'radiates out in man's heart', in which moment the 'religion of
the Bible and its revelations are something so completely a unity
and so clear' that 'one may leave the understanding of the
content of the gospel to the individual's heuristic knowledge
and experiences'.

But if religion and theology are concerned with the gospel of
Jesus Christ and if Jesus is a person who appeared at a certain
time and in a certain place, if in other words he is a fact of
history, then the gap between his life and ours simply cannot be
ignored. Hence the gospels need historical knowledge and
critical reflection for their correct understanding.

Already at the age of eighteen Harnack confessed to a friend
something that was to be quite characteristic of his mature
theological position. His biographer describes this as 'the inward need to understand Christianity historically and to set it
into a living relation to all historical events, the decision to
push through the dogmatic and the traditional to the innermost
content of the Christian truths'.[10] Then again, in 1888, three
years after the appearance of the first parts of his *History of
Dogma*, he wrote to a government official: 'I am convinced that
we shall not be led into a healthy progress and into an increas-

ingly purer knowledge of what is original and valuable by exegesis and dogmatics alone but by a better comprehension of history. Not exegesis and dogmatics but the results of Church-historical research and their acceptance generally will break the chains of burdensome and confusing traditions . . . We are confident that with this method we shall not demolish but build up.'[11]

In 1916 he maintained the same insistence on the historical approach to the gospel. Writing to Friedrich Loofs he questioned the tenability of his thesis that 'the life of Jesus was not a purely human one'. 'Your thesis . . . can mean only this: there are in that life aspects for which we can find no analogies in history. A scientist can and may not use any other formulation. Only this one is possible: here was a truly human life and yet faith draws divine power and wisdom from it. Any other way of putting it draws you hopelessly into the docetism of the two-nature doctrine. If Jesus was conscious of being God's Son in a unique way . . . then he was so in a completely humanly conscious way. This is what history tells us, not to mention sense and faith as well. If you declare that Jesus' life was not a purely human one then you take away what is unique to faith, for you make an assertion, even if it is only negative, which even an unbeliever is supposed to accept. You ask for something which to history and the historian is simply a *horrendum*.'[12]

There is no change of view in the 1923 correspondence with Barth. 'I see in historical knowledge and critical reflection the only possible way of grasping the object epistemologically. But in your answers you shatter every possession of the Christian; your description of the Christian's state of mind – only very few will know as the peace of God.' What Harnack had warned Loofs against seven years earlier had apparently come true in Barth – a theology had arisen which asked that the *horrendum* be in fact acknowledged.

Three years later Harnack reiterated what he had maintained for nearly fifty years: 'History surely does not have the final word anywhere, but in the science of religions and of the Christian religion especially it has the first word everywhere.'[13]

To the question which lurked behind the whole correspondence with Barth: 'how can we obtain reliable knowledge of Jesus and the gospel?' Harnack gave this one answer throughout his life: through historical knowledge and critical reflection.

Therefore: the theologian must be a historian, because theology is a historical science. This judgment is supported by Harnack's own understanding of the task of the history of dogma. 'The history of dogma, in that it sets forth the origin and the development of dogma, offers the very best means and methods of freeing the Church from dogmatic Christianity, and of hastening the inevitable process of emancipation . . . But the history of dogma also testifies to the *unity* and continuity of the Christian faith in the progress of its history, insofar as it proves that certain fundamental ideas of the Gospel have never been lost and have defied all attacks.'[14]

Harnack sees in the task of history of dogma the solution to the tension between the essence of the Christian religion and the relativity of all human statements about that essence. 'All knowledge is relative; and yet religion essays to bring her absolute truth into the sphere of relative knowledge and to reduce it to statement there . . . (This is to help religion) to maintain itself before every possible theory of nature and of history.'[15] But the attempt of religion to express its truth in terms of propositions leads to dogmatic Christianity.

Harnack deplores this development insofar as it creates the above-mentioned tensions. 'Religion is a practical affair with mankind, since it has to do with our highest happiness and with those faculties which pertain to a holy life. But in every religion those faculties are highly interrelated to some definite faith or to some definite cult, which are referred back to divine revelation. Christianity is that religion in which the impulse and power to a blessed life is bound up with faith in God as the Father of Jesus Christ.'[16] The interpretation of the knowledge of Christianity, of man's knowledge of God as revealed in Christ and based on the documents pertaining to that revelation, in terms of dogmas is not a true interpretation of the Holy Scriptures as the Word of God. Investigation of the relative statements about the absolute truth of the Christian religion will show that these statements are not simply the exposition of the gospel but rather the superimposition of the intellectual medium of the hellenistic mind on the gospel. These two truths, that of the gospel and that upheld in dogmas, are not identical. They are in tension which can be resolved only if one goes beyond the dogmatic to the essential, to the 'essence of Christianity'.

The historian of Christian dogma must push back his inquiry through the various historical developments of the dogma to the basic truth which the dogma supposedly formulates. In other words, he must ask about the essential reality which does not change and distinguish it from the particular form which changes with the changing knowledge of man. Having answered this question about 'the fundamental ideas of the gospel which have never been lost' in the maze of dogma, he must ask further: What caused the many and decisive alterations in the simple and 'practical affair' which the Christian religion is? Why has the simple teaching of Jesus, the founder of God's kingdom on earth, become so confused?

History of dogma is in fact the phenomenology of dogma. It asks the following questions: 'What have Christians believed ever since the dawn of the Church?' and 'How is this belief related to the essence of the Christian religion?'. In view of these questions and in view of the fact that since 'this religion teaches that God can be truly known only in Jesus Christ, it is inseparable from historical knowledge',[17] it is clear that the task of history of dogma is primarily theological. In the last analysis it is concerned with the absolute truth of Christianity and with its freedom from false accretions. This means that theology grasps that truth historically. If this is so, if the object of faith is grasped historically instead of theologically, then the task of dogmatics is taken over by the history of dogma. And so Harnack turns critically against dogma as the intrusion of metaphysical speculations into theology, and 'replaces it in the inquiry into the essence of Christianity with a metaphysics with a negative sign'.[18]

What is the simple gospel, the essence of Christianity?

'What is Christianity? It is solely in the historical sense that we shall attempt to answer this question here, that is to say, by means of historical science and of the experience of life gained in experiencing history . . . Where are we to look for our material? . . . Jesus Christ and his gospel. Yet . . . we must not be content to stop here . . . because every great, influential personality manifests a part of his essence only in those whom he influences . . . The more powerful his personality is and the

more he touches the inner life of others, the less can the entirety
of him be known only by what he does and says . . . But even
this does not exhaust our material. If Christianity is something
the validity of which is not tied to one particular epoch, if in it
and through it not only once, but again and again, great forces
have been disengaged then we must include all later manifestations of its spirit . . . we may also add that Christ himself
and the apostles were convinced that the religion being planted
here would in future ages experience yet greater things and
behold yet deeper truths than those at the time of its insti-
tution.'[19]

Harnack reflects in this what has since the beginnings of
historical theology become more and more widely accepted:
'the perfect cannot be found at the origin of a thing.' This was
said in 1771 by the originator of the critical-historical method,
Semler,[20] a leading theologian of the eighteenth century and
the Enlightenment, that period, which according to Harnack
had given clarity and maturity to scientific theology. Jesus
himself and the apostles 'trusted the Spirit that he would lead
from clarity to clarity and develop higher forces'.[21] This is the
graduated development mentioned by Harnack in his letters
to Barth.

This method which Harnack adopts in answering the question what the essence of Christianity or the simple gospel really
is, shows his historical positivism, his historicism. He does not
share the Hegelian concept of history as the unfolding of mind
or reason; that is a metaphysical construction of reality. What
he does share with it, however, is that history, when studied
critically, will reflect the essence of man's spirit and its supreme
relationship to God. The interest in the historicity of a phenomenon in its historical appearance and development, is kept
alive and made the force behind the scientific investigation of
it by the conviction that there is an interconnection between
the essence of the phenomenon and its history. When Harnack
writes that 'we shall do justice to the Christian religion only if
we take our stand on a comprehensive induction which must
cover its entire history',[22] he suggests that our knowledge of the
fundamental, unchanging ideas of the gospel derives from an
imaginative retracing of those ideas as they appear in history.
Through that retracing one does in fact grasp what is funda-

mental or essential, what is accidental and what is supple-
mentary, what is kernel and what is husk.

'The gospel contains something which, under changing historical forms, is permanently valid . . . We shall see that the
gospel within the gospel is something so simple, something
which speaks to us very powerfully, that it cannot be easily
mistaken . . . Whoever has an eye for what is alive and a true
sensitivity for what is genuinely great, cannot but see it and
distinguish it from its contemporary integument.'[23]

We recapitulate: if it is the task of theology to grasp its object
as fully as possible, if this object is the focal point of the Christian religion, namely God as revealed by Jesus Christ, and if
theology is the science of the Christian religion, then theology
is a science which analyses the course of the Christian religion
from its inception up to the present day with the tools of history
and psychology in order to describe as precisely as possible
what the gospel as the focal point of the Christian religion
really is.

But what is Christianity? It is 'the simple gospel out of
which Jesus himself told his understandable and comforting
parables for the salvation of souls', as Harnack wrote to Barth
(above, p. 38). Harnack's popular lectures on *The Essence of
Christianity* set out to answer that question.

The gospel of Jesus Christ is the primary material to be
analysed for that question. Harnack, however, makes a distinction at this point between the gospel of Jesus and the gospel
about Jesus. The distinction is outlined in an essay entitled
Das doppelte Evangelium in dem Neuen Testament.[24] The gospel of
Jesus is 'the joyous news to the poor, the peaceable, the meek and
the pure in heart, the news that God's kingdom is near, that
it will soothe sorrow and anxiety, bring justice and establish
man's childhood in God in addition to giving all good things.
It is a new order of life above the world and politics.' The
gospel about Jesus is 'the proclamation of the incarnation,
death and resurrection, redemption from sin, death and devil
– in a word the realisation of God's redemptive plan. It includes the news of the kingdom, yes, but only within the faith
in Jesus Christ as having died and risen. Christ's own preaching
together with the messianic conceptions of Judaism at that time
and Paul's theology plus certain pagan myths have led to the

expansion and solidification of the second form of the gospel. The first gospel, however, is about the values of the kingdom and its ethical demands.'[25]

This distinction is important for us, for, as we shall see later, the second form of the gospel, according to Harnack, led to Marcionism, dogmatic Christianity and sectarianism, all of which he rejects and all of which he finds in Barth. The first form of the gospel according to Harnack is that which Jesus preaches and which he thinks is what the Church must proclaim and scientific theology must grasp epistemologically.

This gospel is 'simple and also so rich'. Jesus gave it 'calm, simple and fearless expression, as if it were a truth one could pick off trees. For it was just in this that his peculiar genius lay, that he uttered the most profound and most decisive matters so perfectly simply as if they could not be otherwise, as if he were saying something self-evident, as if he were recalling what everyone knows because it lives in the innermost parts of their souls.'[26]

What then is this first gospel? Harnack conceives of it under three headings, although he speaks of the whole under each one. The first is the kingdom of God and its coming. The second is God the Father and the infinite value of the human soul. The third is the higher righteousness and the commandment of love.[27]

When Harnack speaks of the kingdom of God he speaks of it in idealistic terms rather than in those of eschatology. He abhorred the eschatological. But he did not pretend that it did not exist. He knew that Jesus' proclamation of God's kingdom was an eschatological proclamation. Jesus knew and spoke of two opposing kingdoms, the kingdom of God which is to come and the kingdom of evil which is to be overcome.[28] In this struggle Jesus speaks of the last hour – 'the last hour has come'[29] – but, as Bultmann points out in his preface to the 1950 edition of *What is Christianity?*, Harnack seems not to have seen the import of that utterance.[30]

To the question 'which of the two aspects of the kingdom of God, the eschatological or the ideal, is of greatest prominence in Jesus' gospel?', Harnack answers unequivocally: the latter. 'The other view, that the kingdom of God does not come "with observation", that it is already there, was really his own.'[31]

We called this view an idealistic view of the kingdom. This
is because for Harnack the coming of it does not constitute the
end of history. The *parousia* is not taken to be the cataclysmic
change of the world into the world of God. 'The kingdom of
God comes by coming to the *individual*, by entering into his *soul*
and by being grasped by him. The kingdom of God is the *rule*
of God, yes, but it is the rule of the Holy God in the individual
hearts, *it is God himself in his power*. Everything dramatic in an
external and world-historical sense is gone here, gone also is
the quite external hope for the future . . . God himself is the
kingdom. It is not a matter of angels and the devil, of thrones
and principalities, but a matter of God and the soul, the soul
and its God.'[32] The kingdom is something supernatural, a gift
from above, beyond nature, but it is for us in nature. 'It is . . .
not a product of ordinary life. It is a purely religious blessing,
the inner union with the living God. It is in the nature of a
spiritual force, a power which sinks into a man within and which
can be grasped only from within . . . "It is not here or there, it
is within you".'[33] In other words, the kingdom is not of the
future, but of the present; it is equally close to all men in every
age since Jesus. He, therefore, who wishes to be a part of it
must 'grasp it'[34] as a religious blessing, as a supernatural gift
to his soul.

In sharp contrast to this, Barth speaks of hope and a promise
of God in relation to man's appropriation of the kingdom. 'Are
we saved in a way other than in hope? Does not faith live by
being faith in God's promise?' (above, p. 34). That is to say,
he reintroduces the eschatological aspect Harnack had rejected. This lets us just see how Harnack interprets man's
laying hold of the kingdom. It is at hand, he claims, not an
aeon in the future, a gift, not something yet to be given although
already promised. Thus Harnack says: 'Those of us who possess
a more delicate and therefore more prophetic sensitivity [i.e.
'inner openness'] no longer regard the kingdom . . . as a mere
Utopia.'[35] This means that God's kingdom, this idealistically
interpreted spiritual gift and religious blessing, is grasped by
man in a way identical or at least analogous to the way we
grasp such gifts and blessings as Goethe's *Faust* or Beethoven's
Ninth Symphony.

The gospel from the second vantage point is the Fatherhood

of God and the infinite value of the human soul. Jesus proclaimed 'the living God and the nobility of the soul',[36] a nobility which consists in the fact that the soul 'can and does unite with God'.[37]

One must not underestimate the great affirmation made here by Harnack about the irreplaceable value of the individual. In an age of political, economic or scientific ideologies and positivism, in which man is often seen only as a part of evolving nature, in which majorities are the standard for evaluating truth, in which man is sacrificed for all kinds of ends – this affirmation, couched in the dominical saying, 'What shall it profit a man when he gains the whole world but loses his soul?', must only be applauded.

Yet how is this nobility conceived of? How does the gospel, in Harnack's view, speak of this nobility?

'The value of the truly great man consists in his increasing the value of all mankind . . . in having enhanced, that is, progressively given effect to human value, to the value of that humanity which has risen out of the dull ground of nature. But it was through Jesus Christ only that the value of each human soul came to light . . . it was he who raised humanity to this level.'[38]

The soul's nobility, first brought to light by Jesus, is inseparable from its relation to God the Father. This means that Jesus made us see that in view of God's Fatherhood every single person is of value. If everyone is to pray to God as a Father, then God himself confers upon every man that high value of being someone personally regarded by God. This was true of the human soul even before Christ's coming, because God is really a Father, but it was the purpose of the gospel to show man the intrinsic value of every soul.

We see here that the gospel is for Harnack a message of 'essential elements which are timeless'.[39] One of these essential elements is that God loves, that he is love. He is like the prodigal's father, for he waits in unchanging love for the lost child. Another is that through this love for man the soul of man is of infinite worth. This was certainly Jesus' meaning: 'the eternal appears, the temporal becomes a means to an end and man belongs to the side of the eternal'.[40]

Yet the gospel must also be summarised as 'the higher righteousness and the commandment of love'. One may speak of the gospel as of 'an ethical message without devaluating it'.[41] Earlier we saw the emphasis Harnack put on the kingdom of God as being 'within' man. The sphere of faith or religion is 'the sphere of pure inwardness'.[42] Here Harnack claimed to be following the example set by Jesus himself when he severed ethics from the external forms of religious worship and the pursuit of good works for an ulterior motive. Jesus went to the root of things, to man's intentions, to the 'depths of the heart'.[43] Ethics became love. Love is the only motive for man's actions but this love, according to Harnack, does not come with programmes or platforms for the external transformation of the world; 'its purpose is to transform the socialism which rests on the basis of conflicting interests into the socialism which is founded on the consciousness of a spiritual unity'.[44]

Several times in this section of *What is Christianity?* Harnack declares that this aspect of the gospel is new in religion since Jesus. ' "It was said of old . . . but I say to you." The truth was something new; he was aware that it had not been expressed before with such consistency and sovereignty . . . In expressing his message in such a way, Jesus defined the area of the ethical in a way in which no one had ever defined it before.'[45] The new element is the combination of religion and morality in such a way that the former is the soul of the latter which on its part is the body of the former.

It would seem unfair to label this aspect of Harnack's thinking a sophisticated moralism. He unites religion and morality at the decisive point of the love of God *and* the love of man. Indeed this is for him 'the heart of the gospel', 'the close union, indeed the equivalence of the love of God and the love of one's fellow', as he wrote in his fifteen questions (above, p. 29). 'In exercising this virtue men imitate God.'[46] Here we must point out that this may mean two things for Harnack. Either we may be called by Jesus to take God as our example of merciful relations with others and like him love others as ourselves: if so, this love and mercy are powers of our own; or it may be that our love of the neighbour is not merely analogous to God's love for us, but is in fact its product. This seems to be borne out by what Harnack has to say about *humility*: 'Jesus made humility and love one. Humility is not a virtue by itself but

rather a pure receptivity, an expression of inner need, the plea
for God's grace and forgiveness, in a word: openness to God.'[47]
Does he mean that humility, the hunger and thirst for righteousness, the poverty in spirit are pure receptivity, the expression of an inner need and the plea for God's forgiveness and
grace? Does this not suggest that this ethics of Jesus is not one
that speaks solely of man's achievements? Is it not then an
ethics of good works? Or does he make faith itself into a work
when he writes that 'this humility is the love of God *of which we
are capable*'?[48] Is the openness to God in our love for him, like
mercy, a virtue? It may well be that since Harnack was a
follower of Ritschl that we must opt for an affirmative answer
to the last questions. But the quotation itself is not simply a
testimony to the ethicisation of the gospel.

Under those three aspects: the kingdom of God and its
coming, the Fatherhood of God and the infinite value of the
human soul, the higher righteousness and the commandment
of love, Harnack describes the gospel of Jesus Christ. It is for
him the simple gospel, the first form of the gospel found in the
New Testament; this is 'Jesus' gospel'. Its content is the
bringing to light of the unity between God and man. Even though
this unity is not fully apparent, even though it is often threatened or broken, it is there nonetheless, for it is grounded in the
Fatherhood of God. Jesus Christ did not make him our Father
but showed us that God is Father. Through Jesus' actions,
words and passion there shines the timeless truth that God is a
loving father. The unity, however, derives also from man. It
is not simply a natural, perhaps pantheistically conceived, unity,
it is the outcome of a struggle. Man must strive to free himself
from all that would hinder him from entering into union with
the eternal, the spiritual or the superhuman.

Religion is man's endeavour to overcome with the help of a
superhuman being or force which man worships the contradiction in which he finds himself. This contradiction arises out
of man's participation in nature, his dependence on it and even
his subjection to it. But as a spiritual being, man seeks to
remain independent of it and to subject it to himself. In this
tension religion arises as the faith in a spiritual power greater
than nature which will aid man's powers in freeing himself
from nature and gaining dominion over it. 'Religion is an

instinct concerned not so much with the empirical ego or earthly life as with the innermost core of the ego and its true home, the other world, the world of freedom and of the good.'[49] Religion directs man to God in worship because God upholds man's spiritual self-confidence against those forces in nature which draw man from the world of freedom and the good to the merely physical and material. 'The gospel . . . is based upon the antithesis of Spirit and flesh, God and the world, the good and the evil . . . This is a dualism the origin of which we do not know; but as moral beings we are convinced that, as it has been given us in order to overcome it in ourselves and bring it to a unity, it also points back to a unity of origin and that it will eventually find its reconciliation everywhere, in the realised dominion of the good.'[50] No matter whether this dualism or antithesis is described in terms of God and world, the visible and invisible, matter and Spirit, physics and ethics, man knows by experience of a unity underlying them. He also knows that the one can be subordinated to the other and that a unity at least proximate in nature can be achieved.

Freedom from the physical and unity with the spiritual, however, are the fruit of a struggle. He who masters himself overcomes and frees himself from the force which binds all beings, says Goethe, and Harnack quotes it with approval.[51] Man's self-conquest through the higher righteousness and the commandment of love overcomes the antithesis in which he lives and leads him to the unity which is the kingdom of God, where God is the Father and every human soul has infinite value. In other words, the gospel speaks of the *homoousion* of God and man. 'The forces of the gospel direct themselves to the deepest foundations of human existence and only to them; there and there alone is their leverage applied. Whoever can not go down to the roots of humanity, and has no feeling for them and no understanding of them, will not understand the gospel, and instead will try to profane it . . .'[52] (This is what Harnack accused Barth of doing, misunderstanding and profaning the gospel.)

If the gospel is about *homoousion* of God and man, the metaphysical concepts, i.e. doctrines of dogmatic Christianity, are superfluous and even dangerous. On the one hand, they cannot reveal the God who blesses man with his love and Fatherhood, and on the other hand, they give rise to 'a state of mind which is no longer the presupposition necessary for all Christian humility' – which is man's receptivity, expression of inner need, the imploring of God's grace and forgiveness, man's opening himself to God. Dogmatic Christianity is really irreligious since it misses the goal of man's spiritual longings. The determination of the goal, which is that final unity, 'is in no way propositional, it can therefore not unite our space-time knowledge and our achieved inner unity into a philosophically unified theory of the world'.[53] But dogmatic Christianity does this and is thus to be rejected. The simple gospel of Jesus on the other hand shows this unity to be an inward, living reality, for which reason 'it is . . . religion itself'.[54]

The second form of the gospel – the first step in its disfigurement

What is the second form of the gospel? In the essay about the twofold form of the gospel in the New Testament (cited above, p. 76) Harnack had maintained that the second form was about the incarnation, redemption, death and resurrection etc. It is the gospel about Jesus and the realisation of God's redemptive plan. What is significant in that essay for us now is how Harnack continues, for he leads us on to Paul and through him to the beginning of dogmatic Christianity and Marcionism – of which he accuses Barth.

'The second form of the gospel is untenable in the categories of the doctrine of the two natures, for it contradicts historical and in fact every possible kind of knowledge. Every statement about Jesus Christ which does not remain within those limits, which denies anything to him other than his humanity, must be rejected since it is in opposition to the historical picture of Jesus. This admission does not negate what is affirmed in the second form of the gospel. But just as it is certain that no God appeared, died and rose again, so it is equally certain that our senses and our knowledge of nature do not inform us about God in any way. The personal, higher life and morality are the sole areas in which we may be able to encounter God. God is holiness and love. If this is in fact so, then he becomes revealed to us in personal lives, that is through people . . . The first form of the gospel contains the truth, the second the way, and both together, life. It is, however, in no way necessary that everyone be fully conscious that Jesus Christ is the way by which he came to the truth. Christ is also Christ when a brother becomes a Christian to another brother. It is always personal life in God which is mediated to the knowledge of another through which new life is created. But behind it stands Jesus Christ. He who has found God belongs to him. He who has found him will – as he progresses – surely progress also in the knowledge that Jesus is the Christ.'[55]

The gospel about Jesus Christ is clearly secondary as a source for man's encounter with God. It may even be a dangerous form of the gospel since it uses categories of speech which refer to events which certainly never happened: incarnation – but no God appeared; death and resurrection – no God died and rose again; redemption of the world by faith in Christ as having died and risen – but God acts, redeems and perfects through people.

Paul is associated with the second form of the gospel and he is therefore the root of its disfigurement as it spread throughout the ancient world.

Harnack's discussion of Paul begins with the assertion that 'Paul was the one who understood the master and continued his work'.[56] He is the missionary of Christ, who showed more than anyone else that the gospel was in fact religion itself. It is he who removed every particularistic element from the gospel so that it could and did become 'the universal religion'.[57]

Paul conceived of the gospel as the message of the world's redemption which has already been effected and of mankind's salvation which is already present. Jesus Christ, the crucified and risen Lord, has given us access to God and through that we have righteousness and peace. He furthermore placed that message into the scheme of spirit and flesh, of inwardness and outward existence. Lastly he gave that message a language which made it generally intelligible and thus united the gospel with the wisdom of all ages.

'Without doing any violence to the essential, inner features of the gospel . . . Paul transformed it into the universal religion and laid the foundations of the great Church. But as original limitations fell, new barriers of necessity made their appearance which modified the simplicity and strength of a movement which was from within.'[58]

Paul proclaimed the message of the suprasensible community of Christ, the heavenly unity that comes from within but he also founded the Church which took visible shape wherever people lived and believed that message. For Jesus the outward appearance of a community bearing his name created no problem, he could be 'quite unconcerned with externals and devote himself to what really mattered – the question of how and in what forms the seed would grow did not occupy his mind'.[59] But Paul had to answer that question; the seed he planted could not remain in a bodiless condition as it began to grow. There had to be forms of worship and life which embodied the values proclaimed. And this does not happen without the danger of the forms assuming what belongs solely to the values. 'The danger of this is always so imminent because the observance of the forms can always be controlled or enforced, whereas the inner life evades all effective control.'[60]

Here arises the need for doctrine; the community now growing needs to maintain itself in its uniqueness over and against every other *Weltanschauung* or ideology. Paul showed the absolute character of the Christian religion clearly in his Christology, in the way he spoke of Christ's death and resurrection, yet his formulations had of necessity a logic of their own which was in danger of concealing the real, the true meaning of religion. Once a doctrine is taken out of the sphere of personal experience and inner reformation, it is simply a metaphysical proposition and no longer a saving truth.

Why is this so? If the formulation of the truth of the gospel or the formation of a correct theory assumes importance – and in view of the attacks of other religions and theories on Christianity such formations are necessary – then the right knowledge of the truth can easily displace the right relation of the soul to God.

Christ's gospel directed everyone to the all-important point in confronting every man summarily with God. The gospel about Jesus as Paul taught it, however, exercised an influence in the wrong direction, in the way in which the religious conceptions were ordered. Harnack attributes that order and conceptuality to 'Paul's speculative ideas' and goes on to say that 'it is wrong to make Christology the basic substance of the gospel, however tempting it may be'.[61] Paul himself has moved in that direction because he was the author of the speculative idea that Christ had some heavenly nature. From this notion others developed the idea that the redemption of the world *is* the appearance of Christ, of the divine being in the world. Paul himself still saw the incarnation from the ethical point of view, but this peculiar Paulinism soon overtook what was once the real value of this conception and led to perversions of the gospel. If Paul held such views, what is to restrain his successors from doing likewise in the circumstances in which they found themselves?[62]

Nonetheless Paul is one of the spiritual giants among men. 'He has worked with the most living of all words and has kindled a fire.'[63] But what of the lesser spirits who also worked with this message? Harnack's verdict is that they allowed 'an original element to evaporate' and 'Hellenism, the Greek spirit' to become united with the gospel.[64] The latter Harnack believed could happen because of the former and did in fact happen in about A.D. 130.[65]

Marcion, Paul's successor, speculative preacher and transformer of the gospel

The date A.D. 130 draws our attention to Marcion, the Christian who taught the 'gospel of the strange God'. This phrase is the subtitle of Harnack's book on Marcion. We shall turn to it now in order to see how the proclamation of a speculative dualism leads to results Harnack thinks occur also when scientific theology is transformed into the pulpit-ministry.

At the time of the correspondence in 1923 Harnack was working on a second edition of that book, which had appeared originally in 1920. By comparing certain sentences in it with other sentences in the correspondence it becomes obvious why Harnack thought Barth to be a Marcionite.

Marcion was a 'founder of a religion' (*Religionsstifter*). However, he was not aware of this since he wished to preach, like Paul, the God who had appeared in the crucified.[66] Again and again Harnack emphasises that it was Marcion's firm intention to follow Paul's aim and teaching. 'There can be no doubt that Paul would have perceived with sorrow and indignation the growth of Christian syncretism. It is equally unquestionable that he would have approved the more important aspects of

Marcionite criticism of Christianity. He also would have regarded it [i.e. Christianity] as a misled and lost flock. *He would
have seen a genuine disciple of himself in this man who arose here as a
reformer.*'[67] But without doubt Paul would have also recoiled
in horror from this blasphemous teacher who rejected the Old
Testament, denied the birth and reality of the carnal existence
of Jesus Christ. 'It would surely never have occurred in any
way to Paul to ask whether he himself was responsible or not
for these earthshaking errors of Marcion.'[68]

Nevertheless it was Paul who had brought together the conception of the unknown God or the strange God of Greek philosophy, the God who cannot be named and who is not one of
the *di patrii*, and the God who created and now upholds the
world, the God who, in other words, was known by his revelation in the world, in history and in Jesus Christ. This is the
syncretism of Paul: the unknown, nameless God became known
and his name was 'the Father of Jesus Christ'.[69]

This is the place where Marcion begins. This is the God he
wishes to proclaim, only him and in an appropriate way, so
that the Church might really worship him. But then it was
just as impossible for him as for other Christian gnostics to
uphold a connection between the Father of Jesus Christ and
the God who created and now upholds the world. The concept
of God's unknowability became very prominent again with
him. 'On the basis of experiences and their observations, which
impressed themselves on these men more and more forcefully,
they were less and less able to relate the pure, good and exalted
God found in their hearts to the external, corrupt world. In the
end the link broke completely. The unknown God was now
said not to be the Creator of the world. That is why he is
unknown. The attributes: spirit, holiness, goodness, drawn
from the sphere of inwardness, raised God so much above the
world that he was no longer to be thought of as its Creator and
Ruler. At this instant, however, the world lost all its positive
value since not only the valuable, but also the real is to be found
with the unknown God. The world is the prison, it is hell, it
has no sense, it is a mere appearance – a disgusting one at that
– indeed the world is the Nihil.'[70]

Harnack thinks that this point of view derives from Paul's
preaching, as a further step in the syncretisation and hellenisa-

D

tion of the gospel. But the dualism is the outcome of the way
the Greeks interpreted Paul's gospel. Even if Paul left himself
open to such an interpretation, it is important to see how
Marcion fits what is the essential gospel for him into this cos-
mologically and anthropologically negative Pauline dualism.

Marcion wants to teach that even though the Father of Jesus
Christ is unknown, even if he cannot be grasped from worldly
or human data, even if he is strange to us because nothing links
him to us and the world, he is nevertheless the good Redeemer.
'As the strange Guest and Lord, strange in every sense, he enters
into this world.'[71] Here is the negative world-view of gnosticism
and the positive belief that the unknown God does become
involved with the world he did not create. 'This is the fantastic
paradox; religion itself must be regarded as a paradox if it is
to be the genuine religion and not a false one.'[72]

If this religion preaches the grace of an unknown God who
redeems the world, which is not his, and leads man, who does
not belong to him except for some spark of light, to a new, and
unknown homeland out of his real home which is the present
evil and wicked world, then this is a religion of inwardness.
And Harnack says that 'Marcion has taken this inward religion
to its utmost consequences'.[73]

Herein lies the reformatory aspect of Marcion's work. When
the gospel entered the hellenistic world it was forced to confront
and engage in dialogue with that world's wealth of thought.
But it was also concerned to maintain its identity, and by
attempting to communicate its absolute truth in the relative
conceptuality of man's thought-systems, it fell victim to a logic
which made its religion into a philosophy of religion. 'Whatever was divine revelation was given a logical unity and validity.'[74] The result was that the gospel became 'a complex of
opposites'. This must be purified, the real gospel must be peeled
out of this ideology. This is done by returning to the 'definitive
Paul'. Showing the same 'noble seriousness and holy enthusiasm'[75] as Paul, Marcion set out to proclaim the good Redeemer as the unknown God. What Paul had preached on
Mars Hill, Marcion did now; he taught that the Redeemer of
the world is the God beyond the Creator. But his gospel is
bedded in the dualism which denied any link between the
Creator and the Redeemer. 'The justification for combining

the view of the unknown God as the good Redeemer and the dualistic world view seemed to be given by Paul himself. In his epistles are many references to God, the soul, the spirit and the flesh, the God of *this* world, mysteries of the world and of history, etc., which a Greek would hardly regard in a different way from that dualistic system. But there were also speculations in them not very different from his own speculations about aeons.'[76]

Yet this combination gave no clear, no transparent religion or theology. Paul's concept of God is still burdened with Old Testament ideas. That is to say that at least the epistles attributed to Paul are thus burdened and in Marcion's opinion most of them had been tampered with by the pseudo-apostles and Judaising missionaries.[77] Harnack himself is convinced that for Paul 'the Father of Jesus Christ is in no way simply identical with Christ the Redeemer. He is not only the Father of mercy and the God of all comfort, but he is also the unsearchable, who lives in unapproachable light, the Creator of the world, the Author of the Mosaic law, the sovereign Ruler of history, especially that of the Old Testament, and finally the angry and punishing Judge, who waits outside the door with the day of judgment.'[78]

Still, Paul's central concept, both Marcion and Harnack agree, is redeeming love. On it and on it only Marcion builds his gospel. He eradicates every trace of Old Testament thinking and imagery, so that in the end his clear and transparent systematic theology is about the gospel of the amazing, yet incomprehensible because unknowable God of love who redeems man. The Pauline antithesis of gospel and law is gone. Instead Marcion forges a principle which unites all higher truth in the opposition of gospel and law, a principle which then dictates a doctrine of being. The key factor is grace freely given, a paradox beyond solution. Religion must therefore also be paradoxical, as total devotion to him whom one does not know, cannot know. This devotion is flight from the ugly, repulsive world; it is the hope for one's redemption and entry into the alien, unknowable world of the Redeemer.

Marcion rejects the Old Testament in its entirety, rewrites Paul's epistles and the gospel accounts in order to have a document of the genuine gospel of the redeeming God. One of his works, *The Antitheses*, shows what the gospel of this God looks like in comparison with the gospel which claims that the Father of Jesus Christ is the Creator of the world. Marcion points us to a gospel burdened with the concept of law and with a righteousness of works. Both these he eradicates from 'his' gospel. The work begins with the elated exclamation: 'O wonder beyond wonders, rejoicing, power and amazement that one can say nothing about the gospel, neither think about it nor compare it to anything.'[79] Then follow thirty statements in which the antithetical nature of the two gospels is shown. Marcion's theology may be deduced from it.

Harnack cites four items which, as he says, 'inform us excellently about Marcion's basic Christianity'.[80] It would appear from the opening phrase that for Marcion the gospel is something totally new in content and in form. Thus Tertullian refers to the following: '*new* and unusual way of proclamation', '*new* kind of endurance', '*new* forms of sermons'.[81] Obviously Marcion was aware of a great *mysterium tremendum et fascinosum*, Harnack states, even though all elated feelings resulting from the contemplation of the world and its history are irreligious. He thinks of the gospel as something light and dark at the same time; he stands before the only really new in the world and its history with trembling and silent devotion.[82]

Another quotation given is: 'this one deed suffices for our God, the fact that he has freed man by his own supreme and extraordinary goodness which is to be preferred to all riches'.[83] Here Marcion states the exclusiveness of the gospel as object of religion. The gospel brings redemption, nothing can touch its immeasurable goodness, nothing must be made part of it for it is sheer goodness. The God who brought this gospel of redemption must not be regarded, therefore, as author of other deeds, especially of the creation of the world. Redemption is a new creation, nothing remains of the old.

Thirdly, Marcion held the experience of transformation (*metabole*) of the believer in the crucified Christ to be the basic notion of Paul's *Romans* and *Galatians*. In this faith the justified person receives redemption and eternal life out of God's love.[84] Here it becomes evident how Marcion conceived of the historical facticity and appropriation of redemption. To grasp Jesus Christ, his death and resurrection by faith is the inward transformation. Within redemption and the new, eternal life, Christ is all in all, himself the beginning and the perfection of faith.

Lastly, Marcion referred to Christ's Beatitudes as the very maxims of Christ by means of which one may gain insight into his real teachings.[85] They are Christ's edicts. Redemption is already accomplished, but the believer must know that it is his only as a certain hope through the Holy Spirit. As long as he is in this world, the redeemed must be poor, must weep, mourn and be persecuted. He must not become involved with this world. That will make him a hated man. He will know the blessedness of salvation only by faith, own it only in hope. 'No greater contrast is thinkable than the one in which the Marcionite believer lives; on the one hand he knows himself redeemed not only from sin and guilt, or death and the devil, but also from the evil Creator-God of this world; on the other hand he still lives in that world as one hated and persecuted by the God of that world.'[86]

It therefore became necessary to bridge the hated involvement in the world and the blessedness of faith. Like Paul, Marcion makes use of a peculiar and dialectical method of education for the redeemed in terms of the Adam–Christ antithesis. It was a dialectic of sin and grace, sin and law, guilt and redemption, and life and death.[87] (This dialectic is not to be interpreted, however, as a dialectical dualism for Paul. There is no contradiction in principle for him between the God of the law and the God of the gospel, but it is for Marcion who mistakenly believed that Paul had drawn a distinction between them and that later interpolations had blurred this distinction.)

The pronounced features of Marcion's position seem to be these: (1) A dualism of an evil world from which one must withdraw and a good redeeming God who comes to draw man to himself. (2) The gospel of this God is absolutely new; it could not have occurred to anyone before Christ, who brought the gospel. It is an unknowable gospel because the loving God enters this world as a stranger from a sphere unknown to us, in order to bring us into that unknowable world. (3) Because of its otherness in origin and goal, it is open to our understanding only through the sphere of inwardness. There we comprehend the gospel of redemption as our new creation and transformation. (4) It is a gospel, however, inseparable from Christ, in whose crucifixion the redeeming love of God became apparent. As God's Son and self-revelation Christ must not be regarded as a part of this world; he was not like us a creature of the Creator God. We know him therefore only through faith and not from any data of the world or man or of the world's or man's history. (5) It is in this faith that the hope of man lies and the Holy Spirit's assurance to man of redemption is to be found. Hope is thus the link between the hated world in which the redeemed lives as a persecuted outsider and the new, unknown home of the Father of Christ. This hope requires a dialectical education and knowledge, because relational knowledge is not possible here simply because there are no links from the world to God. Our speech regarding God can therefore be only paradoxical and dialectical.

Marcion was a man who preached a gospel which rejects the claims of the Judaising Missionaries, which rejects the Old Testament as a canonical document of the Church, and rejects the Mosaic law and the righteousness from works – in a word a gospel which rejects completely the God of law. But such a rejection leads to a dualism. In the world there are two kingdoms, one of matter and flesh, and the other of spirit, morality and justice. They are opposed to each other but still inseparably intertwined. This demonstrates how weak the Creator God really is. Even though he is spirit and moral power, he could do no better than to create the world and use matter in the process, to which by nature he is opposed. In that world there is man, driven by carnal desires, offspring of a despicable act of man and woman, bound to his flesh and thus dragged down to egoism and the heathen level of the material. But this is not the will of the Creator who has endowed man with a sense of goodness and justice. How does this work out? On the one hand he aims at a strict and meticulous righteousness which seeks to permeate the physical and moral spheres by adopting prohibitions, rewards and punishments, and tries in this way to overcome what is base and merely natural. On the other hand there is the spirit of the ten commandments, with their authority and demand for obedience. In this situation, however, only a servile goodness is possible, a struggling order which is apparently moral. But it is so burdened with harshness, terror and often senselessness that the ideal it upholds is a sad one. And what is more, righteousness here, especially where it appears in its purest form and seems to have overcome the physical, is really immoral because it is void of love. It places all under compulsion and thus leads to sin which means that it does not liberate at all.

Man thus must choose; either he refuses to obey the God of that law and lapses into libertinism, invoking his wrath; or he obeys him and becomes a man of righteousness and lawfulness which means that he has mastered what is base, but is really no further ahead since he is immoral. Evil is basically not the enemy of good. The two are incommensurable and the former can be overcome. The real enemy, however, is a forced, self-righteous morality, which knows neither love nor the freedom of real salvation.

This leads to the dualism mentioned above. The God of the law, the Creator God is not the Saviour proclaimed in the gospel. It is the unknown God who is the Saviour. 'The law cannot reveal the true God to us'; these words of Luther could well have been Marcion's. Jesus Christ alone shows us the true God, he and no other in this world. 'The Christian religion is thus nothing but faith in the revelation of God in Christ. Every recourse to religious capabilities is rejected, man is really "like a piece of wood or a stone" (Luther) before the news of salvation,'[88] Harnack comments. This news is the gospel of the strange God.

Marcion's religion is completely un-Jewish and un-hellenistic. He rejects Judaism and the cosmological, metaphysical and aesthetical judgments which were characteristic of Hellenism. 'Void of all links with higher humanity, with the sphere of geniality, with the prophetic and speculative, void of all links with moralism, legalism and authoritarianism – what a transformation of values and what a dissolution of culture this brought.'[89] The concept of God as pure love is combined with an understanding of him as the wholly other, as someone totally strange, someone subjectively and objectively new. Marcion preached this divinity in a new and unusual way, as he had experienced him in Christ, elevating the historical realism of the Christian experience to the level of a transcendental realism. He discovered the sphere of a new deity, thus the sphere of a new reality.[90]

At this point Harnack adds a very significant footnote. 'When contemporary philosophy of religion again defines the object of religion – the "holy" – fundamentally as the "wholly other", as the "alien" and the like, and when this definition is made by theologians coming from the camps of Pietism, Reformed Orthodoxy, Roman Catholicism or critical thought (*der Kritizismus*) and when they tell us to avoid all proofs and let the phenomenon speak for itself, then they have every reason to remember the only predecessor in the history of the ancient Church who knew this strange God, called him by name and refuted all proofs and testimonies by which one might come to know him and believe in him.'[91]

Harnack now proceeds to set out his objections to Marcion's teachings. 'First of all there is the expressionistic element in Marcion's orientation about God and the world; it is marked, one might well say, by a kind of withdrawal from thought. It is difficult for a precise thinker today as in ancient times to feel very happy about that. Moreover, his interpretation of reality is in danger of becoming a mythology, because on account of the predisposition of our reason it is possible for us thinkers to be monistic and pluralistic. It is not possible, however, for us to be dualistic without becoming mythologists, that is to say without losing ourselves in fantasies. Then there is his decisive judgment about the world, but with all its justifiable indignation about the way the world lives it still strikes one as being boldly presumptuous. Is it given to man to condemn the totality of reality in nature and history when it is not grace and freedom? Is it the case that "morality" and freedom in the realm of the good are merely opposed to each other and are not graduated to each other? Further, one cannot accuse Marcion of not knowing providence, he only denies its applicability to the course of the world. Yet, he is certain that nothing will separate the redeemed from the love of God, so that he calls for an unshakable patience. But he curtails the life of piety in a very drastic fashion when he refuses to regard cross and suffering as sent by the same God who gives salvation. Furthermore, is it not a false inwardness, in fact a lack of charity, to tell others to renounce the whole world as beyond redemption, to limit oneself to the *preaching* of the gospel and not to try to *do* anything at all about it? Does not every action presuppose that reality is reformable, and contains something basically, originally good? Lastly, and this is closely related to the previous point, no conception of God and the world can be right if, in view of all the evidence, it must push asceticism so far that it prohibits everyone from furthering the propagation of mankind. It only abrogates the fundamental presupposition of all thought, that somehow life is worthwhile. If love not only suffers, but also hopes all things, may one give up the hope that its secret and power, contrary to all appearances, nevertheless embrace the world and its history from the depths and with their misery and sin in order to reform them for the better?'[92]

The application of these criticisms could purge Marcion's teachings of their heretical content and give a solid basis to his *credo*: I believe in God the almighty Father of love. The doctrine of God's Fatherhood, of his nature as love, of redemption and man's salvation into the kingdom of God and the accompanying life of higher righteousness would salvage religion from being lost in the dogmatic structures within which the Church has encased it.[93]

Marcion and Barth – a historical parallelism for Harnack

What exactly are Harnack's objections to Marcion?

(1) Marcion's views are stated in a conceptually inexact, a philosophically and scientifically improper manner, which Harnack calls 'expressionistic'. This is quite unacceptable for a thinker and a *horrendum* for a scientist.

With reference to Barth and 'our contemporary theology', Harnack wrote to a friend: 'how weak it is as a science . . . how expressionistic is its method . . .'[94]

(2) Marcion's interpretation of reality leads into fantasy and mythology because of its dualism. The real becomes confused with what is imaginary.

'We do not know the real, the historical Jesus any more? Then how can we prevent the substitution of the real Christ by an imaginary one?' Harnack asks Barth.

(3) Is man permitted to condemn the world? Even though there is much evil in the world, to answer in the affirmative, as Marcion answered, is presumptuous. If the world and God are in fact totally opposed to each other, like good and evil,

'how is one to escape the sophism that one has to remain in the world since even a withdrawal from it is based on a decision of the will and is therefore something worldly?'

(4) Marcion regards morality and man's freedom to which man has already attained while still in the world, as opposites and not as steps to the real good.

'Between God's truth and ours there is only contrast. The way from the old to the new world is not a graduated process.' This is how Harnack interprets Barth's view on the relation between God and the world.

(5) Marcion's view of providence is restricted to God's love and to those whom it seeks out, namely the redeemed. Providence is not concerned with the world and its course. The redeemed must therefore have great patience in the world and wait for the fulfilments of God's love and their redemption, which are all that they receive from him; all else comes from the Creator God. This is for Harnack a very restricted view of religion and the religious life.

This objection to Marcion is certainly parallel, if not identical with the objection to Barth: 'If the knowledge that God is love is our highest and final knowledge of him, and if we know that where there is joy, love and peace there is his sphere, how can one give autonomous standing to what are only transition-points in Christian experiences and by doing so perpetuate what makes them to be dreaded? This only destroys the Christian confidence and joy and substitutes a religious state of mind which only a few will be able to accept as religion.'

(6) Marcion's renunciation of the world as evil and his restriction of himself to the proclamatory work of the gospel is a sign of an inwardness and lovelessness which denies the reformability of the world and its inherent goodness.

Harnack sees Barth moving along similar lines. Barth maintained that faith in God cannot avoid protesting against this world, because faith is aware of the basic distance and the utter contrast between God and the world. But Barth is a Calvinist, who shows the same lovelessness as Marcion on account of the opposition of the world which he inherited from Calvin. So writes Harnack's biographer.[95] Harnack himself believes Barth to think that even if reality were reformable, the good, true and beautiful in this world are not related to the good of God in

any other way than through the barrier which separates them,
namely God's judgment of the world.

(7) Marcion's asceticism denies all value to life; as such it is
simply negative. It destroys the power and secret of love which,
since it suffers and hopes all things, believes in its ability to
embrace and thus to reform the world, and redeem it from its
misery and sin. Such asceticism does not understand the full
meaning of the commandment of love given by Christ.

Barth also introduces a 'problematical conceptuality' into
the discussion of that commandment, which likewise separates
him from the gospel.

(8) Marcion avoids all use of what makes for higher humanity and geniality. Thus he dissolves culture. By calling God
the wholly other, even though it is for him a Christocentric
conception, he works with a transcendental rather than a historical realism and a sphere of reality which is not that of
history.

Barth's point of view 'can be understood only as a radical
denial of every valuable understanding of God within the
history of man's thought and ethics'. He does exactly what
Marcion did, 'severs every link between faith and the human'.

It is clear for Harnack that a religion, the truth of which is
fraught with so many objectionable features, does not lend itself
to a scientific theology. On account of its inwardness *out of
which its truths are drawn* it can only be a devotional religion and
thus belongs in the pulpit. The concepts drawn out of that
unhistorical sphere of reality: revelation, consciousness of God,
election etc., are not scientific concepts; 'science can neither
draw together under one generic concept nor explain in terms
of revelation . . . the paradoxical preaching of founders of religion and prophets (and religious experiences in general)'.

Harnack's conclusion is this: in order to grasp scientifically
what Marcion and Barth wish to preach, namely that God is
love and that he is revealed in Jesus Christ, and that our faith
comes through the preaching of the Word of Christ, *one must
stay* within the reality of history.[96]

Marcion's *gospel* is heartily applauded by Harnack, for that
preacher wanted to proclaim only the love which is not of this
world. It is a love, seen in Jesus Christ as the love of God, a
love which does not judge but helps. It is Christ the beginning

and fulfilment of the new, liberating power of God, through which man ascends to the eternal truth and the true eternity given in the love of God and in the love of one's fellows.[97]

Thus Marcion has in fact led religion through the heart of the gospel, the close union, indeed the equivalence of the love of God and the love of one's fellow-man, to the very object of religion, the holy. Augustine also had preached this liberating love, and so did Luther. Thus Harnack does not hesitate to follow Neander in calling Marcion the 'first Protestant'.[98]

Some comments are needed here on Harnack's own views on that book which Marcion so roundly rejected: the Old Testament and its retention as a canonical book in the Church. The actual thesis of Harnack's on this issue is of no import for our discussion, but it does allow us a glimpse at what he considers his own ancestral line in scientific theology, that line which since the eighteenth century attained to such clarity and maturity.

Harnack's thesis states that 'the rejection of the Old Testament during the second century A.D. would have been a mistake, which the great Church rightly refused to make. Its retention in the sixteenth century was a fate from which the Reformation was not yet able to extricate itself. Its conservation as a canonical document for Protestantism since the nineteenth century is the consequence of a religious and ecclesiastical paralysis.'[99]

Marcion had diametrically opposed its canonicity.[100] It is quite fruitful to read and historically important, but of no consequence to the religion of the unknown God. Its use of law and its depiction of the horrible acts and demands of the Creator God, are dangerous for the understanding of the God who as Redeemer has shown himself in Jesus Christ. Gospel and law cannot be united in this religion. The unholy must not be given the veneration due to the holy. Hence Marcion's rejection. The Church did not follow him in this, it rather regarded that book as a stage in religious development toward the higher religion of the new covenant, the religion of Christ.

Augustine, and especially Luther, upheld the Pauline–Marcionite difference between gospel and law; the law cannot show us the true God. The law is a phase of religion now overcome. Even though he saw this clearly and actually took a very similar step in regard to the sacraments in his *Babylonian Captivity*, nevertheless Luther was not able to deprive the Old Testament of its canonical status while giving it its real due – an honoured and high place in history.

Tradition was too strong for him. He was still bound religiously at this point. The law is helpful in awakening man's conscience. For him, unlike Marcion, it retained a place in the order of salvation. The fate from which he could not extricate himself was that the Bible occupied a position much stronger than that of doctrine. Biblicism was gaining strength and even though one may be sure that Luther was not lacking in courage and in strength to oppose it, his own position was not clear enough for him to take that step.

This ambivalence gave biblicism a strong boost, especially in Anabaptist and Calvinist Churches. 'Here the Old Testament, given an equal status with the New Testament, had a disastrous effect on dogmatics, piety and Christian life . . . it produced a new kind of Judaism and promoted legalism consistently. These effects were made worse by the gradual disappearance of the allegorical method of exegesis, which had at least softened the most inferior and worrisome features of the Old Testament. Had Marcion come back in the days of the Huguenots and Cromwell, he would have encountered again in the very midst of Christianity the warlike God of Israel, whom he despised. The reaction could not but set in and it did so in that very part of Christendom in which room had been made so unthinkingly for the Old Testament spirit: in Calvinism.'[101]

In the early eighteenth century, English deists again raised the question of the Old Testament's place in the Church. Tindal and Thomas Morgan showed by means of historical-philosophical conceptions that the God of the Old Testament must be rejected, that its law is a disfiguration of natural law, and that its people, clinging to this God and law, were doomed to atrophy. Christ taught mankind the natural law as it is purified through revelation.

In these men Harnack sees the beginning of a universal and positive-critical philosophy of history. This philosophy developed and corrected the insights of the English Enlightenment. Early next century Hegel and Schleiermacher offered a religio-historical clarification and analysis of the meaning and uniqueness of the Christian religion. The manifold data were studied and the conclusion reached was that while, formally, ideas are immanent in reality and the truth develops in the course of history, materially it is the cognition of the distinctive Christian conception of God *sub specie Christi*. It became quite obvious that the Old Testament is good and useful for the believer's perusal, but it cannot claim canonical authority. Jesus himself declared that from now on all knowledge of God goes through him. Once these conclusions are understood it is a profanation of religion to continue to regard the document of the pre-history of Christianity and the document of Christ's religion as of equal standing.

Christianity since Hegel and Schleiermacher must therefore know that its knowledge of God is Christocentric knowledge, the truth or content of which is to be seen in the course of history, since truth is immanent in reality in which it develops itself. The Christian theologian must be a historian in order to grasp epistemologically what the gospel of Jesus Christ really is. As a scientific thinker he must keep to the truth of history.

The study of history and its significance for faith

Does history offer certain knowledge? Is keeping to the truth of history sufficient for religion? How must history be studied if an affirmative answer is given to these questions?

These questions are now to be put to Harnack. We turn to the last of them first. The basic prerequisite of any scientific method is that it be objective. This does not only mean the absence of subjectivity, which Harnack defines as 'the bringing to bear of one's powers of mind and soul upon the object studied in order to recreate it artfully',[102] but also means the absence of outside interference. Yet in his aim, the pure representation of the object with the strictest objectivity, the scientific theologian faces a dilemma. The object, the gospel of God in Christ, is one to which man's faith witnesses. It is an object of great importance to his existence. And faith has a two-fold form as history shows. 'On the one hand faith is ecclesiastically bound, on the other it is personal and free. Bondage represents a stage of religion in which obedience is demanded, which as such makes a relationship with God impossible or at least

questionable. Only complete freedom permits such a relationship; the desires of the soul are satisfied only through freedom.
In its highest stage religion affords the greatest freedom. An
authoritarian faith and highly developed religion are incom-
patible. For this reason the science of theology and the Church
must agree to a *modus vivendi*, to a compromise. The spirit of
dogma contradicts the spirit of theology even though dogma
comprises a vast amount of history, philosophy and ethics,
which theology must consider, and which it cannot afford to
neglect.'[103]

Nevertheless even though the theologian strives to be and
must be objective, he cannot as a theologian be unconcerned
with the authoritative and the subjective aspect of faith. He
must go to it in order to determine what the object really is to
which that faith in its subjectivity testifies, so that in turn he
may go beyond it and contribute to the higher form of religion.
This is behind Harnack's remark to Barth in his 'concluding
postscript', 'Paul and Luther are for me indeed not primarily
subjects but objects of scientific theology as is Professor Barth
and all those who express their Christianity as prophets and
witnesses like preachers, whether they do it in biblical commentaries or in books of dogmatics etc.'. They are indeed expressions of faith and as such are to be studied as historical
manifestations of Christianity, but the scientific theologian is
concerned to examine the reality to which they bear witness,
and to relate it to the gospel of Jesus so that theology may in
fact show forth the pure gospel.

This is then the theologian's dilemma: if he is to be the intellectual analyst and interpreter of the object of religion he must
submit himself to the subjective experiences and the heuristic
knowledge of those who profess that object. These experiences
arise in the context of man's search for the life in God. As a
subjective matter this is analysable in terms of an inner openness, that is the kind of subjectivity which allows the object to
be recreated for objective study. Harnack had pointed this out
when he asked whether on the one hand it was enough to have
historical knowledge of dogma in order to understand the
religion of the Bible (a question addressed to Orthodoxy) and
whether on the other hand mere inner openness, mere subjectivity, was enough for that understanding (a question addressed

to biblicism and Pietism). Harnack's own view was that one needs both and must face the dilemma, which, when kept in mind, will lead to a correct view of the gospel. His method therefore draws on both of these 'tools'.

But it is a historical method, one which 'lets the history of Christianity define those questions whose very formulations, in the first instance and most completely, disclose the nature of its origins'.[104]

We asked how history was to be studied so that a sufficient answer regarding the truth of religion might be given. Harnack never answers this systematically. But a study of the following essays of his will allow us to show fairly precisely what steps Harnack himself followed in his scientific study of the gospel. They are: *Über wissenschaftliche Erkenntnis*; *Über die Sicherheit und die Grenzen geschichtlicher Erkenntnis*; *Was hat die Historie an fester Erkenntnis zur Deutung des Weltgeschehens zu bieten?* and *Stufen wissenschaftlicher Erkenntnis*.[105]

All science is the knowledge of reality but knowledge with the intent of acting purposively. Knowledge for its own sake is empty – Harnack held this to be so important that he made it a proviso for all scientific study.[106]

Scientific knowledge is reached in four stages. It begins with the identification, analysis and organisation of the phenomena of reality. Then it proceeds to the determination of their inter-relation. This is followed by the study of the architectonic ideas and purposes of life. The last and highest stage is the cognition of man and his spirit.[107] Although it is only in this final stage that the human spirit meets with the absolute Spirit, the ultimate unity behind all reality, where history really comes into its own, nevertheless the historian is always bound to the facts which are established in the lower stages, and through them to the truth of reality.

Those facts are divided into three categories. The first includes the elemental setting of the phenomena studied, the geographical and climatic conditions surrounding it and the natural as well as the given physical and mental conditions impinging on it. The second includes cultural factors such as the state, the Church, schools and the institutions society creates for itself. Examples of these are legislations, constitutions, declarations, treaties, liturgies and economic structures.

All these influence the phenomena of history. The third category comprises those factors which relate to individuality, to the talent and genius of great men. Great ideas and institutions reflect great men.

To these three categories corresponds what the historian can establish as certain knowledge. There are first of all the great events of history, such as the Persian Wars, Napoleon's conquests etc. Then there are the monuments of various epochs, i.e. the remains of bygone ages, buildings, inscriptions, coins, manuscripts. From them the historian reaps rich knowledge of religious, cultural and private life, public actions or private feelings. Thirdly, there are the fruits of the development of history, the residuum of man's spirit. Harnack thinks here of laws, standards of conduct, authorities and the expressions of men's perception of reality.

From this material which he gathers, the historian must deduce the direction, strength and achievement of an epoch. It falls to him to establish standards of value valid for his own time, assessing what is positive and what is negative in its impact on life. That is the fourth stage of the historian's task, in which he makes a cross-section of the epoch being studied. Only when he has done this can he proceed to a longitudinal section of history to determine its development. Together these sections then help him to use the mass of verified and categorised facts for purposeful action.

As soon as one determines the spirit of an epoch and observes the development of the spiritual in history, *Geschichte* becomes *Geistesgeschichte*. If it is accepted that the spirit is one, as it is by Harnack, then it is one and the same spirit which is operative in all historical phenomena and in us. Obviously the facts of the first category mentioned above are to be excluded here, but all cultural, individual and spiritual factors are caused by or can be traced back to ideas, for ideas are spirit. Through the spirit a deep unity between all events and our own essence, our spiritual life is established. 'I am man; nothing historical do I regard as alien to me . . . All that has taken place in history, all that still takes place in it, *is you yourself*. It all depends only on whether you grasp it consciously. This is why the historical is not only more comprehensible to us than nature and its processes, but it can also become our inmost possession and can fuse with our higher, personal life perfectly. Because of this we may illuminate history with our own experiences and with what we have learned from life, convinced that we shall be able to understand it from this basis more and more since the spirit unveils itself to spirit in this way ... We must – like Faust – enlarge our own ego into the ego of the world. This is done by appropriating with noble appetite the whole course of history and all its great and good personalities and by making them extensions of one's own essence.'[108]

This method offers reliable knowledge because history deals with man and the effects of his higher life. Now the purposive action intended by science must follow. The spirit has been seen, its direction determined. According to Harnack that direction is the preservation and enhancement of life as something valuable.

'History teaches unmistakeably that life is preserved only by that direction and power which frees man and mankind "from the power which puts all beings into bondage" (Goethe) or, as the Bible puts it, "from the service of what is transitory", that is from the servitude of the natural and one's own empirical ego ... No statement is confirmed more definitely by the course of history than the word of Jesus that he who wants to save his life will lose it.'[109]

The direction and power for the liberation of man from the merely natural tend to comprehend and unify the various aspects of life they touch. This unity is culture which, once it loses its tendency to comprehend and unify everything, becomes mere civilisation which leads to the decay of its dying members until barbarism takes over. The more fossils it contains of what once was a treasure of culture the more terrible the barbarism is.

Yet in the power to rise above the natural the historian perceives the paradoxical fact that all valuable events in history, in other words, all things which preserve and enhance life are determined by a mysterious One who is sought by that power. 'There is no doubt about it, mankind operates in history "as if God existed", as if, deriving from a higher source, it had to return to it through purposive action and draw all its members into a unity in the process. Religion interprets that action as the love of God and the love of one's fellow-man.'[110]

Not only does history show us the trend of the spirit, the signs of cultural enhancement or decay, it also shows in great individuals the devotion to the good, the true and the beautiful. 'By introducing us to people who stand higher than we, people whose cognition goes deeper, whose purposes go deeper and whose striving is more forceful, history in its biographical work brings us together with them by means of a secret bond and lifts us up to them and fills us with respect and reverence for them . . . Upon closer examination, however, it becomes plain that there are only a few from whom all mankind as a growing unity has received imperishable gifts.'[111]

When man faces such an individual of beneficial influence on mankind as a whole and as his reverence for him is kindled, he is enabled to lift himself above the material. With purposive action, with love for God and man, he can become free to live the higher life.

Let us summarise briefly in a systematic way the scientific method followed by Harnack.

(1) The first step is the pre-condition for historical study. It is the practical wisdom of the historian. It is the 'experience of life gained by studying the actual course of history'[112] with which the historian can set all things into a living relationship. Without that wisdom he will be an analyst, a categoriser and perhaps an interpreter, but not a scientific historian for whom knowledge leads to purposive action.

(2) The actual work begins with the systematic study of the sources. This involves textual criticism, philological analysis, verification of their genuineness, establishing their dates, place of origin, etc.

(3) The historian then studies and categorises the environmental, cultural and personality factors involved in his analysed sources.

(4) This is followed by the identification of the spirit of the epoch from which the sources derive. The direction, purpose, power and values of that epoch are to be established here.

(5) Then the overall interpretation of the period into which one's sources fall is to be made so that its meaning and actual significance can be determined.

(6) The historian may not delete this next step if he wishes to be true to his craft. For now he must propose purposive action. Having learned from his study what history teaches

about the overall value, namely life and its enhancement, he must propose ways in which that value will be upheld and the embodiment of it, culture, will be protected against its decline. The purpose of the proposed actions must be to assist the striving of history itself toward the life of the spirit, the life of superiority over matter. This striving is the essence of religion. The task of the historian is to show how mankind is to live the higher life of the spirit, how to defend culture against barbarism, how to prevent the life of religion from deteriorating into a life of atheism.

This last step is really the historian's value-judgment about the process of history and his communication of that value to us so that we might also share in it and thus live with, not just in, history. He fulfills this task by confronting us with the impressive, worthwhile and noble aspects in which he sees greatness to be reverenced and emulated. If we do so we shall be lifted above the material and attain to the higher life. What the historian really does is to educate us in goodness, that is in godliness, through his historical knowledge and critical reflection.

The meaning of history is therefore its value to its children. They have to incorporate that value into themselves and assimilate it into their inner being. ' "He who does not know what the last three thousand years mean to him remains in darkness, ignorant; let him live just one day at a time . . . If anyone restricts his life to his own experiences alone, he is like an animal in meagre pasture tethered by an evil spirit so that it can only move in a restricted circle, cannot see the rich, green meadows around it" (Goethe) . . . It is not only a part of education to enlarge oneself in harmony with the inner life of our spirit. We shall remain beggars and slaves if we do not go beyond ourselves; we shall become rich and free if we enter every door of history and make ourselves at home in its spacious rooms.'[113]

Enlarge ourselves! How? By looking for the valuable. The meaning of the great is its value. In relation to Jesus Harnack can say therefore that 'the community of Christian believers . . . bore witness to the impression which the person of Jesus had made on it . . . The image of Jesus and the power which proceeded from it were the things (this community) really possessed . . . It is thus the historian's first duty to signalise the overpowering impression made by the person of Jesus on the disciples, which is the basis of all further development.'[114] But 'the enquiry about Jesus can take only this form: ask what we and the world would be without him.'[115] Or again, in a letter to Ritschl, dated 6 January 1882, Harnack writes that the correct position in Christology is that Christ has the value of God for us, a position which is based on historical examination.[116]

The Christological question, 'Who is Jesus Christ?', leads the historian, once he has grasped the impression Jesus made on his followers, to ask: How can I become his follower, since Jesus has the value of God for us? What would the direction and power of the higher life be today without Jesus?

How is this answered in the terms of the six steps outlined above? First there must be the practical wisdom, the knowledge and experience of life, the ability to reflect critically. With them the historian approaches the sources which in this case are the gospels and any other document in which is recorded the impression Jesus has made on men. The historian must then establish with critical-historical analysis the date, setting and genuineness of the sources. Then he categorises the environmental, cultural and personal factors involved. When he proceeds to the fourth step, to the enquiry into the spirit of the time he is studying, he must be aware that – if he is dealing with the gospels – some of the factors established thus far do not have an immediate bearing on his further study. 'Concepts such as God, revelation, sin, redemption, eternal life, etc. . . . are research hypotheses for pure science, but pure science cannot comprehend the fullness of reality. The researcher must therefore know precisely where pure knowledge ends and the wisdom of life begins.'[117] With this knowledge and aware of this distinction, the historian will be able to grasp life, its purpose, direction and value. Only then can the fourth step actually be taken. Harnack suggests the following rule for it: 'Anyone who wants to determine the real value and significance of any great phenomenon or mighty product of history must first and foremost inquire into the work it accomplished.'[118] Christ accomplished man's redemption; the gospel he preached shows us the love of the Father as the power which overcomes the anti-spiritual, a power available for us so that we might also overcome matter.

Then the next step can be taken, the meaning and value of the gospel can now be declared, as it is upheld by the image of Jesus Christ. 'There has never been progress in history without the marvellous intervention of a person. It was not what he said which was new . . . it was rather how he said it, how his words became in him the power and strength of new life and how he made it grow in his disciples. Mankind looks up reverently to all great spirits, which have been given to it, the explorers, artists and heroes, but it venerates only its prophets and founders of religion, for it senses that a power was active in them, a power which sets free from the world and lifts up above the base course of events . . . But the spiritual content of a life, of a person is a historical fact the certainty of which is in the effects it creates. It is here that we are bound to Jesus Christ and he is bound up with piety itself. About the content of his life it is rightly said that even if one were unable to refute all objections to the Bible, religion would nevertheless remain unshaken and intact in the hearts of those Christians who have obtained an inner feeling of the essential truths of that religion.'[119]

In this step then the accidental truths of history are bridged with the essential truths of reason. The significance of the gospel, made powerful by the person of Jesus Christ, is seen and our reverence for him is kindled.

Then there must follow purposeful action as the last step, and life must be enhanced. Here we become disciples of Christ, through the power of his personality. 'Where do the strength of the strong and the action of the active come from? Why is it that a helpful insight, a saving thought is passed on from generation to generation as if it were a useless and barren rock until someone picks it up and makes it spark? Where does the procreation of a higher order, that marriage of a thought and a soul come from, in which they become one, belong to each other for ever and master the will? Where does the courage come from that conquers the dumb resistance of the world? Or what is the source of the creative power which convinces?'[120] From the person of Christ himself. What is great in history, what has led to goodness, truth and beauty, what has given us culture comes from the impression he has made. He has the value of God for us. His gospel is pure religion, religion itself.

It is the higher life, that which enhances life and creates the noblest embodiment of it in culture.[121]

Through history then the theologian arrives at the nature and meaning of the gospel. The Bible is for him the source for his formulations of the Christian position. It is evaluated historically, for critical reflection and historical knowledge establish what is the heart of the gospel and what is merely husk.

The Harnack of the correspondence

Our analysis so far has shown us Harnack's theological method and what he believes the object to be which this method is to study. We have discussed briefly what he considers to be the actual gospel the Church must preach and how that gospel became falsified through Paul's concepts and Marcion's speculations. We also saw that Harnack believes Barth to be a modern Marcion in the sense that he is as speculative and dualistic as that ancient heretic who really did not want to be one.

This examination allows us to determine why Harnack asks his questions, what he affirms and what he rejects in the despisers of scientific theology.

The religious question of contemporary man is 'How do I come to know God?' It is no longer Luther's question of how one might find a gracious God. The former question and questioner go further. The answer to both questions, however, is basically 'through faith in Jesus Christ'. But here the answers become different. 'The Bible says' is an insufficient and indeed deficient answer, as is 'leave it to your experience'. The Bible is not so plain in its meaning that one may forego all ancillary methods for its understanding. A certain openness of mind is needed along with scientific tools so that its true affirmations may be clearly grasped. Given these tools the gospel of Jesus can be taught in such a way that faith in him is awakened and God is experienced.[122] This experience confronts man with the love of God for man and elicits a reciprocal love for God on man's part. This love is channelled in purposive action toward other men. The gospel makes these two loves equivalent so that man's experience of God is the experience of that power by which people are united in a life of love, one for the other. In a union of this kind they uphold whatever is good, true and beautiful, and whatever is virtuous, because in so doing they foster that unity one with another and in it the higher life which is theirs on account of their experience of God. Here too we have an answer to the question as to how one may come to know God, namely, 'through the participation in the higher life which is created by God's love for man, a love which founded man's desire to seek unity with mankind'.

The higher life is the life of culture which must be protected against irreligion, atheism, and cultural atrophy or barbarism. Whatever enhances the cultural values will strengthen the experience of God because he is to be found wherever there is love and peace and joy. Moreover in the development of culture there is discernible a continuous deepening of man's perception of God. The deeper therefore one's knowledge of the true values of culture goes, the deeper is one's experience and thus knowledge of God.

But critical-historical reason is required to give us a clear grasp of the religion of the higher life, the religion of the Bible. It is not enough to leave the object of faith as a *mysterium tremendum et fascinosum*, to define the holy merely as the numinous. In order to comprehend it, even as the numinous, and to uphold it in its uniqueness the activity of reason is essential. Otherwise occultism and gnosticism result, as history shows. They are caused by a mistaken picture of Christ, a picture not firmly bound to the historical person of Jesus. It was through Jesus' personality that the disciples had access to God. It is thus of the utmost importance that we know him as the disciples did and recapture for ourselves what impressed them in him. We need this knowledge lest we venerate an imaginary Christ. Scientific theology, using the critical-historical apparatus of *Geistesgeschichte*, is able to give us precise knowledge of him who has the value of God for us. This theology which studies Christianity as a part of the whole history of man's spirit, applies laws which are valid in the analysis of every endeavour of the spirit, to the theology of the gospel.[123] But theology must maintain its close ties with all sciences in order to be able to depict adequately the object of man's faith.

Barth's answers to the initial questions aroused specific criticisms and further questions which Harnack expressed in his open letter. At the same time he admits that he did originally have Barth in mind especially when those initial questions were raised.

One of the main issues in their public discussion, the concept of revelation as Barth speaks of it, 'is wholly incomprehensible to me', says Harnack. Revelation is not a scientific concept because religious experiences do not form such a unity that they can be drawn together under one generic concept. At best revelation is a research hypothesis and a hypothesis cannot claim to comprehend the fulness of what it refers to. But Barth speaks of it as something so objective that the processes of human reason are not needed for its understanding. Either Barth understands revelation as something which communicates itself totally and is thus beyond misinterpretation or as something which cannot be grasped by any human faculty so that he is forced to wait until it radiates in man's heart. Both these views are to be rejected by scientific theologians.

Once again then we shall turn to the open letter he wrote to Barth and, drawing on the results of our analysis of those works which illuminate Harnack's 'scientific theology', outline in detail the Harnack of the correspondence.

The title of the questions and question 15. To Barth contemporary scientific theology appears unstable, transitory and too far removed from its actual object. It has for him no greater value than an opinion. Harnack counters that it uses scientific epistemology which has been sharpened and tested by the last two centuries of theology. This is the critical-historical method, based on the ontology of history. Since it strives for complete objectivity and sets aside all subjective influence it is believed to be in a position to deal positively with the facts of history, much as the natural sciences do in relation to their particular objects of study. The realm of theological cognition is man as he appears objectively in the history of the spirit and its effects and concrete embodiments. This is the result of the insights of idealistic philosophy since the Enlightenment. But Harnack adds also the insight of Herder, that pure science cannot grasp the fulness of reality. There is a point where pure knowledge ends and inner wisdom of life begins, where spirit confronts Spirit. Hence one must add to the categories of historical knowledge those of psychological analysis, which are experience, inner openness etc. Yet these two disciplines, history and psychology, have been strengthened since the Enlightenment and have given theology tools which assure it a scientific character. Now it can operate with generally valid historical, psychological and theoretical principles of knowledge.

Barth on the other hand identifies the task of theology and that of preaching. To be sure they are not precisely identical. Theology has two forms, each of which has a different purpose and thus a different task. One is charismatic and must edify or build up devotional life; it has to confess Christ and show how we are to be his disciples in that confession. This depends on the other form, which like any other science has as its sole task the pure cognition of its object. This calls for an objectivity which excludes the kind of 'objectivity' found in the inwardness pertinent to the experience of God. The objectivity of theology as science is critical, analytical, an objectivity the intention of which must not be devotional edification. If it were it would only lead to confusion since it derives from a confused understanding of the revelation of God in Christ. The aim of theology is the correct determination of objective revelation.

Those who have denied this, Harnack argues, have led the Church toward dissolution. History shows that. Some have used that approach to call the Church back to her task; they have meant their work to act as a ferment. But such work has never become the theology of the Church because it is really a complementary effort which, even though it is valuable, has not much effectiveness. But one must not intend one's work merely to act as a ferment. Those who have the courage to be objective and to bear witness must know that this involves the separation of the spheres of theology and preaching.

Questions 2 and 3. Barth's answer to them suggests that no human faculty whatever is to be applied to the understanding of biblical religion. That must be left to faith and faith is not identical with one's experience of God. This opens the way for faith to be transformed into uncontrollable fanaticism, since it is not answerable to any rational control. It is incomprehensible for Harnack how anyone can return to the kind of inwardness which allows only the proclamatory aspect of religion, which has often turned into the fanaticism that condemns the world and man. Faith of that kind does not enhance life and

strengthen culture, even though it derives from the preaching
of the word of Christ and is said to be the means through which
the gospel is understood. Moreover, the use of 'the Christ' in
this context is reminiscent of the dogmatic interpretations of
Jesus Christ which have caused severe misrepresentations of
him and have side-tracked the real issues of the gospel. Harnack sees in this a re-emergence of metaphysical orthodoxy, the
intrusion of transhistorical objects, the dogmatism which is
concerned with the relation of Christ to God, the *a priori* confession of Jesus as the Christ.[124] He rejects that Christology as
docetic. Metaphysics is for him not able to speak about reality.
He abhors any attempt to give a metaphysical significance to
a historical fact; it draws into the domain of cosmology and
religious philosophy a person who appeared in time and
space.[125] Metaphysics of this sort necessarily leads to an imaginary Christ and obstructs confrontation with the Jesus of the
gospels. Paul himself was responsible for the development of a
Christology in which that Jesus was lost to view. The two-
natures doctrine replaced our knowledge of Christ according
to the flesh, for according to it the historical Christ is no longer
knowable. Does our understanding of Christ really derive from
subjective, inward experiences, and not from generally valid
historical, psychological and theoretical principles of knowledge? What is this but Marcionite modalism, gnostic docetism
or Overbeckian *Kritizismus*?

  Question 4. Barth's answer is devious, but speaks of the protest
of faith against the world, a protest made necessary because
faith is hope for the invisible. It is true that faith overcomes the
world, and that the spiritual is set free by it and related to God
in the higher life. However, since it is in faith itself that there
takes place the struggle against the world in so far as it is merely
material or barbaric, this means that faith is also the hope and
conviction of the redeemability of the world. Faith is the power
of culture. To protest against the world is justified in the first
instance, but false in the second, unless one has that absolute
inwardness and lovelessness which denies the world any relation to God. Harnack thus demands that Barth be specific on
this issue.

  Question 5. The gospel proclaims the redemption of the world
through Jesus Christ, through God's love. By speaking of this

love in coordination with the love for one's fellow, it shows us how this redemption – the freedom from the material, and the barbaric – is accomplished. Culture is the concrete embodiment in the world of this power of religion, the love of God and of man, to transform the enslaved world into one free from the material. Barth tears the two loves apart and declares that their coordination in the gospel signalises their separateness which only God can bridge. This view is not in accordance with the gospel.

Question 6. Harnack sees in Barth's answer the same dualism which led Marcion to sever the human from faith. Faith was the knowledge of man's redemption of the world and of his eventual presence in the home of the unknown, the strange God, of whom one knew nothing on the basis of what is merely human. Even the highest morality is of no value, since reality and value are both to be found in the unknowable. If the world is the *nihil* and if religion is inwardness to the absolute degree, no link can exist between even the highest morality and goodness in the world and the godliness of the alien unknown sphere of God which is open to faith only. This standpoint is not that of the gospel. Faith is the *fides historica* and *fiducia* in God and his redemption of the world through love. However, since the higher life of the love of God and man, that is, of morality, is what religion teaches and what history itself strives for, education in culture or the higher life is directly related to faith and in fact based upon it.

Questions 7 to 9. Can culture give us any correct understanding of God? Can ethics? Are Goethe's pantheism, Kant's conceptions helpful? Barth apparently does not think so. His insistence that the gospel is neither helped nor hindered by those valuable insights results from his Marcionite understanding of God as the wholly other.

The person of Jesus Christ, the revelation of God is the fountain of life and of all culture. The purer our knowledge and veneration of him are, and the closer our culture is to him, the deeper is its insight into God. Its conceptions of God will thus approximate to those of the gospel, even if they do not become identical to them. The gospel is inseparable from its fruit in the higher life of culture. Cultural treasures uphold the godly and protect against the ungodly. To deny this is to sow the seed of cultural decline and of barbarism, just as Schleier-macher had maintained.

This understanding of culture implies that with the heighten-ing of the cultural life and in its development, there occurs a development in the understanding of God. In human life there is a parallel deepening of one's understanding of God. The life of the spirit is attained through the various advances and set-backs experienced in one's attempts to become free from the material. This excludes the notion of any contrast between God's truth and our truth as well as any immediate, total under-standing of it, because the idea that God cannot be known by man and is inaccessible to his perceptive faculties is rejected.

Questions 10 and 11. God is love. This is the central affirma-tion of the gospel. It is the essence of the Christian religion, and indeed of religion as such. This knowledge allows us to see the redeeming love of God grasping the whole world with its misery and evil, and working in the world for its reform and ultimate redemption. The attainment of that final insight gives man a joy and confidence and peace in which the blessedness of the victory over the world is real. The task of the ministry is to hasten realisation of it and a life corresponding to it in every man.

This peace is the peace of God, so that the joy and the love experienced in the life of godliness indicate the presence of his kingdom. But where these are embodied there is the power which leads men on to the higher life. The treasures of culture, the good, the true and the beautiful, are therefore related to the peace of God and are to be pursued most actively because of that very relation.

If this is denied, what 'solid joys and lasting treasures' does the Christian possess? His joy becomes a make-belief, his con-fidence in his and the world's redemption is illusory, his hope subject to frustration. How can a state of suspension between godlessness and final insight into the love of God be regarded as a foundation for the humility and gratitude of the Christian on which his responding love to God and his outgoing love to man rests?

Question 12. Barth's return to the doctrines of the fall, of original sin and the corresponding doctrine of man's salvation by faith and by grace alone, appears to Harnack as a falsification of the gospel. He rather applauded Marcion's affirmation that the Sermon on the Mount comprised the normal maxims of Christ by means of which one may gain insight into his distinctive teaching. It is simple, straightforward, to the point, free of ambiguities and dialectics. Above all it does not involve one in a departure from the truth of history, whereas those doctrines involve one in paradoxes which necessitate a confusing method.

The gospel is about redemption through love, about the forgiveness of sins. Both have to do with the same thing – man's freedom from the antigodly, his freedom for the godly life. Paul and Luther knew that and in weighty words proclaimed that very freedom. They preached the love that helps because they rejected the concept of a God who condemns. Barth on the other hand re-introduces the notions of judgment and obedience, and those other doctrines which are detrimental to the conviction and practical demonstration of the Christian's freedom.

Question 13. Harnack does not really reply to what Barth had said in relation to the subject raised in the original question. He merely states that it can be shown that the despisers of reason will erect a 'theology' that leads to sectarianism and from there to a complete decay in occultism. He reiterates here the warning against the dangers of speculative religion, which he had given to Barth during their meeting at Eberhard Vischer's house in Basel, April 1920. Barth wrote to Thurneysen about it. 'Toward the end of the conversation Harnack said that I was a Calvinist and an intellectualist. Then I was dismissed by him with the prophecy that according to all experiences of Church-history I would found a sect and receive inspirations.'[126] Harnack now sees that prophecy fulfilled in Barth's thought.

Question 14. Undoubtedly for Harnack faith in God cannot do without knowledge of the historical Jesus, while that knowledge cannot be gained without the critical-historical method of exegesis. Harnack sees Barth doing away with it and fears that because of it the Church will once again be plunged into an era of fanaticism and theological tyranny, from which the Reformation and the Enlightenment had freed it.

He is aware of Barth's dependence on Overbeck whose radical biblical science and accompanying historical criticism challenged Harnack's own historicism. Here is an emphasis on something other than historical effort to establish real knowledge of Christ which strikes Harnack as a blow to theology as a science. This is because he is convinced that the moment theology ceases to investigate its object historically it also begins to do what it is not meant to do. Faith then lays itself open to the charge that it is based on an illusion and that its truth is imaginary.

Harnack suspects a spiritualism or gnostic occultism which is out of touch with reality. It is quite unable to grasp reality epistemologically and to gain any true knowledge of it. Its transcendental reality is not the reality of the gospel. It is mythology.

Theology is a science. But how can science be what it is meant to when it is built up on fantasies? Science can be pursued only in the certainty that man is in fact building on the truth and on his real knowledge of the truth. Therefore the knowledge of man's sin, of his 'being lost in a god-likeness which ends in death' cannot be the basis of theology. Theology must be rid of paradoxes and whims. Critical-historical knowledge alone can do this by providing a reliable basis of certain, assured facts. In view of the possession of such knowledge, in view of the universal validity and reliability of our knowledge of the gospel, the task of theology as the science of the Christian religion is, as Harnack said in 1901, to safeguard the highest good which mankind possesses, to protect it in its purity against misunderstandings and to bring its historically knowable features into an ever growing understanding which is to be put into action.[127]

The objectivity of theology is upheld and guaranteed by the method employed by the theologian. For Harnack only the critical-historical method does this.

Harnack concludes his open letter with a note of regret and of fear that, should Barth's way of theologising become predominant, the gospel will again be falsified and theology lose its status as a science. The highest good of mankind would again be disregarded by the despisers of religion.

What actually does he mean by the phrase 'despiser of scientific theology'?

We may find an answer to that question in Harnack's open

letter at the point where his sensitivity and subsequent criticism
are aroused. 'We do not know the historical Jesus of the
gospels any more? How am I to understand that? According
to the theory of the exclusive inner word? Or according to one
of the many other subjectivistic theories?' This was Harnack's
reaction to Barth's statements about radical biblical science
and its results regarding our knowledge of Christ 'after the
flesh'. Harnack discerns here the influences of Overbeck's
radical biblical criticism and of his historical scepticism, and
his expert knowledge of history led him to draw certain historical parallels. What Barth calls the knowledge of Christ
according to the Spirit is a Paulinism which had given rise to
the speculations of gnosticism and the docetism of Marcion.
These positions had always neglected a precise study of the
historical Jesus and eventually aroused fanaticism. By definition, however, fanaticism is the opposite of science.

Furthermore, Barth had spoken of the identity of the tasks of
preaching and theology. This point of view Harnack regarded
as directly opposed to his own conception of theology as critical-
historical science. 'Scientific theology and witnessing cannot
remain healthy when the demand to keep them separate is
invalidated', he writes in his postscript. Barth does invalidate
it and by doing so neglects the essential task of science, the pure
cognition of its object. What else can one conclude from that
but that Barth is not concerned with the legitimatisation of
science in the faculty of theology at the university? 'What you
say in regard to biblical science may be formulated like this:
the most radical biblical science is always right and thank
heaven for that, because now we may be rid of it.' This pushes
theology as a science aside and opens the door to theological
dictatorships which are wild fantasies.

This is precisely what Harnack meant to oppose. The
objectivity of theology is threatened when its scientific method
is challenged in this way and its sphere is shifted into subjectivity. Those, therefore, who in conjunction with historical
scepticism seek a source of religious knowledge apart from
reason, apart from history and who reject the critical-historical
method, thus basing themselves on speculative ideas derived
from a gnostically falsified Paulinism, must be regarded as
sectarians who by the very definition of science cannot be taken

for scientists. Indeed, Harnack sees in the works of Barth and others like him 'all kinds of paradoxes and whims' and 'sublime metaphysical and psychological' speculations which are in no way in keeping with the free enterprise of science which, void of presuppositions, pursues its task objectively. These speculations imply a false attitude to reality and indeed contradict it entirely.

Harnack claimed to belong to that reformation of the Church which, beginning with Luther, but constituted primarily by the Enlightenment, had sought to anchor man's knowledge of God in Christ. This Christocentrism in theology came to be determined by a concern for the Jesus of history, but all this, Harnack felt, would cease if Barth's theology were to become predominant. For him this would be the end of the pure presentation of the gospel, which with its Christocentrism depended on the critical-historical theology as Harnack exercised it.

The questioning of Harnack's idealistic-scientific theology and the transformation of it into a theology from within – a subjectively anchored and charismatic affair – is what Harnack calls contempt or scorn for theology as a science: those who take this line are 'despisers of scientific theology'.

<h3 style="text-align:center">BARTH</h3>

Karl Barth's answers to Harnack's questions begin with a statement which in summary form expresses the charge which the so-called 'despisers of scientific theology' were making against their teachers: your theology has moved away from its theme more than is good. The great sixteenth century Reformers were the last to state that theme clearly, whereas the theology deriving from Pietism and the Enlightenment, which has dominated the last half-century or so, has served to narcotise, to lull to sleep.[128] Later, in his reply to Harnack's Open Letter, Barth states clearly what the charge against Harnack and his kind of theology actually involves. It is 'the foregone conclusiveness' with which the task of theology is emptied, that is to say the way in which a so-called 'simple gospel', discovered by historical criticism beyond the Scriptures and apart from the Spirit is given the place which the Reformers accorded to

E

the Word, the correlation of Scripture and Spirit. Such a gospel can be called 'God's Word' only metaphorically because it is at best a human expression of it (above, p. 42). Or again, the meaning of the charge may be expressed in terms of two opposing concepts which Barth, following Luther, used in an address given just six months before he first answered Harnack: *theologia gloriae* and *theologia crucis*. The former is a theology which knows itself to have arrived at its ultimate destination; it is a theology free from struggle (*Anfechtung*) because it is a theology possessing eternal life now, by the strength of God and in his sight, in Harnack's terminology. Such a theology must guard its possession since it holds in its hands essential religion, religion free of any particularistic elements. Barth calls this liberal theology, because it desires to be free from the distress and the struggle which arise whenever the question of God is really asked. Liberal theology flees 'from the question which God puts in order to give it his answer'.[129] *Theologia gloriae* has salvation, possesses final insight, it no longer needs hope. Barth protests against it in the name of *theologia crucis*. This is a *theologia viatorum*, a pilgrim-theology on the way to a promised fulfilment which it is not given to man in his pilgrim state to possess but which he may lay hold of only in hope. This theology lives between *Not* and *Verheissung*, between distress and promise, because it has nothing in its hand to possess. It 'arises where man has let go even of his highest and best, where he has submitted it to judgment and in so doing grasps the promise, where he does this on the strength of faith and of faith alone because he himself has been grasped by the unsubstantiated, self-substantiating mercy of God, because Christ the crucified is . . . the bearer of the promise'.[130] It is a theology which in its poverty can only pray for the Creator Spirit to come.

Yet the description of Harnack's and Barth's opposing positions in terms of these two concepts of theology is too broad to be really adequate to either. Harnack had asked specific questions to which he received specific answers along which the discussion continued.

Barth's objection to 'scientific theology'

The theology of the Enlightenment and of the late nineteenth

century can no longer be regarded as being appropriate to the
actual subject matter of theology, the one revelation of God to
man, or to its central theme that God himself became man.
This revelation can be known to man only through God himself and not through specific methods of study or clearly outlined experiences. Indeed these human 'faculties' contribute
nothing to an *understanding* of revelation. The Spirit gives that
understanding through faith; it comes by the self-communication of God to faith which God himself must awaken in man.

The scientific methods of theology described by Harnack are
certainly essential in man's transmission to others of the content
of this revelation, but in themselves the methods cannot bring
about God's self-communication. Between that communication
and those methods there is a barrier which is insurmountable
from man's side. The repudiation of the existence of such a
barrier is indicative of the loss of the knowledge of God as
Creator. That is the barrier found in the cross by which the
oneness between God and man is established. This means that
there is no other way appropriate to God the Creator in which
man can consider that oneness except through the cross. It is
in the cross that God has surmounted the barrier, in and through
the death of the cross that there begins the life of the final
oneness of God and man. God gives that life through Christ;
through him man is born anew to the 'life in God'.

Because the new life begins with death, with the cross which
is also the barrier between God and man, it is not possible to
speak of our attainment of that life as a gradual growth into it.
It also means that statements about God based on considerations of culture (including the statements which define culture
as Harnack does) cannot be equated with the statements the
gospel makes about him since they ignore the barrier. Genuine
statements are made only when one is aware of being confronted
with the barrier, face to face with death and judgment. Here
and only here does there arise true speaking about God – as the
Bible speaks of him.

Since all things come under judgment, and we must give up
everything to it, can we ever presume to possess final knowledge
here and now? Is not our knowledge a knowledge born in hope
and sustained by hope because what we have is given us only
by way of promise? Barth denies that we have any final

possession here and now, since we must all pass through the insurmountable barrier, through man's crisis, through death. The barrier was said to be insurmountable both because God is the Creator from whom man derives his very being and because man's sin, his being lost in a deadly god-likeness, virtually pushes him to death and judgment. That is not a barrier which can be bypassed by a higher morality, reverence and love, because of that 'ontology' of man as sinner. Only the free and self-grounded mercy of God revealed in the cross, in the barrier itself, can avail for man at the barrier.

The knowledge of the meaning of the barrier as God's mercy, the proclamation of which may have to follow ways which are not simple, is based solely on God-awakened faith. Our critical-historical methods of study are helpful in establishing this fact. They are of great service in ridding us of bases of knowledge of God which, because they bypass the *one* revelation of God in Jesus Christ, are utterly inadequate as bases for our knowledge of *God*. We no longer know Christ according to the flesh, we know him through the Spirit who is identical with Christ. But since Christ as God's one revelation is on the other side of the barrier, theology must be satisfied with witnessing to Christ: therein lies its appropriateness, its task, its *raison d'être*.

What exactly does Barth affirm and repudiate in this?

The first affirmation is this: that the reliability and universal validity of the knowledge of the person of Jesus Christ can be only that of a God-awakened faith. This Jesus Christ is the one whom we know through his own Spirit and therefore no longer know according to the flesh. The corresponding repudiation is this: that the Jesus shown to us as the fruit of critical-historical and psychological research, the so-called 'historical Jesus' of the gospels, is a banality which is proclaimed loudly, but in vain, as a pearl of great price. What those scientific methods establish is (to borrow Harnack's words) 'an imaginary Christ' and not the real one. The real Jesus Christ is the one revelation of God and the actual theme of theology.

The second affirmation is found in this statement: 'the task of theology is at one with the task of preaching. It consists in the reception and transmission of the Word of Christ.' This does not mean for Barth a rejection of scientific methods, it means rather a different interpretation of their place in the understanding and proclamation of the gospel. Those methods, especially the historical-critical method of biblical and historical research, are to be fitted into theology and its work in a meaningful way. Barth affirms the critical-historical method but also distinguishes it from the way in which revelation is actually understood. It may well be of preparatory service for the task of theology but it cannot lead to or create the understanding of revelation. This then is the corresponding repudiation: that the historical method is not exclusively the avenue toward man's understanding of God's Word, for theology is not identical with history. Since theology is not able to grasp or lay hold of revelation, and since it only receives and transmits revelation, its task is basically proclamatory, i.e. preaching.

Here we meet with Barth's third affirmation: that theology is the *witness* to revelation. Its objectivity lies in its reference to God's Word, and is evident in its courage to let itself be reminded that Christianity began with testimony. Theology is objective when it is directed to an ultimate reality beyond itself and knows itself to be *en route*, to be a *theologia viatorum*. It is not objective when it assumes that it can speak from a fixed *stand*-point (in the terminology of two of Barth's earlier addresses, *The Christian's Place in Society* and *The Need and Promise of Christian Preaching*). This is exactly what makes up the corresponding repudiation here: that the gospel is not a thing, an object, knowledge of which is derived in the objectivist manner attempted by the positivists in science or history. One cannot take up a merely analytic attitude to the gospel in the belief that one can understand it in this way. Theology is concerned with 'an object which once was subject and which it must become again and again' if we are to know it as it really is. Because this object is also a subject, we cannot have it at our disposal nor know it directly. This subject-object is none other than the transcendent God.

This brings us to the fourth affirmation made by Barth: that theology is a science which operates from within its object. Its knowledge of the object to be known is in fact the presupposition on the basis of which it proceeds to ask its relevant questions. It is a condition of man's knowledge of God that he does not stand outside or over against God, but that he is grasped, comprehended, addressed by God from within. Barth repudiates the claim that this position constitutes the denial of science, or that it is unscientific and sectarian and that it makes *tabula rasa* with human reason and man's other cognitive faculties.

Within these four positive-negative guidelines we may discern and discuss Barth's position as it is developed in response to Harnack's questions and subsequent answers. Barth expands his position in his lengthy reply to Harnack's Open Letter.

Barth's affirmation and use of critical-historical analysis

The 'tone' of Barth's position in that reply is set by the reference to the fathers of the Reformation. The fundamental point of departure of their theological thinking represents a material superiority over the theology prevalent since the Enlightenment, says Barth, because it was still aware of a determinative object of theology, whereas the latter theology is preoccupied with the authority of method. For this reason the Reformers could speak of the theme of theology clearly, something that has not been done since.

It is not the intention of this juxtaposition of the Reformers and recent theologians to discredit the latters' methods. Such methods, however, need to be fitted into the actual work of theology, which is the study of the determinative object. The objection is thus not against the methods used but against the way in which they become the instrument with which that determinative object is bypassed and replaced by something that is not the actual concern of this science. For Barth the concern of theology is with the Word of God. He distinctly rules out everything that is no more than a human impression of it, for such impressions, if they are taken to be the object to be studied, bypass the Word and empty theology of its proper content. There can be no truth beside the truth of the determinative object; the preacher must speak of it and not of his experience or reflections; the theologian must seek it, and not what remains in his sources after the appropriate basis of cognising the truth, which is given in that very truth itself, has been eliminated. Because of the nature of the Word of God and its demand upon us, Barth says that the tasks of theology and of preaching are the same. There are certainly differences in the execution of those tasks, but that does not alter the fact that they are both concerned to seek and proclaim the same truth.

Harnack had objected to this. Barth on his part now objects to Harnack's identification of theology and history on the ground that it empties theology of its actual task. The critical-historical study of the Bible is involved in these objections. Harnack had maintained that any side-stepping of the analysis of the Bible by means of this method leads to sectarianism, and to merely edificatory-subjective views of the truth of God. Barth maintains that the analysis of the Bible by this method leads to an understanding of the words used by the biblical authors but not of the Word of God which they seek to proclaim.

Harnack's objection misses Barth's point, for Barth is not interested in separating the scientific study of the Bible from the work of theology nor in opening the door to biblicism. A glance at Barth's exegetical work shows this. In view of Harnack's objections to Barth on this issue, however, it is difficult to say conclusively that Harnack knew Barth's *Römerbrief*. It is much more likely that, since he did not at first have Barth in particular in mind when asking the original fifteen questions, he had not gone deeply into Barth's exegetical work. It is worth noting that Harnack's colleague Jülicher had written an extensive review of Barth's major work in this area, so that Harnack may well have relied on it.[131]

In August 1918 Barth wrote that the historical-critical method of biblical study has a rightful place in that study because it gives us a very necessary preparation for the understanding of the Bible. This says – with a less provocative flair than the preface to the second edition of the *Römerbrief* – that this method assuredly has a place in the study of the Bible but that it cannot give understanding of what the Bible does in fact say. The method alone will not lead us beyond the place of the spectator to participate in what is being said.

Three years later Barth made this even clearer. The explication of what is written in a biblical text in terms of translation from one language into another and the subsequent philological, archaeological, historical and linguistic analyses are proper and necessary. But that is not the same thing as the attempt to penetrate through the text to the real meaning of the author, to an understanding of what he wants to communicate. Those using the critical-historical method should be more critical. A critical approach to a document cannot stop short at the point where it determines what was actually written in the document. That is only the first stage of its operation. It must rather proceed from there to seek the Word in the words, and pass on to the point where the riddle of the document is solved and its substance is made indubitably clear. Barth respects the critical-historical analysts, yet he feels compelled to ask them whether they are aware of the cardinal question which the exegete must ask and answer: the question about the Word in the words. It would not seem so, Barth thinks, for apparently the task of explaining biblical texts, together with the instruction of how one goes about the 'pure presentation of the Christian's task as a witness', is left to practical theology. That is to say, while Barth recognises the need for critical-historical study, he insists on distinguishing it from the theological exegesis of the Scripture.

This distinction leads us to the very point where Harnack insists that Barth is totally incomprehensible to him when he says in connection with his 'concept of revelation' that no critical-historical or theological method can establish what the Word in the words is.

Barth claimed that man cannot have this Word at his disposal, since it 'is a series of free divine acts . . . which never hardens either in the thesis or in the antithesis, nor stiffens anywhere into positive or negative finalities'.[132] To Harnack this appeared to be the end of theology as a science since human speaking, human perception and human comprehension are eliminated from its operation. Barth's point, however, is that even though exegesis cannot do without that method, its introduction as 'the only way of grasping the object epistemologically' has led to the idea that the actual object of theology can be called God's Word only in a metaphorical sense.

According to Barth that Word is the correlation of Scripture and Spirit and is communicated by God himself. This communication is revelation, the actual content of the gospel, but this means that the object of theology is that Word which is comprehended only by a God-awakened faith.

For Harnack, however, this was no more than a pious platitude; 'believe a little harder' seemed to be the advice Barth gave. If the task of theology is to get intellectual control of its object then the particular dialectics which Barth calls in is clearly an attempt to cover up the weakness which arises when he is asked how that Word is comprehended. All this 'leads to an invisible ridge between absolute religious scepticism and naïve biblicism – the most tormenting interpretation of Christian experience and Christian faith' (above, p. 53). By keeping us constantly 'between door and hinge', constantly in motion, the weakness might not become apparent. Harnack's own method, the historical approach and the emphasis that theology is history, does not know such a weakness, for theology occupies a stance within the interpretation of culture and operates in the belief that history is able to give certain knowledge for our understanding of the world and its course.

For Barth, however, there was a noticeable discrepancy between the fruits of the research done in the name of 'scientific theology' and the dimension of truth in which man lives.

The first objection of a *theologia crucis*, or a *theologia viatorum* to a Harnackian *theologia gloriae* is that it claims to be able to yield final insight into the truth of God, and to be able with its 'scientific' tools to transcend the barrier which stands between the Creator and the creature, between God the Lord and man the sinner, but that in that claim the actual object of theology has become lost.

The second objection is to the cultural analysis and the 'historical pantheism' which precede Harnack's exegesis of the gospel and profoundly influenced his view of it.[133] In his eighth answer to Harnack Barth had indicated why he thought these two factors affected the understanding of the gospel. 'Real statements about God are made only where one is aware of being placed under judgment instead of believing oneself to be on a pinnacle of culture and religion.' The objection is that the 'simple gospel' avoids this element of judgment, this *skandalon*, and seeks to bypass it or neutralise its effect.

The objection to this pantheism of history is that its representatives believed the results of critical-historical study to have absolute validity and to be able to lead us to a vision of the real Jesus on which our faith can then be built up. But such validity cannot be imputed to historical conclusions because historical factors are all relative insofar as they form part of a larger interrelated and contingent whole. This is the reason why Barth contrasts reality with the data of history. Thus he

says that the existence of a Jesus of Nazareth which can be discovered by historical study is not the reality of which the gospel
speaks. A historically discernible simple gospel, discernible
because it is humanly plausible, simple because it causes no
scandal, would not be this reality. A word or deed of that Jesus
which would be no more than the realisation of a human possibility would not be that reality either. The 'simple gospel' is
assumed to speak of this reality because it is believed that God's
revelation may be perceived in that larger interrelated whole
in history by humanly plausible methods.

But then we saw that that is what Harnack in fact believed.
He maintained that the religious forces in man enable him to
rise above nature to culture and that in the persons who were
and are the leaders in this spiritual process the divine may be
perceived. History as a process of graduated ascent toward
culture – in Harnack's sense – is thus regarded as a unity, as an
inclined continuum of nature and culture. Since the forces of
religion – the love of God and the love of one's neighbour – lead
from one to the other, those who exemplify these forces are the
revelation of God. One may therefore make direct statements
about God on the basis of these religious people.

Here God is spoken of in terms of an elated discussion of man,
and a pantheism of history is proposed. Historical study pur-
veys certain impressions of persons who are religious, exhibits
certain acts done in the name of the love of God and of man,
and shows us people's faith in God or their consciousness of the
love and 'holy majesty' of God, but the error of historicism is
that these phenomena are taken to be acts of God. Thus the
consciousness of forgiveness on the part of those people is taken
to be an indication that God loves and forgives us also. Against
this, however, Barth argues that mere credence in historical
facts is no basis for faith in God. Herrmann had driven that
point home to his students. The basis of faith is rather the
obedience a man gives to a human word which testifies to the
Word of God as a word addressed to him, as if it were itself
God's Word. What Barth objects to, then, is that historical
pantheism, on the ground of a oneness of the spirit manifest in
history, proposes direct knowledge of God from history.

Harnack's argument went like this: all institutions of history
are born out of ideas. Ideas precede all historical achievements.

Ideas, however, are spirit. Thus all history is in essence history of the spirit and the spirit is one. This spirit is active in all the results of historical processes and in us. Here we see the unity of all events and our own spiritual essence. The immanence of ideas in reality (which is for Harnack the reality of history, as may be seen in his critique of Marcion) and the development of truth in the course of history were the formal results of the philosophy of the Enlightenment. The higher life of man in God and his life in the world are a continuum because the spirit is one and the same in both spheres. The divine is immanent in history. God and man are correlated.

For this reason Harnack's historicism may be called a pantheism of history. But it bypasses the scandal of judgment, for the otherness of God and his transcendence are ignored, or at least repudiated. Because of this Harnack cannot understand why Barth maintains that God's confrontation with the world means his *NO* to man and man's history, that it means crisis.

Barth raises similar objections to Harnack's cultural analysis. It, too, bypasses the *skandalon*. That argument was that religion interprets the forces of culture which lead man from the lower to the higher life as the love of God and man. The 'cultured' Christian is he who makes the ideals upheld in Christian ethics determinative for his everyday activities. As such this ethical standard of the Christian must not be denied: morality must be given the 'highest valuation' 'gladly', Barth said; but are we really capable of loving our neighbour, and of loving God? The objection is against the view that worldly aims – such as pacifism, Christian socialism – are in fact identical with the kingdom of God. This is probably behind the perhaps somewhat cryptic answer 13 in Barth's first set of replies. 'Which theological tradition is it that, having begun with the apotheosis of feeling has apparently landed happily in the swamp of the psychology of the unconscious? Who thought that a special religious source of knowledge could be opened up apart from critical reason? And – *ad vocem* gnostic occultism – which theology is at every moment notoriously close to the danger of losing its ablest devotees to Dr Steiner?' The answer might be: that theology which believes that our worldly actions of love toward the neighbour, that highest morality and culture are in fact our service of God. It is the theology which – unaware of the transcendence of God – believes that what we do within the world can justify us before God.

Such actions, however, do not bring us to God but rather up against the laws operative in the sphere of immanence, i.e. the sphere of human-practical life, of what is good, true and beautiful. The assumption that highest moral action is as such the work of the kingdom of God is a denial of the scandal of the Word of God, of the crisis which links that kingdom and the sphere of man. Every valuable insight into ethics and culture and each corresponding action stand under God's judgment – including Goethe's *Faust* (the annual performances of which at Dr Steiner's 'shrine' at Dornach, Switzerland, are the highpoint in the life of anthroposophy). The point is that even our cultural analysis does not grant direct cognition of God, and that our highest moral life is not in itself direct service of God. Neither a world-affirming attitude, which seeks to reform the world, nor a world-denying attitude, which leads to protests against the world and a withdrawal from it, can establish the kingdom of God. Rather must it be given absolute precedence, for the kingdom of God is the big *NO* preceding our little no, the big *YES* preceding our little yes. It is the ultimate ground out of which our theses and antitheses arise. The transcendent is the origin of all these immanent movements.[134]

Cultural analysis and historical pantheism constitute a prior frame of thought or a pre-understanding which, according to Barth, have the effect of replacing the real object of theology – God's one revelation – with a 'simple gospel' which really cannot claim to be appropriate to the matter of which the Bible speaks. Genuine theology is emptied through this pre-understanding, and in fact, as Barth says, Christ and man are betrayed.[135] The betrayal consists in the fact that theology takes up a position or assumes a standpoint from which it can dispose over the content of the gospel.

Against this Barth holds that theology is not to be regarded as having a *stand*point, so much as a *view*point, a *mathematical* point on which one cannot stand.[136] 'Our position is in fact an instant in a movement, comparable to the momentary view of a bird in flight, aside from which movement that position is utterly meaningless, incomprehensible and impossible. By movement . . . I mean *that* movement which penetrates all

other movements vertically from above as their hidden, transcendent meaning and motive, *that* movement, in other words,
the origin and aim of which are neither in space nor in time
nor in the contingency of things and which is not a movement
beside others: I mean the movement of God's history . . . the
movement the power and significance of which are revealed
in the resurrection of Jesus Christ from the dead.'[137]

Theology cannot depict what its object is; it cannot depict
this movement. All attempts to do so are as ridiculous as 'to
draw the bird in flight'. Barth admits that at this point he is
weakest,[138] but because 'it is *God* that we are about, the movement *originating in him* and our being moved by *him* and not
religion',[139] he claims that the absence of a standpoint is not a
weakness at all for theology is itself in motion, as life and
testimony.

Here we recall the distinction between the experience of God
and the awakening of faith. The concern with religion and its
experiences is occupied with the derived and fragmentary form
of the divine, with the 'more distinct and more confused symptom of and testimony to the awakening of faith'. The Immediate
and Original is never experienced *as form*, it is not a type of
godliness. The form may very well be a reference to the content
and even though the two, form as the experience of God and
content as that which is known by faith through the action of
the content, are not the same; the former which man sees and
may analyse historically and psychologically may distinctly or
confusedly point away from itself to the latter. It can help us
to become aware of something other than man but the analysis
of that awareness alone cannot determine what in fact it is man
is aware of. This is because the object of that awareness is God
(such at least is claimed by the believer) and God is not correlated with experience.

The content is not 'a new godliness . . . [It is Christ] the
absolutely new from above, the way, the truth and the life of
God among man, the Son of Man in whom mankind becomes
aware of its immediacy to God . . . The way from there to here
. . . is the miracle of God's revelation'.[140]

The gospel as man's witness to God

'But at this point arises your categorical declaration that my concept of revelation is totally incomprehensible to you. You have asked how one might find out what the content of the gospel is . . . I answered . . . that the gospel itself tells us that this understanding occurs exclusively through an action of this very content' (above, p. 43). Barth then proceeds to specify what he means by this. According to the gospel its proclamation is about something that man cannot hear, see or perceive *unaided*. Indeed the gospel by itself cannot communicate its message; the content of that message must make itself known, must come to man and create in him the capacity to hear and see what is being said and shown. The way to that content is created for us by the content itself, while all the other ways of investigation we attempt fail to lead us to it. The way to the content and the content itself are identical; God proclaims himself.

That this is so is indeed puzzling, incomprehensible, for we cannot imagine that to God's way to us there should be no corresponding way that originates with us and leads to God. God's way to us turns out to be our only way to him. But is that not precisely the meaning of revelation, Barth asks, that the way from man to God is exclusively God's way to us? That revelation is something one cannot believe? That one may well acknowledge it yet not comprehend it? That revelation involves something which cannot be reduced to a sublime or profound but nonetheless possible human discovery?

What is this so-called content of the gospel, what is its message? 'It is the totally incomprehensible, inaudible and un-believable, the really scandalous testimony that God himself has said and done something, something new in fact, outside of the correlation of all human words and things, but which as this new thing he has injected into that correlation, a word and a thing next to others but still this word and this thing' (above, p. 43f).

How this testimony is to be accepted is another matter; what is at stake now is that theology be aware that this is the *testimony* with which the Church began its historical existence. This testimony Barth identifies with the Scriptures. Every scientific technique available to help us discern that testimony must be brought to bear on it, but this will not alter the fact that the Scriptures are testimony to the incomprehensible, inaudible and unbelievable new fact of God's Word and deed.

The Scriptures witness and proclaim and refer to that divine reality, as theology and preaching do in their way. For Harnack, however, the Scriptures were rather a source-book. He readily acknowledged this. A reviewer of his *History of Dogma* suggested that Harnack used Christianity and the biblical texts as material for the study of religion, or sources from which to distil the essence of Christianity. Harnack agreed that this was exactly what he meant to do.[141]

This view of the Scriptures is either unaware of or ignores their testimonial character, but Barth maintains that this involves also unawareness or ignorance of the reality to which the Scriptures testify, which is the very content of the gospel. But since this content, as the revelation of God 'vertically from above', not only confronts all events, words and deeds of history as unique truth, word and deed in history but is also placed as such into the correlation of historically discernible words and deeds, it is *as this truth* also a truth of history beside all other truths of history. This is what the historian Harnack ignores or is unaware of.

The testimonial character of the Scriptures was evidently foreign to Harnack. 'It was a weakness of Harnack . . . that he failed to realise the importance of the so-called religious-historical school, and never became sympathetic to it . . . Harnack somehow never clearly saw nor understood the eschatological character of the appearance of Jesus and of his preaching of the imminent advent of the kingdom of God. Moreover, Harnack never gave due consideration to the eschatological consciousness with which the early Christian communities and Paul were suffused. In fact, Harnack never even caught a glimpse of the utter strangeness of the image of primitive Christianity disclosed by the religious-historical school . . . Can the paradoxical situation of primitive Christianity hovering "between the times" . . . be at all viewed as valid after the eschatological expectations of the first Christian generations were extinguished? Is Christian life, perceived and prescribed in the New Testament as a "transcendental" life, viable? The author of *What is Christianity?* was never worried by such questions . . . and it is characteristic of him that the Pauline "as though not" played no role in his thought.'[142]

This weakness, as Bultmann calls it, is due to Harnack's conviction of the ability of history to give final insight. Related to this conviction is another matter of interest to us now: the failure to distinguish between source and testimony.

Harnack had maintained that the question about the essence of Christianity is to be answered historically. 'That is to say he let the history of Christianity define those questions the very formulations of which, in the first instance and most completely, disclose the nature of its origins.'[143] The question is preceded, as we saw above, by an analysis of culture and a pantheism of history, by a prior frame of thought. The answer to that question is thus moulded by a definite world-view, indeed in the case of Harnack Christianity becomes 'an Enlightenment doctrine or an ethical appeal'.[144] This is precisely what engrossed Harnack's attention so that what is testimonial in character was taken to be a historical expression of a particular world-view and thus a source to be probed for the reality behind it.

And yet it may be right to ask whether it was a blindness in Harnack or his aversion to Overbeck which prevented him from seeing this kerygmatic character of the gospel. Harnack knew that what Barth called critical-historical study in his fourteenth answer was the biblical scepticism exercised by Overbeck. This study, said Barth, 'signified the deserved and necessary end of those foundations of this knowledge (of Christ) which are no foundations at all since they have not been laid by God himself. Whoever does not yet know that we no longer know Christ according to the flesh should let the critical study of the Bible tell him so. The more radically he is frightened the better it is for him and for the matter involved!' Harnack's reply to this made it clear that such scepticism in the study of theology endangered its scientific nature. One reason for this is that Harnack is convinced that faith is dependent on the knowledge of the real historical Jesus, so that our faith in God through Christ may have a solid, because historically real, foundation. It had been the merit of the Enlightenment to show that our knowledge of God is irrevocably Christocentric. Once this was grasped it became naturally imperative to establish precise knowledge of Christ; the Church depends on it. Troeltsch made this point very clearly in his statement that for the Church 'there is indeed a dependence on scholars and professors, or better, on a general sense of historical reliability which is created by the impression scientific research makes'.[145] Anyone who does not care for the exact determination of the historical Jesus of the gospels seems also not to care for the scientific nature of theology.

But there is another reason for this fear of Harnack's. He considers the Bible to be a condensation first of a near-Eastern (lower) religion and then of the (higher) Christian religion. How can one understand what the religion in the Bible is? he asked the despisers of scientific theology. Religion was *Weltanschauung* for Harnack insofar as it was the power which helps man 'to free himself from that force which enslaves all beings', the power with which man ascends from the lower life in the world to the higher life in God.

Overbeck's critique is very much to the point here: the gospel is neither religion nor world-view. Christianity is not a historical entity, for 'neither Christ nor the faith he founded have had historical existence under what is called Christianity'.[146] How then can one want to give Christianity a historical basis? Yet exactly this attempt 'has given rise to the question whether Christianity is and can be more than a riddle, a problem namely of fundamentally mysterious nature which questions everything in history'.[147]

'Christianity began by denying itself a history, which then, however, it suffered against its own, originally stated will ... It shows us that there is no chance for it to allow itself to be defended on the basis of historical knowledge. If one subsumes Christianity under the category of the historical, one admits that Christianity is *of this world* and that it has lived in this world – like all life – only to run its course to its end.'[148] The locus of Christianity is therefore not history. Because of its uniqueness and particularity Overbeck calls its locus *Urgeschichte*. 'Christianity means nothing but Christ and the faith in him; it is something supratemporal ... I believe that no attempt of recent times to show historically what primitive Christianity really was has proved the contrary. After Jesus' death Christianity withdrew from every historical comprehension of it, since Christ's followers became something wholly incomprehensible, something which scintillates ambiguously between being and non-being ... Only a clouded mind will let

Christianity begin with the historical person of Jesus Christ.'[149]

Christianity in this sense can be understood only in terms of non-historical concepts, it can be comprehended only through non-historical means of cognition. 'History and *Urgeschichte* are to be distinguished on principle formally and materially. Formally, because they are passed on differently, materially, because their content is different. The objects dealt with in both belong to different worlds or to different series of development.'[150] Overbeck's distinction refers to a qualitative difference. *Urgeschichte* is not merely primordial history, it is a history which is temporally different from history, but it is a history. The conclusion Overbeck drew is that 'Christianity not mysterious', that Christianity 'the centre of which is the historical person of Jesus', is an illusion and self-deceit.[151]

'Long before the religious-historical school moved primitive Christianity out of the bourgeois familiarity of pious ideas into a distant and fantastic world Overbeck saw and pointed out this phenomenon in its original and frightening otherness. Religious-historical research has confirmed his view. Overbeck did not minimise this phenomenon by a clever distinction of suprahistorical meaning and historical form, of temporal appearance and eternal content with which the essence of Christianity could be grasped and determined; he rather allowed primitive Christianity to say what Christianity is.'[152]

It is important to note that Overbeck came to his conclusions regarding *Urgeschichte* on the basis of historical analyses. These were made through a secular methodology which allowed him to see more clearly than his contemporaries that one would neutralise Christianity if one were anxious not to 'hand over to the secular sciences' what is holy. His method made quite clear that faith in Christ and faith in the historical person of Jesus are two different matters, that the latter is in fact against the self-interpretation of Christianity as found in the gospels and that the synthesis of Christianity and culture is a betrayal of Christianity. He made it plain that the 'close tie and the blood-relationship of Christianity and science in general', the aim of which is to make faith acceptable to its cultured despisers and theology to its fellow-disciplines at the university, should be cut, since it can only serve as an apologetic which deceives everyone about Christianity.

According to its own declaration Christianity is not of this world, says Overbeck; it is otherwordly.[153] There is a difference between its world and the world as such. This difference becomes apparent when we see that Christianity 'in all seriousness refers us to the last things, that is to say, it refers us beyond ourselves'.[154] It never envisioned any effects of Jesus in history.[155]

This Christianity cannot be represented by a theology which does not 'rid itself of all historical or scientific claims on Christianity'.[156] On the contrary such a 'representation cannot be based on anything other than the very heart of the matter which is non-historical Christianity'.[157] (This is the point Barth made when he wrote to Harnack that 'historical knowledge could tell us that the communication of the gospel can be accomplished, according to the assertions of the gospel itself, only through an act of the content of the gospel. But critical reflection could lead us to the conclusion that this assertion is founded in the essence of the matter and is thus to be taken seriously.') 'The eternal aspect of Christianity can be spoken of only *sub specie aeterni*, that is, from a point of view which knows nothing of time.'[158] The reason for this is that 'religion does not give us knowledge of God – (where do we have such knowledge?) – it rather wishes to assure us that God knows us. Our knowledge of God as such could not help us if we were in need of help; everything would rather depend on his knowledge of us.'[159]

This so-called radical biblical science or the historical scepticism of Overbeck had demonstrated the otherness of the gospels of primitive Christianity, an otherness which, because it pointed beyond the horizon of history, did not allow the merely historical approach to the gospel to be a sufficient method for its understanding.

Barth based himself on this insight of Overbeck's when he addressed the student-conference at Aarau in 1920 (*Biblical Questions, Insights and Vistas*) just a short time after he published his review of Overbeck's *Christentum und Kultur*.

The Bible speaks to us of the knowledge of God and the last things, Barth said there.[160] Yet this knowledge of God and of the last things is a knowledge which we are not wholly qualified for nor equal to, because our quest for it is not due to our

natural strength, our religious emotion, our religion. Knowledge of God is rather the antithesis to other knowledge. The
Bible makes this clear by confronting us with 'the fact of election'. 'What is called religion and culture may somehow belong
to anyone, but the simple and universal faith which the Bible
offers is not something anyone may have; it is in no way and
at no time anyone's possibility.'[161]

So far Barth has been quite Overbeckian; the element of the
eschatological is very present in the Bible, an element which,
because of its avowed origin in another world, is not open
directly to our comprehension.

What is this special object, which is 'offered' to us in the Bible?
This literary monument of an ancient racial religion and of a
hellenistic cultus religion is a collection of writings about or by
men who are spell-bound by what they see and hear. They see
the invisible, hear the inaudible, say the unspeakable – something astonishing which cannot be interpreted as religion or
worship or experience. Indeed, these men do not interpret it
themselves; they point to it and bear witness to it. It is 'the
turning of God to man', something which cannot be construed
in this-worldly terms.[162]

The object of the Bible is in fact so other-worldly that man
can do no more than witness to it. 'Its true interpretation must
begin with the understanding that the categories of religious
science cannot exhaustively designate and describe this process
(God's turning to man), much less contribute anything toward
an understanding of it. In the biblical experience there is a
decisive element which cannot be made comprehensible by any
of the means of psychological empathy or reconstruction . . .
Biblical religious history has the peculiar characteristic of not
being religion or history in its essence and its deepest aims –
it does not want to be religion but reality, not history but
truth.'[163]

Overbeck could not have said anything like that. He would
recognise only his own emphasis on the other-worldly nature
of the gospel and the impossibility of grasping that nature
through historical categories. Yet it was this very emphasis
that opened Barth's eyes to the nature of biblical statements, to
their referential, ostensive or testimonial nature. The radical
biblical science of Overbeck which refused to regard anything

as sacred and thus as untouchable for scientific analysis showed
that 'biblical piety . . . points beyond the world, points at the
same time and especially beyond itself. It lives completely of
its object and for its object.'[164]

This is the point Barth makes in replying to Harnack that
the Bible witnesses to revelation, that it proclaims God's turning
to man, that God has said and done something new outside the
correlation of human words and deeds and that he has injected
this new Word and deed of his – vertically from above – into
the correlation of human words and deeds.

That testimony is indeed maddening to listen to, incomprehensible and scandalous, but theology must be courageous
enough to begin with it. One may wish to soften or bypass the
scandalous and use the methods of history and psychology
instead in the search for the historical Jesus. But this misses
the 'content of the gospel' and produces what Barth calls a
spectator theology. The point is that one cannot ignore the
eschatological aspect of biblical 'religion' (which the Blumhardts had emphasised), fail to consider seriously the kerygmatic aspect of biblical statements, or overlook its emphasis on
the other-worldliness of its essence (to both of which Overbeck
had drawn attention) and remain an objective theologian, if
objectivity means to accept a phenomenon as it does in fact
confront man, if to be scientific means above all to respect the
dignity and the uniqueness of the phenomenon to be studied.
The objection is that the theology coming from the Enlighten
ment has moved dangerously far away from its object because
it has entered into a blood-relationship with idealism (the
formal and material findings of which Harnack has applauded,
cf. *Marcion*, pp. 221f) and has made historicism its methodological framework. In its hands theology became history and
made 'by its talents what is incomprehensible altogether self-
evident and transparent once again' (above, p. 46). This
theology is estranged from the kerygmatic character of the
gospels and of its own essence. It therefore distinguishes between scientific theology and preaching, between edifying and
educated thought and speech.

In the place of what the fathers called the Word – the correlation of Scripture and Spirit – there appears the simple gospel,
'the essence of Christianity'. Its authority does not derive from

what might be called the authority of Scripture but rather from its 'inner content of eternal matter'.[165] According to this point of view, it is up to theology to discover that content and thus close the gap between accidental truths of history and eternal truths of reason.

According to Barth the simple gospel may be called the Word of God only metaphorically because it is at best only a human impression of it. The object of that theology is religion, the so-called experience of God. But this experience 'is a wholly derived, secondary and broken form of the divine. Even in the most sublime and purest instance it is form and not content . . . "Experience" is always only a reference to the Original, to God . . . No mental apprehension of the form of this truth, however subtle that apprehension may be, can replace or obscure the real transcendence of this content.'[166] Barth accuses Harnack of identifying the experience with the content, and of making what is witness coincide with the reality to which it witnesses. Society has been betrayed because Christ is not brought to it nor is it brought to Christ through this theology. Here is rather a man-made coincidence of form and content, of the reality signified with the sign pointing to it. This coincidence does occur, says Barth, but only as the Word and work of God.

The Scriptures witness to revelation. They witness to the possibility of God, that he has acted in the form of a human possibility. In the person of Jesus of Nazareth, the Christ, God became human-historical reality. Barth then goes on to say that because it is *this* reality to which the Scriptures witness, the reality of God in the flesh, human-historical cognition may well be able to depict exactly what kind of *man* Jesus was, what he said and did, what he meant to those who knew him, all those things, in other words, which Harnack so ably said about him, but it still remains true that faith alone can see God incarnate in this man from Nazareth. And what faith can see in him is precisely that to which the gospel witnesses.

It is admitted that if God became man then as man he is open to human historical cognition. Barth himself came to speak in later years of the humanity of God and of a secondary objectivity posited by revelation. Where there was *diastasis* in the 'early' period there was analogy in the 'later' one. It is

obviously true that there can be no separation between the
human-historical reality of God and his revelation. But is it
really the case that, when Barth insists that the event of God's
becoming human-historical reality is *not* also object of human-
historical cognition, he is in fact separating revelation from the
human, as Harnack charged? Is not Barth's point *here* rather
that even if one affirms 'truly God and truly man' the divine
and the human are not to be correlated or mixed together in
such a way that the divine can be directly and conclusively
read off the human? Is not the point *here* that Christ as God's
Word has become the object of theology in a context in which
man alone calls for consideration? Again, is it not Barth's
point *here* that the humanity of God, the very human-historical
reality to which the Scriptures testify, is just as much a matter
of faith as the true God in the incarnation? It would seem to
me that here Barth is denying that human-historical cognition
can grasp God in the human-historical person of Jesus because
the very humanity of God is as much a matter of faith as his
divinity. I believe this to be Barth's meaning here also because
of what he goes on to say afterwards.

The apostles are interested in the person of Jesus only as it is
related to the reality, God as human-historical reality, to which
they point. They speak of this reality as revelation. And they
do so in such a way that it is apparent that they rule out a direct,
human-historical understanding of it. In their accounts one
sees again and again that the Word and deed of God is hidden
from direct comprehension. The centre of the gospel is the
risen Christ. We know him indirectly only through this testimony, by way of reference to him. Human-historical means of
cognition can determine precisely what their testimony says
but that does not mean that its objective content is then reality
for us. It is still testimony pointing beyond itself. Only through
the act of God's Spirit and the faith it creates does it become
reality for us to which, then, we on our part can also do no
more than witness. Otherwise the testimony is incomprehensible. This makes it scandalous; any attempt, however, to get
round the scandal in order to ascertain directly the objective
content of the testimony goes astray. One must stand still before the scandal, and believe or refuse to believe the testimony
that is given. No other alternative allows the object of this

testimony its proper objectivity. The merit of biblical science, of historical criticism is that it can show us the kerygmatic character of the Bible, so that we can let it fulfil its proper function in directing us beyond itself to the divine reality.

Does this mean that one must 'forever remain between door and hinge', as Harnack expressed it, and stand still before the scandalous, before the paradox that God became man? Can belief not win through to a direct vision of that to which the scandalous refers and thus resolve the paradox? If not, how can man judge between 'rival' scandals which claim him?

The answer must first of all be that it is surely not a matter of paradoxical *statements* with which the Bible is concerned. The actual scandal or the paradox is the event to which testimony is borne. It is not the statement 'God became man' as such which is the paradox, but rather the inaudible, invisible, unspeakable event spoken of. The fact that the statement 'God became man' is true is no doubt paradoxical for man, but the content of revelation, that God became man, is not paradoxical, else there would be no revelation. The point is that if revelation *as an event which is true for man* were not paradoxical, that is, if it did not cut across man's natural this-worldly forms of thought, then there would be no revelation, and the Bible would simply be a source-book for man's own *Weltanschauung*. It is important, therefore, to let our own forms of thought come to an abrupt halt, so that we can respect and consider what confronts us in its own reality if we are to understand it objectively out of itself. When we do stand still like that before the scandal that God became man, we find that it is not paradoxical in itself but paradoxical for us in the sense that it is contrary to our prior opinions or conflicts with our *Weltanschauung*. There can be no way of dissolving that paradox by appealing to some 'outside' criterion which can allow us to reach an independent judgment about it; the logic of the actual event must be allowed to assert itself and give us understanding of it in accordance with its own nature and reality. Then only will the scandal be overcome.

What is demanded of us is faith, faith as the acceptance of the unbelievable testimony of the Scriptures, of the scandal that God became man. It is an obedience toward a human word which proclaims to us God's Word as addressed to us.

Human words have no authority to do this on their own, so
that this word spoken to us, even though it appears to be God's
Word itself, is really only testimony to it. It becomes God's
Word to us and ceases to be mere testimony through the Holy
Spirit; it becomes reality for us through an action of the content
of the gospel, and thus ceases to be something to which previ-
ously one could only point. The transition from testimony into
reality for us, the scandal which is a paradox, can take place
only through an act of God himself. Faith is different from all
other human functions of cognition. Apart from faith, the God-
awakened acceptance of the testimony, the human word which
tells us of God's Word must remain an incomprehensible, rather
dark and confused human utterance.

The process – if one may speak of it as such – is this: God has
spoken the Word of Christ. It is the object of preaching and of
theology. The Scriptures witness to that Word. Through that
witness the Word is also addressed to me, and through the Holy
Spirit's own testimony I hear – not just words uttered by
apostles – but the Word of Christ and by hearing it also believe
it. This is nothing less than a miracle; it is a new birth, a being
raised from the dead, since the Word is that of Christ who is the
crisis of man and the world.

The possibility of knowledge of God

The objectivity described in the concept of the correlation of
Scripture and Spirit is turned critically against the objectivity
alleged to be in the scientific theology of Harnack.

It opposes the assumption, made in the belief of an immediate
knowability of God, that God is a given 'entity' which may be
known through direct observation. Against this Barth states
that God is knowable only when he acts and reveals himself;
our knowledge of him is not identical with the knowledge we
have of his creatures. It is not a knowledge comparable to that
derived through experience, inner openness, heart or feeling.
Such 'faculties' establish a direct grasp of the object, and enable
man to have or possess knowledge. But man cannot have or
possess God. God is not known through man's intellectual
control or possession of him. The God whom man seeks to
know through that kind of possessing, whether he is 'had' in
man's experience or conscience, or in the supreme achieve-

ments of cultural creativity, or in the development of the spirit in history, or in the 'life-force', or in the abyss of being, in the crisis of man or the world – in all these he is too much like the projection of man himself which Feuerbach denounced as illusion. Barth, however, is equally aware that God is not to be 'had' in the critique of this intellectual control over him, or in the critical protest against this possessing of him. He is not grasped epistemologically in the *NO*, in which God rejects the adequacy of our conceptions of him; man cannot have God, but he can witness to him. This witness is said to be objective since it acknowledges the distance between Creator and creature, the *vis-à-vis* of God to man, his transcendental otherness.

Real knowledge of God is said to arise where man is confronted by God in revelation and is thus placed under judgment along with all that he thinks he has or can conceive of God. The only cognitive unity of God and the creature is through the cross, man's crisis and death and his new birth, for there God makes himself known to man in such a way that he is radically called in question by the divine revelation.

'The forces of the gospel direct themselves to the deepest foundations of human existence and only to them; there and there alone is their leverage applied. Whoever cannot go down to the roots of humanity, and has no feeling for them and no understanding of them, will not understand the gospel.'[167] No, Barth answers, we come from the truth of man to the truth of God only through a new birth, from death to life (above, p. 33f). 'But who can, without a deep sense of panic, speak and hear of him who, as the men of the Bible see and perhaps we also see from a distance, must increase? When we turn our backs on the merry circus of the history of religion, we are surrounded by something of the oppressive stillness and solitude of the desert which arouses awe and nothing but awe, the desert which in the Bible is not for nought such an important place. It must indeed be a *mysterium tremendum* which draws the men of the Bible before our eyes more and more to the edge of time and history, of experience, thought and action and impels them to take their stand in mid-air, where one can obviously only fall. Would it not be better for our peace of mind to turn back here? Shall we dare to follow with our eyes the direction of the pointing hand of Grünewald's Baptist? We know where it points.

It points to Christ. But to Christ the crucified, we must add here right away. There it is! is what that hand says ... The only source for immediate and real revelation of God is death. Christ has made it manifest. Out of death he brought life to light.'[168]

Man's knowledge of God means facing judgment. Harnack regarded this view as first of all a denial of every valuable insight culture believed itself to have about God and secondly as a scepticism of the world which is characteristic of sectarianism. It also meant for him doubt as to the cognitive powers of human reason. But Barth speaks of this crisis in revelation in relation to man's sin. Sin is more than a lack of reverence and love, it has entered the very structure of man's being, his being lost in a god-likeness which leads to and ends in death. Sin is man's self-assertion over and against God in which man in fact tries to raise himself up to the level of god-likeness.

The re-emergence of the notion of God's wrath and judgment annoyed Harnack. He really seems to be enthusiastic in discussing Marcion's conception of that wholly other God's love. If we remember that Harnack was preparing the second edition of his book on Marcion during his public discussion with Barth, the parallelism in his formulations becomes more meaningful. The sphere of Marcion's divinity is love which drives out all fear. Humility alone can receive this love. This concept of God as love is the supreme, the final concept in our understanding of God. For Marcion such understanding is not speculative but rather the result of Christian experience, for one experiences love in the person of Jesus Christ who is the embodied reality of almighty love.

Jesus Christ is the beginner and perfecter of this new liberating power of God, of almighty love. Marcion preached with magnificent assurance that *Jesus' will to love, that is to say, God's will to love does not judge but helps*.[169] Every motive of fear is excluded from the gospel; the only reaction to sin can be disgust which leads to the renunciation of sin.

Harnack concluded this section of his book with the affirmation that Marcion's way of preaching the gospel meets the situation of today. It answers today's questions. Those among the despisers of organised Christianity who know the soul of the people best, assure us that only a proclamation of love which does not judge but helps has any chance of a hearing. Marcion stands thus right next to Tolstoy and Gorki. And this kind of Marcionism has a great deal more to offer than those who come to us with their *quid pro quo* opinions.[170]

But Barth again spoke of judgment and God's wrath which introduced all kinds of paradoxes and perpetuated that situation which is detrimental to the humility of the Christian – his assurance of God's love which can help him to live the life in God. 'How can a minister talk this way when that sort of talk will not be given a hearing?' asked Harnack. Barth makes faith an illusion when he speaks of the cross and man's crisis as the point of man's contact with God. In the person of Jesus Christ man becomes aware of his childhood in God, the cross only shows how great that love for man was. As such the cross is not at all necessary as a factor in our faith. God is love, this knowledge makes Christianity pure religion. Whoever is re-conciled with God knows that for those who have not yet found God to be that way, he appears to be angry. But this idea of God's wrath is a deception which through Christ is done away with. Thus, we must alter our attitude to God and the gospel helps us in this. The loving Father has always been waiting for us with love; the parable of the prodigal makes this helpful and comforting truth plain.

Barth's understanding of the cross and of sin, of man's being lost in a god-likeness which ends in death and judgment, which is made plain on the cross, speaks not of eternal truth which Marcion, Luther, Tolstoy, Gorki, and then scientific theology since Schleiermacher, have discovered, but of a revolutionary fact, of an event. Christ not only preaches the Word of God, he *is* the Word. The gospel is not that the eternal truth is now 'out' and made public, it is the event of God's love in space and time. To overlook the event-character is to overlook the wrath of God and vice versa. To speak of the gospel as the becoming known of an eternal truth is to rule out as deception everything but the love of God. It is equally a cheapening of God's mercy and grace. Luther, who had 'rediscovered' the truth of God's love, also said that man always stands before that loving God with empty hands, depending wholly on God's grace. To ignore the event-character of the gospel is to overlook its kerygmatic nature, to overlook the fact that it is a testimony to

God's action in man's space and time. Therefore, one may rightly speak of the gospel as *Heilsgeschehen*, as the event – *das Geschehen* – of salvation – *das Heil*.

God's confrontation of man is man's judgment, it is man's standing before revelation where he is questioned and searched, slain and made alive, said Barth. That revelation is Jesus Christ, God become man, crucified and now risen. To know this is to have faith. 'Faith comes through the preaching of the Word of Christ', the Word of man's justification in his crisis and man's obedience to the testimony to Christ. The knowledge of faith is one of ac-knowledgment, cognition is re-cognition.

This knowledge or cognition, this faith is not a matter of man's consciousness insofar as one must admit that the statements of faith are assertions which man could not make on the basis of his self-knowledge or cognition of the world. This impossibility causes faith always to be also unfaith. Faith is not a once-and-for-all, not a standpoint but a movement, the fruit of the Holy Spirit's inward testimony. It is the action of the content of the testimony which Barth calls the miracle of revelation. The miracle is not, however, that a gap between an accidental truth of history and the essential truth of reason has been bridged 'vertically from above', but that God himself acts through his Spirit today in us who hear the witness of the apostles just as he acted in them at the time when they witnessed to his revelation in Christ; the miracle is that God acts in us today in the midst of 'the darkness of our spirit and culture' (above, p. 50), just as he did at the time of those witnesses who spoke of that 'unpleasantly dark history' (*ibid.*), of the particular event to which they testify. The miracle is, in other words, the simultaneity of God's act, of what is 'the essence of the whole matter: his relation to man' (above, p. 31f).

But Harnack replies that Barth cuts faith from the human, since he speaks of the Word of God as something so objective that human 'faculties' can be set aside in the understanding of that Word. Barth's denial that the Word of God can be grasped epistemologically amounts to an erasing of critical reflection etc. in the methodology of theology.

This is a misrepresentation, says Barth. The intention is to dispute the continuity of faith and the human, not to sever them. The human is not to be discredited but must be allowed to appear for what it really is and that means the repudiation of every attempt to divinise it.

Barth does emphasise the discontinuity of revelation and the human, yet the stress on *diastasis* is not to be interpreted as a severing of faith and the human. Still, the insistence on the latter is only half convincing. It is clear that the 'natural-titanic presumptuousness of the *homo religiosus*' (above, p. 48), which had identified the 'thing signified with the sign pointing to it' (above, p. 48), must be repudiated. However, the insistence on discontinuity raises the question of how man is involved in revelation, a question which in view of the overstressing of this point is not satsifactorily answered. Eventually, Barth rectified this issue.

Man's faith may be described as inner openness, experience, religion, and the like, but one must not believe that this describes the divine. Those things are, in their way and actuality, the created realities which testify but do no more than testify to the uncreated absolute. Faith is therefore also a psychologically-historically discernible indication of the miracle of God. The religion in the Bible is a witness to the historical reality of God's revelation, but it still remains a fact that we can know it only through faith.

Barth explicitly denies the possibility of positing something relative as the absolute. He asks not 'how *do* we speak of the absolute?' but rather '*can* we speak of it at all?' and answers that because we are human we cannot do that.[171]

It is precisely with this impossibility that Barth's theology begins. In his review article of Overbeck's *Christentum und Kultur* he said that it was Overbeck's merit to have shown that only the impossible can help us out of the impossible.[172] The impossible which can help us is the reality of God's self-revelation which as such is the event in which there is posited the reality acknowledged by theology. The impossible possibility, namely the coincidence of time and eternity, occurs as God's deed in which the opposition between each of the poles mentioned is not abrogated so that a continuity between them results. But if this coincidence posits itself and precedes our speaking of God then our question about God is, as Overbeck put it, identical with the fact that we have already been answered by him. We ourselves cannot give that answer. In-

deed, even our question about him arises in the first instance
because it has been begotten in us by him as the wholly other,
and is not the result of any continuity with the divine immanent
in us. By giving this answer to the question '*can* we speak at
all of God?', by uttering a loud *NO*, Barth attempts to point to
the reality, to the truth which posits itself and speaks to us in
the correlation of Scripture and Spirit, or of the testimony to it
on the part of man and its own self-communicating activity.

How is man to speak of the reality of the testimony?

This question leads to the actual concern of Barth's 'early'
theology. It was expressed in the identification of the tasks of
theology and preaching and is dealt with explicitly in the
address *The Need and Promise of Christian Preaching*.

For Barth the concrete responsibility of theology is the reception and the transmission of the Word of God. To say that the
question regarding the understanding of the Bible and its
proclamation, that the horizon marked by the text of the
Scripture and by the sermon, is the origin and goal of theology,
is indeed to characterise Barth's 'theological existence' and the
premise of his whole theology.

Barth contrasts the 'chaotic business of the Faculties today
for which the authoritativeness of the method' has become the
all-absorbing task with the 'idea of a determinative object'
(which has become strange and monstrous to Harnack and
other scientific theologians). He confronts Harnack with his
criticism of the question as to 'how do we do this?'. For Barth
theology operates on the road between text and preaching,
between witness to God and proclamation of what is witnessed
to.

The problem for theology is that as theologians we ought to
speak of God. But we are human and as such cannot speak of
God. We ought to acknowledge both our obligation and our
inability and by that very acknowledgment give God glory.[173]
The problem arises since the theologian must speak of God and
not of something intermediate or penultimate but of something
final. He must proclaim the truth which is of God. Because
of this the situation of the theologian 'is eschatological . . . that
is to say, when this situation arises history, all remaining his-

tory, comes to an end and an ultimate desire of man for an ultimate event becomes authoritative'.[174] However, this desire for an ultimate event, this questioning on the part of man is answered by the Bible, from which the theologian took his starting point, in terms of an even more radical question put to man. 'The Bible quite simply takes its place beside the man who has been awakened to an awareness of his position (that his certainty is wavering) and asks with him . . . is it true, really true, that there is a meaning to everything, that there is a goal, a God? – But the Bible differs in two aspects from the awareness of this awakened man. In the first place it confers on his question a real depth and significance and does so in a way which once again leads even the most frightened, most humbled, and most despairing man to the edge of an abyss of which he had no idea; . . . in a way that we must all see that all our questioning was only a preparation and practice for the serious question: namely whether we are asking in dead earnest, whether we are asking after God?'[175]

With this desire for an ultimate event, with this question for the final truth man is, however, already in that event even though the event confronts man in terms of the question for it. Man cannot give himself the answer, cannot bring about the event, he is at best suspended between recollection and anticipation of it.

This is why the situation of the theologian, commissioned but unable also to speak of God, is a situation of need and promise. God's answering is not at man's disposal, it rather takes place between the need and the promise of Christian preaching. The event is God's speaking in human words between the Scriptures and the congregation, between the text and the sermon, between testimony and theology.

'This is the promise of Christian proclamation: that we speak the Word of God. Promise is not fulfilment. Promise means that fulfilment is assured to us. Promise does not do away with the necessity of believing but establishes it. Promise is man's part, fulfilment is God's.'[176] Man's part is his expectation of fulfilment. Fulfilment on the other hand is more than expectation insofar as it is the event itself which goes beyond what we ask or expect, so that the answer God gives really elicits our question for him.

This is characteristic of Barth's thought. It is not our existential questions only which are answered by God, so that the
important thing is really to ask the right questions and then to
look for the answer. It would appear that even then – 1922 –
Barth refused to make man's questions normative. Man might
perhaps never want or even dare to ask the question which,
when answered, meant his crisis. In his Elgersburg address,
October 1922, he put it this way: 'When people come [to the
minister] for help, what they have on their heart is not their
existence, but the beyond of their existence, God's existence . . .
Man as man cried out for God, not for *a* truth, but for *the* truth,
not for *something* good, but *the* good, not for answers, but for
that answer which is identical with his question. For he himself, man, is the question and so the answer must be the question, he himself must be it but now as the answer, as the
answered question. Man cries out not for solutions [*Lösungen*]
but for absolution [*Erlösung*] . . . But this answer, this reality
(which is the subject of all the predicates, the origin of all the
abortive beginnings in which man finds himself), this subject,
this meaning, this origin is there, beyond, not here. The
answer is not the question. He who is there, beyond, is not he
who is here. When man asks for God he asks for the answer
which as such would be his answer, he asks for the infinite,
which as such would be finite, he asks for him who is what he
is there, beyond, also here, he asks for God who as God is also
man.'[177]

The answer is God's to give and man's to point to. But
precisely this questioning, this situation between Scripture and
congregation is an ontological situation because it is a question
for truth. What Harnack relegated to scientific theology, the
question as to the ultimate truth about God, Barth regards as
the final concern for both theology and preaching.[178] It is
Barth's understanding of revelation as an act solely of God
which makes him relate the ontological question to the situation of preaching. If the question is answered (and only God
can do so) then it is in the situation between Scripture and
sermon – hence the definition of God's Word as the correlation
of Scripture and Spirit. But the answer is promised to us; we
do not possess it, we grasp it in faith, in the hope that God's
promise to fulfil it will come true. 'Yearning and supplication

F

will always be the first and the last thing for us', writes Barth
to Harnack (above, p. 34), and the meaning of that is that
man's prayer for that fulfilment is the closest he can come on
his own to the event in which fulfilment is given by God. Similarly Barth described his theology as the sigh *Veni Creator
Spiritus*, the sigh which points to the situation of theology
between Scripture and Spirit.[179]

Yet, since theology must speak of God but is unable to answer
the ontological question, how are we to speak of God? How
are we 'to give God the glory in the knowledge of our obligation
and our inability?' Or how can we speak of God appropriately
when the objectivity of our theology is determined by the act
of God which set in motion our very question and search for
him but which is an act over which we cannot dispose? How
can we speak of the truth, or reality, when the Word of God,
that truth and reality, cannot be subsumed under a general
epistemology? Given this kind of ontological premise, what
hermeneutics does one develop? How is theology to speak of
that history, that event which, as God's actual speaking to man,
as his Word, is *promised* to man's proclamation but not *given
over to it*, that event which occurs as an act of God *in* but not *of*
man's preaching? Harnack answered that this is 'a dialectic
which leads to an invisible ridge between absolute religious
scepticism and naïve biblicism' . . . and claimed that it was
unable 'to create community' and rather destructive of whatever presented itself 'as Christian experience' (above, p. 53).
But then he had already conceded that Barth's concept of
revelation was totally incomprehensible to him and that he
could not discuss things which he did not understand. His
estimation of Barth's hermeneutics, his dialectic, rests in the
confessed inability to understand Barth's point of view. That
alleged inability is, however, inability to accept and not in-
comprehension, it is disagreement with that point of view.
Harnack could not accept that an understanding of God's Word
is possible only within the event of God's addressing man,
within the act of the 'content' only. That concept of revelation
is one of pronounced actualism, as the emphatic *NO* to Harnack's questions 5 to 11 shows. Harnack's own replies indicate
that he regarded actualism as speculative dualism. By repudiating any extension of revelation in history and culture, Barth

left nothing but a 'vacuum, a crater created by the impact of revelation', as he said elsewhere.[180]

Before we pass on to a consideration of Barth's dialectic we must look at the actualism of that period.

God is *totaliter aliter*, he is the wholly other.[181] Harnack had correctly interpreted this emphasis of Barth's thought, except that he had considered it to be Marcionite.[182] God and man are not on the same level and every attempt to overcome this separation apart from God's event of speaking his Word is rejected – hence the sharp renunciation of religion. 'Religion, as we know it in ourselves and others, is a human possibility which, as such, is the religion of the highly problematical attempt to depict the bird in flight. Religion in every conceptual, comprehensible and historical sense must be regarded and rejected as an appearance of the world of man.'[183]

If the Word of God is understood in terms of the event of its self-communication, theology can speak of an intersection where the different levels of God and man meet. This point has no extension on our level of existence.[184] The resurrection from the dead is the point of intersection. 'The resurrection is revelation, the discovery of Jesus as the Christ, the appearance of God and the cognition of God in him . . . In the resurrection the new world of the Holy Spirit touches the old world of the flesh. But it touches it as a tangent touches a circle, without touching the latter world. Precisely because it does not touch it, the world of the Holy Spirit touches the world of the flesh as its boundary, as a new world.'[185] This geometrical figure shows Barth's concern to depict the either-or character of God's truth *vis-à-vis* man's. It indicates the rejection of every assumed continuum between God and man on the basis of which one might speak directly of God. ('I explicitly deny the possibility . . . of going from testimony to direct statement . . . which is and must remain, in the most exclusive sense, God's concern', Barth had written to Harnack (above, p. 48).)

Revelation is dialogical, it is God's addressing man; this is an irreversible sequence. 'The "instant" is and remains something unique in comparison to what preceded and what followed it, it is different, strange, does not extend itself in what follows, nor does it have its roots in what went before. It stands in no temporal, causal or logical relation, it is always and everywhere the absolutely new, always the being, the having and doing of God . . . Life comes always only out of death, beginning only out of the end, Yes only out of the No . . . Between us and God there stands and there will always stand the cross, uniting but also separating, full of promise but also full of warning. The paradox of faith can *never* be bypassed and is never removed. *Sola Fide, through faith alone* man stands before God . . . the faithfulness of God can *only* be believed because it is God's faithfulness.'[186]

Even if we describe Barth's concept of revelation as the event of God's Word being spoken and say that it is an actualist concept, even if we show that in it Barth's criticism of every attempt to speak the truth of God on the basis of what is possible for man manifests itself, it is important also to state that Barth himself does not want to use the categories of pure actuality, eternal future and event as adequate or appropriate terms by which revelation can in fact be described. This would only be establishing a new kind of continuum in which the free Word of God is again 'at our disposal'.[187] These terms as much as the method of speaking – even the dialectical method – fail in the end, for neither can do what only God can do, namely speak his Word. Both are testimony only, both are parabolic, neither is standpoint, but 'a pinch of spice in the food'. Neither our concepts, the form of the divine, nor our method of speaking can bring the Transcendent to us.

Such actualism, restrictive as it is *vis-à-vis* Harnack, is intended to safeguard the sovereignty and freedom of God and his grace towards man. That which is promised to Christian preaching cannot be fulfilled by man; actualism is meant to show that and is thus negative. But it is positive also insofar as it leaves our understanding of God's Word open for the reality promised in the testimony to God's Word, namely salvation, the good itself, that reality which, in other words, is beyond our possibilities.

The dialectical relation between revelation and man's speech concerning it

But how then does one speak of God's revelation? 'To speak of God would, if it were meant to be serious speech, mean to speak on the foundation of revelation and faith. To speak of

God would mean to speak God's Word, that Word which can come from him only, the word that *God becomes man*. We can utter those three words, but have thereby not spoken God's Word in which that fact becomes *truth*. Our theological task would be to say that, to say that *God becomes man*, but to say it as *God's* Word as in fact it really is *God's* Word.'[188]

Barth sees three ways in which the attempt to speak that word can be made. All three will, however, end up by seeing that they have failed. These ways are: dogmatism, self-criticism and dialectics.

In its attempt to speak of God the first way leans on the Bible and develops the ideas embodied in the christological, soteriological and eschatological dogmas. Such dogmas show a great deal of objectivity in their basic treatment of the conception in which they rest, namely that God becomes man. But the difficulty with dogmas arises at the point where the descriptions given in these dogmas are taken to be the very things described. A christological truth is not Christ, a soteriological dogma is not salvation and an eschatological concept is not man's hope or God's kingdom; these descriptions are an objective witness at best to God, but are not identical with revelation. This way does not speak of God as it was defined.

The second way is a radical self-abnegation: all of man is surrendered so that he becomes sheer receptivity to the being of God. Man as man is overcome by placing himself under the judgment, all titanism is done away with, man dies to himself so that every obstacle is removed. It is asserted that the utter negation before which man stands, the abyss he falls into here is God. God, in other words, is spoken of here in terms of a very loud negation of man, or in terms of man's radical self-criticism. But this way does not lead to the question of what is ultimately positive beyond the negative. God, however, cannot be spoken of when man is denied. God's Word is addressed to man in his concrete existence. 'The cross is erected here, yes, but the resurrection is not preached in this way for which reason it is then not really the cross of Christ which is erected here, but another one. The cross of Christ does not really need to be erected by us.'[189] When God enters into our emptiness with his fullness, into our No with his Yes – then we may speak of God.

The third way is the way of dialectics. Barth says that he travels on this way, since it 'repudiates every continuity between hither and yonder. It refers to an identity which cannot be established nor presumed by us' (above, p. 49).

On this way then the question of our commission and obligation to speak the Word of God is to be answered. Here we are to explore what is involved in that promise that God's Word shall be proclaimed in man's word. This obligation brings theology to the event between testimony and proclamation. The hermeneutical question is determined by the event-character of the Word of God, so that right from the beginning the question 'what does the text say?', 'what is the meaning of Scripture?' is led through the critical-historical method of exegesis to the movement from God to man which, like the bird in flight, cannot be depicted. The task of hermeneutics is thus not only to verify human expressions, human testimony, but also and above all to question the text so that the answer promised there may in fact elicit the right kind of questions as to truth, reality and salvation. But this cannot be done when the text is taken away or abstracted from the event of God's Word. Barth said this to Harnack when he remarked that for the understanding of revelation, occurring through the Spirit, critical reflection, historical knowledge, etc. are of preparatory value and thus necessary. But they cannot bring about that event itself. Similarly, the real Jesus Christ cannot be depicted by historical analyses; they rather come up with an 'imaginary Christ', not the one to whom the New Testament witnesses.

Harnack had then asked: how is scientific theology possible if its object is not open to scientific methods and cognition? His question actually was: how can one have a science if its object is not open to *direct* insight?

(In her biography of Harnack Agnes von Zahn-Harnack writes that philosophers would not be able to regard Harnack as a philosopher. Even Harnack's friend, Dilthey, knew that his ideas and Harnack's were worlds apart. She writes that Harnack thought differently, not in the sense of disagreement but rather in the sense of moving in a different sphere. It means that he did not really follow what Dilthey and others had to say. In our context it would indicate that he did not ask the question of the presuppositions of human cognition, of human thought the way Dilthey and others, for example Troeltsch, did. Harnack's late essays about human understanding reveal that he did not see the same problems as Troeltsch did in his *Der Historismus und seine Probleme*. Because Harnack did not raise such questions he could not see the distinction between a science that claims direct insight and one which sees the need for dialectical speech in order to express its insights. In the natural sciences the concept of complementarity became necessary shortly after Harnack and Barth had this discussion.)

In that 'staggering address' at Aarau, Barth said in Harnack's hearing that 'it is abundantly clear that intelligent and fruitful discussions about the Bible begin beyond the insight into its human, historical-psychological character'.[190] Later in their correspondence Barth charges Harnack's historical analysis of the gospel, desirous of being founded on nothing but historical facts, with being predetermined by his doctrine of culture and his 'historical pantheism' which are in fact ontological constructs preceding and determining that analysis of the gospel.

But criticism does not answer the question of how one speaks of God between one's obligation and inability to do so. The point of the criticism, however, is to show that this speech cannot come from any assumed relationalism[191] but that it comes from the event of God's self-revelation in the testimony of men to him. This event makes our speech possible.

Barth's presupposition for theology is this event of revelation, the history which God's Word makes for itself. It is precisely that which precedes hermeneutics, the event of the Word, God's free self-communication, that this method emphasises, but for this reason it is aware that it cannot achieve or bring about the event on its own, and cannot relate it to cultural, personal or historical factors in such a way that it might gain control over it or reproduce it.

Theology is, therefore, obliged to follow the movement of the event which takes place between the text and the proclamation, between Scripture and theology. It is the task of theology, therefore, to follow the thinking in the text of the Scripture. 'It is the peculiarity of biblical thought and speech that they flow from a source which lies above religious antinomies such as creation and redemption, grace and judgment, nature and spirit, earth and heaven, promise and fulfilment. Of course, they enter now on the one then on the other side of those anti-nomies, but they never bring them pedantically to a conclusion, never come to a halt in the consequences, never harden either in thesis or antithesis or solidify anywhere in final affirmations or negations. Biblical thought and speech have no "antenna" for what our ponderous age calls "an honest either-or". It is concerned with the Yes just as much and as little as with the No, for the truth does not lie in the Yes nor in the No, but in the understanding of the beginning out of which the Yes and the No arise. They are thought and speech which are original, thought and speech coming from the whole and going to it . . . They want to be understood but never just accepted . . . They are dialectical through and through . . . The Bible has just *one* theological interest and that is purely objective: the interest in God himself.'[192] Theological speech must correspond to bib-lical speech.

Thus, we return to consider the way of dialectics. 'Right from the beginning this way seriously undertakes to develop positively the idea of God on the one hand and the criticism of man and all things human on the other; but neither of these must be done independently but in constant regard of their common presupposition, the living truth which, of course, cannot be named but which lies between them in the middle and which gives to both the affirmed and the negated their meaning and significance. That God (but really God!) be-comes man (but really man!) – that is understood there as the living truth, as the decisive content of any true speech concerning God. But how is that necessary relation of both sides to the living centre to be established? The true dialectician knows that this centre cannot be apprehended or beheld, so that he will allow himself to be drawn into giving direct information about it as rarely as possible, knowing that all such information be it positive or negative, is *not* information *about it* at all but always *either* dogma *or* criticism.'[193]

For Barth this centre is the 'centre of the gospel', the 'essence of the matter (namely the relation between God and man)'; it is the oneness of God and man in Jesus Christ. This centre is not at man's disposal, it can only be witnessed to by a continu-ous process of affirmation and negation. Neither side of this process can claim finality because they are parabolic only.

But parabolic statements are based on the presupposition that somewhere between question and answer there lies the promised truth, the reality of God. 'The assertion on the right [that which is affirmed] sounds unambiguous as does that on the left [that which is negated], but the concluding assertion that both in the last analysis assert the same thing is very ambiguous.'[194] But how can such ambiguous speech carry meaning and bear witness? When it does succeed in this it is because the living centre has asserted itself and has created both the right question and the right answer. This the dialectician cannot do; God speaks not as a part of the dialectical process but when it breaks off. The method cannot bring about the event on which it is based and to which it points.

On the one hand, this dialectic is *critical* insofar as it *repudiates* every continuity between the world of man and that of God. Because everything here is said in reference to God only, this third way makes it very plain that the truth is painfully absent from all three ways as such: truth arises at the point where they come to an end and must point beyond themselves. But on the other hand it is *constructive* insofar as it does indeed *refer* to the event of God's presence, the miracle of God's addressing man. It points to the synthesis which precedes thesis and antithesis in the dialectic. But that thetical-antithetical way of speaking is all we have. 'God is one, the God of Jacob in eternity who reveals himself as God to man. But we can understand that we cannot *understand* God other than in a duality, in the duality of dialectic, in which one must become two so that two are really one.'[195]

With this inadequate way we, who are obliged but unable to speak of God, are to give him glory, precisely because in it God remains God and is not a dogmatic dictum or an imaginary deity.

This dialectical thought and speech corresponds to biblical thought and speech, to the need and promise of Christian preaching. The locus of real speech and thought concerning God is between Scripture and preaching, thesis and antithesis, and since it is the event of revelation which, as the synthesis, sets in motion this dialectical way, one cannot speak as a spectator who from outside makes his observations and comments but as an insider who has been addressed, claimed and laid hold of. Or, in Barth's words, our questions are not answered until the answer, given in revelation, has re-made our questions and thus opened the door to the real answer. 'How can one hear, understand and know the answer in any other way? But the answer is the primary. It would be no question if it were not the answer.'[196] The fact that we go to the Scripture with the question for the Word of God, to which the Scripture claims to witness, presupposes that the Word has been spoken in it; the Word testified to in it leads to the question for that Word and in correlation with the Spirit becomes event between Scripture and testimony. 'We are inside and not outside, inside the knowledge of God, inside the knowledge of the last things, of which the Bible speaks . . . The question of God is the last inevitability and it is evident that our very asking is full of the answer, that we are pressed hard and taken captive by a pre-supposed original Yes.'[197]

Barth had expressed this to Harnack in their correspondence 'in many and diverse ways', but we shall now try to gather what he had to say into a connective form. The gospel is communicated through an action of its own content – the one revelation of God in Christ. The content of the gospel is God become man, subject, and this is really understood as an utterance of God only in the event when he becomes subject again and thus confronts us. This event cannot be reproduced through critical-historical study or methods nor is it an experience which can be analysed psychologically. Whatever we study critically-historically and psychologically is only indirectly indicative of the event. Direct statements about God are not possible since there is an utter contrast between God and man which only the cross of Christ, man's judgment, bridges. Yet this contrast, this either-or, is also the unity of God and man, the overcoming of the contrast and the salvation of man from judgment. The No to man in the cross is also the Yes to him. But the knowledge of this content and thus of man's salvation is knowledge of things promised in the Bible, while the fulfilment comes from God only in the event of his speaking in fact his Word to me. Outside of the sphere of this event, outside God's judgment and his No, one can only speak as a spectator and thus cannot make real statements about the Word addressed to man. Such statements would rather empty faith; they do not speak of God but replace the Word with something which is at best only an associate effect of it and thus only indirectly indicative of it.

The event cannot be brought about by man. If there is a way to it then the content of it must be that way, the speaking voice must also be the listening ear. God alone is the way to it and the goal of that way. Revelation as a concept already implies that one cannot go from here to the beyond. The Bible itself indicates this since it speaks of God, of the beyond, of salvation, etc., in a testimonial or kerygmatic fashion. It speaks of it as something new outside of the correlation of human words and deeds but injected precisely as such into that correlation, so that it comes as the new, incomprehensible thing of God clothed in human words and deeds.

This testimony is the Scripture through which by the action of the Spirit, of God himself, God's Word speaks to us and this the Scriptures claim may occur when it is proclaimed today.

The Scriptures witness to revelation, to the incarnation of God's Word in Christ. It does this, however, by hiding this reality from every desire to speak of it directly. There can be no direct historical comprehension of the historical reality of revelation witnessed to. This witness refers to the resurrection, to the risen Christ. He is the Word of God which we cannot pronounce the way God pronounces it.

This Word can only be believed. This unbelievable testimony is known by faith only insofar as one accepts it by obedience to the testimony, which declares – as if it were God himself speaking – that it does in fact testify to his Word and that this Word is addressed to us. Through the Holy Spirit the miracle of transformation takes place and the testimony, when proclaimed, becomes in fact God's Word addressing us. Faith is thus God working on us.

But faith itself, our acceptance of the testimony, does not produce that miracle, for it needs to be correlated to the inward testimony of the Holy Spirit in order to confront us with the Word. Yet, the fulfilment of this correlation is not a human possibility. When it does happen that the correlation is fulfilled and the miracle takes place, we who cannot hear God's Word are given to hear it, we who cannot believe it are given to do just that, we who cannot find God are given to find him, awakened from death to life. The miracle of revelation confronts us with God's Word and we hear it and we are confronted with Jesus Christ, the risen Christ, so that we in fact stand before judgment and grace, death and resurrection, our own judgment and death and God's grace and his gift of life.

However, since this event and its content cannot be produced or expressed by us, we can only point to it. Our human faculties are indeed incapable of understanding the gospel, so that there is no inherent link between them and it. But this statement is not meant to discard those faculties. The human may move between the memory and the expectation of revelation. It may indeed be symbolic or parabolic of the gospel, of faith, of revelation. The human may and thus does testify to the divine.[198] And because human faculties, words and deeds with all their relativity may witness to God they are very much involved in our communicating the gospel, in theology. They are essential if our witness is to be a witness to God's Word and not to something else. Otherwise one might land in the 'horrid swamp of the psychology of the unconscious', represent 'gnostic occultism', end up with an 'anthroposophical chaos of faith and occult possibilities' against which theology may well be helpless.

Theology must be satisfied with its testimonial character. It cannot provide the link between the human and faith, or between history and revelation. It can point to their identity by dialectical speech but cannot establish or presume that identity. The human must be made free from its false sacredness. If we see in it its true secularity we can honour it in its kerygmatic possibilities.

This is the point where the extension of the historical interest of Neo-Protestantism to its ultimate conclusion by Overbeck comes in. It was the merit of liberal theology not only to have given depth and greater clarity to our knowledge of history but also to have sharpened our critical outlook. Bultmann writes that 'it was an education for freedom and truthfulness'.[199] The concern for radical truthfulness, for freedom from traditions and thus from dogmatic determinations is apparent in Overbeck's work. For him the point of historical criticism is to bring about that freedom for scientific cognition and to make clear that the sphere faith seeks to grasp cannot be grasped by scientific methods. His own method, the 'radical biblical science' to which Harnack refers, was thus a secular one. It is obvious why Harnack feared that Barth or anyone else who adopted Overbeck's method would 'hand over to the secular sciences what is known as theology'.

If we regard human statements as being in fact testimony, if we see that 'Christian biographies, pedagogy, and protests against the world' are parabolic only of the divine, if in other words this radical biblical, this 'negative science' has shown us *a posteriori* that the relative cannot be posited as the absolute, theology will avoid ideologising the object of its study. If theology were again to begin by reminding itself that its own beginning was by way of testimony to God's Word and if it again were to have the courage to witness to that Word of judgment, of revelation, and of God's love, it would once more be objective and scientific.

Thus, Barth goes on, God is absolutely not like anything said about him on the basis of culture and ethics. Goethe's pantheism and Kant's conception of God, resting on the moral argument, are not statements about God. This No can be said only through faith in revelation, for this No, stripping the relative of all pretensions to absoluteness, allows the recognition of the true absolute. But that means that the No, posited by revelation and uttered by theology – if it is objective – can be comprehended in its affirmative character. For the No, pronounced by revelation over all that is relative, is also the Yes, secretly and deeply.

Thus, revelation is the crisis of the human. In this sense it is a negative concept inasmuch as it forbids all identifications between here and beyond; only God can do that. But it is also a positive concept, since it gives to what is here significance and promise, significance, by making it parabolic for the beyond, or by opening it out really to point to the divine and not to idols, and promise, by freeing it from an unreal consciousness of absoluteness, or the illusion of living in God, in eternity. This No frees theology really from metaphysics, from illusions, from frivolity in faith.

Theologia crucis *and* theologia viatorum

Barth had said that he regarded his theological statements as a *theologia crucis*. It is also a *theologia viatorum* because it has no fixed standpoint on which it rests. It is a theology which claims that it 'does not pretend consistently to be in possession' of final knowledge of God. It is rather a science bound by its object insofar as its activity begins not with man's search for and discovery of God by means of an appropriate method but rather with man's being confronted, addressed and instructed by God, for which reason its cognition is re-cognition, its knowledge ac-knowledgment, its thought re-flections. Its *cogitare* derived from the *cogere* of revelation, as Barth was to say later in his *Christian Dogmatics*.

Its task is to testify to God's Word. That is to say, its life is the ever new reception and subsequent transmission of that Word, so that it really consists not in being a particular methodology appropriate to its object or a particular ontology of the world and man – all these may be 'fruits that fall into its hands later as a reward' (as Harnack put it, above, p. 52) – it consists rather in prayer for the Holy Spirit as it points like Grünewald's Baptist to Christ.

Instead of saying that theology is a bound science one may say that its stance toward its object is obedience. This is because God's Word, as the object, must again and again be heard anew, for man cannot comprehend it on his own. Theology is addressed by this Word and through this confrontation it is sct into motion from testimony to proclamation. The theologian is therefore not a spectator but a witness, he is not outside the event, but inside it, drawn into it by the Word.

In this sense it is a *theologia viatorum*: being addressed it obeys, hearing it speaks, speaking it witnesses, witnessing it prays for the Spirit – it is always in motion; it cannot stand still and attempt by a prescribed method to depict what is in motion, it cannot attempt to become a *theologia perennis*. Theology cannot accomplish what only God can do – reveal himself. Thus its activity, the testimony to God, keeps it constantly on the road only toward the 'final and supreme knowledge of God'.

But this means that theology has no possession of its object nor any assurance of its findings. It has no more than the promise of God's Word that it will in fact hear and proclaim that Word. It hopes and waits for that fulfilment. The fulfilment itself is in the hands of God because it is the answer he gives to man in the situation of being addressed by God, in the Word-event. (Barth never ceases to emphasise that God's Word is not a mere object, but a subject actively confronting man. The Word is never separated from the God who speaks it so that the object – the Word – is always the subject – God – and vice versa.) In other words, theology must expect to receive from God and from nothing else what it cannot give itself or get from anywhere else.

Why is this theology *en route* a *theologia crucis*? In his Aarau address Barth depicted eloquently the source of theological speech. Using the illustration of John the Baptist in the Isenheim Altar, he says: 'The only source for the real immediate revelation of God is *death*. Christ unlocked its gates. He brought life to light out of death ... It is natural that the Prince of Peace, the Servant of God among the nations, the heaven-descended Son of Man of the Old Testament can be no one else but the crucified who occupies the centre of the New Testament ... Out of *death* life! *Thence* comes the knowledge of God as Father, as the Origin, as the Creator of heaven and earth. Thence comes grace as the first and the last, the thoroughgoing, decisive and inexpressible Word from the sovereign, kingly relation of God to estranged humanity.'[200] Its wisdom is wisdom of death, *Todesweisheit*, according to Overbeck,[201] a wisdom which, because man has sacrificed his wisdom to God's judgment so that he may lay hold of God's promise, has been given to man through the bearer of that promise, Christ the crucified. As a theology without possessions but with great hope, without fulfilment but with the promise of fulfilment, without the contentment of having arrived at its final destiny but with the expectation of 'death being swallowed up in victory' (above, p. 50), it is a theology in temptation, a *theologia crucis*.

We may stop here and close the circle. Harnack accused Barth of a docetism which, because it avoided the critical-historical study of the gospel, preached an imaginary Christ. Therefore it was not theology Barth was engaged in but preaching, a 'theology from within' which in its testimony acted as a ferment but went about it as if it were genuinely scientific theology, *theologia gloriae*. Barth replies that the so-called 'theology from without', based on an idealism which perceived Reason in history and culture, thus speaking of objectified revelation (these phrases are all Harnack's, above, p. 110, n. 123), in fact empties theology because it bypasses the cross. *It* is a *theologia gloriae*, not the theology which Barth would like to see taught. Genuine theology would rather have to be *theologia crucis*, not an assured speaking from an arduously won, scientific point of view, but rather an impassioned prayer for the Creator Spirit, which, as Barth says, is for us always the first and the last thing (above, p. 34).

Barth now breaks off the exposition of 'his theology'. And the few pointed questions he poses show that he feels that there really was no discussion with understanding between them. Barth admits the relativity of all theological utterances as well as the need for him to rethink and restate his own views. But he cannot allow that Harnack's charges against him are to be accepted as correct; his own study is therefore to continue in the same direction as before.

Harnack replied briefly to Barth and also suggested that the discussion be discontinued. What he was to express systematically four years later in a guest-lecture at Bonn, entitled *Die Entstehung der christlichen Theologie und des kirchlichen Dogmas* he now stated thetically. Theology is one thing, preaching another. For this reason those who witness are in themselves objects of theological study. Their work acts as a ferment, as a guideline to scientific theology. But because it aims basically at edification its objectivity is not scientific objectivity the aim of which is only the pure cognition of its object. 'Educated' and 'edifying' thinking must not be mixed together for both suffer from such a commixture.

And again Harnack the historian, drawing on his immense knowledge of history, judges Barth's theology to be destructive for the community of Christian believers because of its dialectics and its concept of revelation. They push the believer into the dilemma between scepticism and naïve biblicism and allow no alternatives.

Harnack's view, based on historical studies, is this: Barth's theology is a 'very strong and clear expression of a kind of Christian experience not unknown to me, to which experience, however, I cannot give general validity exclusively. I must

rather confess that it is a stage which can and must be overcome . . . One must keep to the reality of history.'[202]

The discussion ended, never to be taken up again by these
two men. Yet even in its incompleteness, does it not have
profound significance for the history of theology?

PART TWO

An evaluation of
the correspondence

AN EVALUATION OF THE
CORRESPONDENCE

The issue in the correspondence between Harnack and Barth is the way man speaks about God. The question asked by both is this: how do we speak adequately and appropriately of God? What are the ontology and the hermeneutics in our speech concerning God? What is the science of theology? In the course of their discussion answers were given. We saw them in the previous section. We also saw that both men reject each other's answers. Harnack accused Barth of not being scientific; Barth accused Harnack of emptying theology of its real task.

Which of these two ways of speaking about God is the right one is a matter we need not settle here. The history of theology since has not declared itself unequivocally in favour of either. Indeed, the very men whom Harnack addressed as despisers of scientific theology parted ways some years after this public debate precisely because they differed in their views about the appropriate way of speaking about God.

Our question here is somewhat different. It is about the way man speaks of God. To speak of him cannot mean in this context an interior monologue of pious self-reflection, but the public speech concerning God on the part of theology and Church. It is the audible conversation between people, a conversation with distinct intentions and expectations. On the one hand it is a speaking which seeks to be understood by those addressed so that they may be able either to agree or disagree with what is said. But to be understood is the intention. On the other hand it is a speaking which expects that understanding to come about, although the creation of that understanding is actually not within the power of that speaking. My speech can facilitate or hinder the occurrence of understanding, but it cannot create it. In the case of men's speech about God the intention is, of course, to be understood in such a way that agreement results. The expectation of it is the awakening of faith. The creation of faith is not within the power of man's speaking about God. The actual understanding of God and faith in him derive from a source outside of man's way of speaking about God.

Harnack and Barth were both aware of this. The former spoke of the experience of God, the latter of faith as that source. And here arises the need for appropriate speaking. It is not enough merely to retreat into atheism or agnosticism and not speak about God at all just because that source is not at man's disposal. Theology rather must move on systematically and scientifically, based on the question: how do we speak and think of God if understanding and faith are our aims and hoped-for results? Or negatively: how must we not speak and think of God when we affirm that the source of those results is not at our disposal?

The answer here cannot be a perennal theology. The theologian and the Church must always '*in* every period of time think *for* that period of time' (Barth, above, p. 41). But the period of time into which this correspondence falls is a time which from the point of view of historical theology is highly noteworthy. This is due to that group of younger theologians whose way of speaking about God was labelled 'dialectical theology'. Their work has led to a far-reaching questioning of theological thought and speech.

Our question may therefore be put as follows: what kind of theological thinking and speaking is manifest in the correspondence which may be said to have brought about changes in theology and Church?

The aim of every theology and every churchman is to teach the gospel and nothing else. It is certainly Harnack's intention. So much so in fact that for fear this aim would not be realised by the younger generation of theologians he approached them with his questions. His concern was reformatory in intention. Only an ever-reforming Church will fulfil this aim. Barth's aim and concern are precisely the same, so that each refutes the other's position for the same reason, thinking that the gospel is not taught and that the Church is not being called to its true destiny or led forward to it by the other's way of speaking about God.

But what is reformation of the Church? Basically it is a new establishing of the Church. It is an attempt to give the Church a foundation on which she can stand and carry out her intention: the worship of God as revealed in Jesus Christ. The foundation itself is not man's to lay but he can and must see to it that he does in fact stand on it when he speaks of God, worships and obeys him. In this sense man can give the Church the foundation for her true worship and teaching. But in order to do this he cannot avoid raising the question about the truths of which or in which the Church speaks and lives, such as the authority of the Scriptures, the sovereignty of God, the validity of Jesus Christ as God's self-revelation, the redemption of man and the meaning of faith. The point of raising those questions is two-fold: one must see whether they are in fact proclaimed without error and, secondly, if they are indeed taught that way, whether the response to them is genuine Christian life and obedience. The question about the condition of the Church in relation to her destiny is a theological and a practical one. It is a question for both the theologian and the preacher, using Harnack's distinction, and it is one involving both the academic and the practical spheres of theology, in Barth's sense.

But it means that the question leads to a decision. One must agree or disagree, that is decide for or against revelation in the sense of deciding to seek God and our source of knowledge of him where he has given himself for our knowledge: in his revelation in Jesus Christ. Since both Harnack and Barth insist that our knowledge of God is knowledge *sub specie Christi* the question becomes: whose decision for Christ as God's revelation is genuine not only in intention but also in execution?

The Barth–Harnack correspondence is too short a document, too specific in its scope for an answer to be given to that question based on it alone. It addressed itself to the matter of scientific theology and what it was concerned with. It is obvious, therefore, that an answer to that question would have to consider the other writings of these men more extensively. We cannot do that here. Yet even though we cannot determine Luther's position as a reformer (to take a historic example) from a study of his disputation with Dr Eck in Leipzig in July 1519, there still emerges from that discussion what is indicative of the recall of the Church to her Lord. Similarly, even though the full theological position of Harnack and Barth cannot be determined from a study of their exchange of letters, those letters are still indicative of a new reformation in the Church. It is reflected in the discussion of the scientific character of theology.

The concern with an adequate way of speaking about God brought theology in the nineteenth century into a confrontation with two different opponents. Facing inward, it had to contend with Orthodoxy and with Pietism. The former spoke of God in terms of metaphysical categories and was accused of thinking about 'revelation and faith without having clearly understood how the reality of salvation encounters man and is understood by him. Orthodoxy has almost completely forgotten that whatever the Church teaches about God, the Trinity, the natures and pre-existence of Christ, does not refer to things in themselves, but rather to a history of God's revelation and his dealings with man. Orthodoxy hardly knows any more that faith does not comprehend God's being in himself but his being for us. Our comprehension of him can therefore be no more than our acknowledgment of Christ as Lord, it can be only the obedience of faith . . . God is unveiled in his effects only. We can partake of salvation only as we experience these effects, only as we are personally grasped by them, which means that we are saved in the active relation of faith in Christ and in the appropriation of God's will by our own will.'[1] Melanchthon's statement from his *Loci Communes* of 1521, 'to see Christ means to see his gifts to us; it is not what they – the scholastics – teach, namely to reflect upon his natures, the mode of his incarnation', had become the guideline in Christology at the time of this confrontation. If we do speak of God as he is in himself, we do not really speak of him as revealed in Jesus Christ, because apart from that revelation we do not know God. Pietism, on the other hand, spoke very much of Jesus, but in such a manner that concern for his historical existence in the first decades of our era was abrogated. The objection against it was that the Jesus Christ confessed here is more an imaginary than the real Christ since both critical reflection and historical knowledge are repudiated and the Bible left to speak for itself. That means however that he who is worshipped is not really the Christ whom the gospel proclaims to us. It rather is the Jesus which the particular individual reads into the Bible. Here one does not go beyond the biblicist view of Christ and since that Christ is one who is at man's disposal it is not the lord who in complete freedom gave himself to man.

Facing outward, theology confronted various forms of positivism, especially that claiming to rest on the natural sciences. It challenged theology to propose a method in which it could speak of God with the same assuredness as the sciences believed they could speak of the objects of their investigation.

Science demands that the object of experience be in fact experienced and that it can be portrayed in its truth and reality by means of a correct method. This would be possible only if the object of religious experience could be studied through the controlled repetition of this experience at any time and at any place. Otherwise one could not speak of a strict scientific method in the proper sense of that word. Even if one could make the demands of the scientific method less stringent, one would still insist that this experience is capable of being verified by anyone, otherwise the deductions made about the object are of no account. The question arising for the theologian in this situation is this: how can one continue one's allegiance to the Bible in this confrontation with science so that justice is indeed done to science and one's heritage of Church and religion? Obviously one must allow science to observe theology in its determination to remove the nimbus from the Bible and thus also remove the scandal which the sciences see in theology: the technical impossibility of demonstrating and proving the existence of its object. Precisely by entering into a very close relationship with science in general and by professing the one scientific task, the pure cognition of its object, theology will overcome this scandal and uphold the relative divinity of the Bible through its very content. This is done by using history and by applying the critical-historical method to the divine in history.

The appropriate method of operation became the paramount concern. It rested on two assumptions: 'The first basic assumption of theological thought lies precisely in a methodological consideration, in the balance between an objective, scientific method and a purely non-theoretical, inward directness to God. And secondly, this method rests on the assumption that between "faith" and "faith-experience" and revelation there exists a perfect correlation or symmetrical relationship.'[2]

Over and against this stand those to whom the results of that method are impressive neither to science nor to faith because what emerges from it is neither a purely human nor a purely divine phenomenon. It is suggested by these critics that the very search for such unified knowledge is basically mistaken because it fails to grasp the unbridgeable distance between the divine and the human. The demands of the scientific method which challenged theology, namely the portrayal of the object of experience in its truth and reality and the verifiability of the experience at any time and place, do not correspond to the nature of faith, of the Christian's encounter with God. It is mistaken to attempt the isolation of a condition in the Christian's life which has transcended the ever-remaining distance mentioned and then to make this condition comprehensible directly to human cognition.

In the final analysis, a science the task of which is the pure cognition of its object becomes a positivism if it assumes that its noetic *ratio* is expressive of its ontic *ratio* univocally. The formal relations established by our ontological concepts and constructs are again and again broken through by that which those concepts and constructs describe as reality, truth, being.

The objectivity of theology as a science derives therefore not primarily from the answer it gives to the question: How can I grasp and present the object – God?, but rather from the answer to this question: What is the reality – God – of which I am to speak? Its appropriateness or adequacy would be 'the assimilation of the mind to the object of its own systematic or scientific search. It is a certain obedience and loyalty to the object of investigation. It is objective in the sense that the method of investigation is a secondary concern compared to the actual understanding of the object. The understanding of the nature of the object actually moulds the method which will be appropriate for investigation.'[3]

But what does objectivity, what does being scientific mean in relation to an object which is claimed to be separated from man by an unbridgeable distance? How is a science of God possible when he is said not to be open to scientific cognition?

Unless one becomes positivistic, what noetic *ratio* is necessary which does not identify itself with its ontic *ratio*?

OBJECTIVITY, SUBJECTIVITY AND COGNITION

The experience of modern physics may serve as an example here because it asked those same questions in regard to its object of investigation. The ideal of classical physics was a strict objectivity which, if the scientist adhered to it consistently, would allow in conjunction with experimental investigation a pure cognition of the object. That this belief was not illusory was demonstrably clear. The ideal of cognition seemed assured when one's subjectivity was totally suppressed and one proceeded without presuppositions to the objectifying, positive cognition of facts. Such cognition would require constant reappraisal with the advance of knowledge.

This method operated with the subject-object dichotomy in relation to reality. It was challenged, however, by the quantum theory of Planck, the principle of relativity of Einstein, Bohr's concept of complementarity and Heisenberg's principle of indeterminacy. Modern physics finds itself unable to speak of reality in an objectifying manner and uphold the subject-object dichotomy. The Kantian forms of cognition, space and time, and the categories of thought, substance and causality, appear in an essentially different light to physics today. The conclusions of its research no longer permit the conception of the world as the mere object of physical or materialistic thinking and of the will of man to manipulate it at his pleasure since it is a machine, as Descartes proposed.

The step from the various fragments of knowledge gained by experimental study to a comprehensive picture of reality as it actually is in itself, which was the aim of that physical or materialistic thinking, can no longer be made. Reality is simply no longer objectifiable in the view of modern physics. 'Complementarity and non-objectifiability mean that the axiom of Western epistemology, the division between the three levels of being, action and cognition can no longer be maintained to be as sharp as it has been hitherto. "The aim of research is no longer the pure cognition of the atoms and their movements 'in themselves', that is distinct from our experimental ways of posing the questions; we are rather right from the start in the very centre of the encounter between nature and man. The natural sciences are only a part of that encounter so that the usual divisions of the world into subject and object, the world within and the world without, body and soul, no longer fit but rather lead to difficulties." The cosmological picture of classical physics, which had become a *Weltanschauung* with its view of the infinity of space, the eternity of matter and the uninterrupted predictability of every course of events, is gone. So is the faith that the world is an object over which man may dispose. Gone is the faith in the spiritual omnipresence of man in the world.'[4]

The total effect of those discoveries and theories of modern physics is – at least for the scientist – the end of the kind of positivism for which the ontic and noetic *ratio* coincide. The epistemological picture of reality since then looks somewhat as follows: The primary level of reality is nuclear reality. Then there is the level of classical physics in which nuclear reality manifests itself and in which the scientist objectifies the former, primary level. (It is obvious that modern physics cannot simply neglect classical physics because it is still in need of solid objects in its experiments. Consequently it works with objectified concepts as a means of speaking of reality.) The third level of reality is the physicist himself as that in which conclusions are drawn about the primary level on the basis of the objectifications made in the second. In the last level, the physicist himself, one speaks of his cognition and his experimental actions, but that division – cognition and experimental action – is only a conceptual one since in practice it cannot be made. The physicist can no longer be excluded from the process of cognition.

In other words, the ideal of cognition held by positivists has undergone a radical change. The pure cognition in a totally objectivist way, a way on which the researcher's person is wholly excluded is no longer the way the scientist approaches reality. Man's cognition is now regarded as indirect cognition. On account of the experimental action to which reality is submitted our statements of reality are never statements about reality in itself, but reality as objectified by us through that action. That means, as Bohr pointed out, that reality as it is in itself lies somewhere between our statements about it; our speech about reality must be complementary speech.

Complementary speech of reality as our noetic *ratio* is the conceptual representation of the scientist's objectivity *vis-à-vis* the superiority of the object, the ontic *ratio*, to which the complementary statements refer. The understanding of reality is a dialectical one. We must speak of thesis and antithesis when speaking about the synthesis which we cannot accomplish and which is not at our disposal.

This means that the supposed continuum of man and reality, on the basis of which direct statements about reality were assumed possible, is discarded. An autonomous construction of reality is, according to Heidegger, not a picture of reality but rather an anthropology. 'The more completely and pervasively the world becomes an object at the disposal of man, the more objective that object appears and the more subjective, that is presumptuous, the subject becomes, the more irresistibly cosmology and the study of the world become a teaching of man, an anthropology. Small wonder then that humanism arises only where the world becomes a picture ... Humanism here means that philosophical interpretation of man which explains and evaluates being as a whole preceding from man to man.'[5]

Modern physics has called a halt to that kind of epistemology and ontology in the realm of science. It appears to me that the theology of Karl Barth does the same for theology for which reason I call it a reformatory theology.

The exact sciences do not as sciences make a *Weltanschauung* part of their system. Nor do they attempt any more to establish an ontology of the universe. Through its methodology science now regards the world and analyses and describes it as a world of man, a world in which the hypothesis of God is no longer needed for its application, as Laplace said. Furthermore the sciences also separate the area of the knowable from that of the unknowable.

Through Overbeck it became clear to Barth that theology has to speak of God in terms of 'secular' language. There is no 'holy' method for the study of the holy. God's revelation in Jesus Christ is revelation in history, in a human-historical possibility, as Barth said. Theology, therefore, has no choice but to describe that reality of revelation in terms of the epistemological means available to it. Surely, this was also Harnack's point; God's revelation is historical revelation and historical knowledge must be used to fathom it.

Where then is the difference? Melanchthon's statement cited above makes plain that God as he is in himself is not knowable to man. God is known when he reveals himself. Thus to see Christ is to see his gifts to us. Kant's distinction between the noumenal and the phenomenal parallels the distinction Melanchthon made. Kant argued that things-in-themselves are not knowable to us; specifically in relation to God we cannot use what is phenomenal to give us knowledge of him. Instead of cosmological proofs the moral argument is to be used in the attempt to gain knowledge of him. But since morality is that life of man in or through which he has access to the divine – and this access is surely the point or meaning of the *beneficia Christi* – morality and thus theology are an aspect of the self-knowledge and self-confidence of the man who has benefited from the gifts of Christ. This view of Kant's, knowledge of God proceeding from man through self-knowledge, has led to the view that theology is just as much as physics a part of a well ordered sphere of human possibilities. Theology has therefore the same basic task: the establishing and cognising of its object.

But Kant's epistemology, even though it distinguished between the noumenal and the phenomenal, still held that real knowledge of the real world is possible. The imposition on sense-data of the forms of cognition and the categories of thought made this possible. That means, however, a knowledge of the world proceeding from man, not in the sense of self-knowledge but in the sense of an assimilation of the object to the mind. The method of understanding actually moulds the object of investigation.

In both cases, physical and theological knowledge, Kant's epistemology establishes knowledge which is humanistic in the Heideggerian sense (above, p. 179). Modern physics, however, finds itself unable to continue using the Kantian forms and categories and calling its knowledge of the world and reality direct knowledge. The objection is exactly as Heidegger put it: the belief that an increasingly growing objectivity in man's epistemological control of the world leads to final insights does in fact lead to a confusion between anthropology and cosmology.

This is because of the superimposition of the mind on the world. Modern physics for that reason goes beyond Kant and the classical physics he helped to shape with his theory of knowledge and speaks of those three levels of cognition mentioned above in which the mind is moulded by the object of investigation.

Theology, says Barth, is in a similar situation. When it states that its method cannot dispose over God's revelation, then it means that it has no knowledge of God unless he moulds the mind of man to become appropriate to the knowledge of him. It means that there is no continuum between man and God, that there is no direct insight into him. Such insight is the result rather of an objectification, as is the insight into reality which the scientific positivism prior to modern physics believed itself to have obtained. Barth labels such objectifications in theology 'impressions at best of the object of the gospel'. These objectifications were made on the basis of that method which, distinguishing between the noumenal (God in himself) and the phenomenal (God's historical revelation for us) and thus proposing the method of obtaining knowledge of God through morality in its wider sense, spoke about God in terms of the anthropology of the man under the *beneficia Christi*. In this method the relative divinity of the Bible – as a source of religious insights – was upheld and the scandal of theology – the existence of its object in the sphere of the noumenal, its inaccessibility therefore to controlled investigation and subsequent inability of proof – was removed.

It is not permissible for theology as a science to bypass the being of God and consider merely his action in the *beneficia Christi* just as it cannot derive knowledge of his being from a general conception of being without considering those benefits. Theology must not therefore proceed in its knowledge of God from man and consider itself a part of a well-ordered sphere of human possibilities, i.e. as an anthropology. It requires an approach to its object in which in fact its mind is moulded by God himself; theology must, in other words, become properly objective, and learn again to speak appropriately about God.

Barth appears to be doing just that in his exchange of letters with Harnack. The revelation of God is not a revelation of propositions but of God himself. He, God the wholly other to whom man has no access through the correlation of human words and deeds, unveils himself by entering into that correlation and revealing himself as he is. This entering into the correlation which, because it is the human correlation, is separated by an unbridgeable gulf from the divine is therefore also God's veiling himself. Human speech of God must correspondingly refer to his veiling and his unveiling of himself. It must be complementary, dialectical speech which admits the limits of human cognition and the ever present need for supplementation. But on the other hand this speech admits the superiority of the object spoken of over our cognition, so that dialectical utterances about God are really the expression of man's obedience to that object, namely the subject God to whom the thetical and antithetical statements refer.

The dialectical method, unable really to speak directly of God, admits that its noetic *ratio* is not identical with its ontic *ratio*. But by referring everything to the ontic *ratio* and by clearly insisting on its inability to do more than that, it creates the situation in which our speaking of God is at least appropriate speaking.

Our speech concerning reality is ideological if we speak of reality and man as in a continuum. Direct utterances about reality are to be rejected as positivism. Dialectical, complementary or indirect utterances concerning reality are appropriate insofar as they acknowledge the indeterminacy of reality as it is in itself in terms of human concepts. The truth lies somewhere 'between' our statements about reality, about God. The epistemological picture of Barth's dialectical way of speaking about God seems to be as follows: the primary level of reality, of God, is the being of God, the hidden God, God in his aseity. God is known through his self-revelation which is an event in history, in creation. This event is the one revelation of God, Jesus Christ, who is the secondary level of reality, of God. Christ is the Word of God which is addressed to man. Man as the hearer of that Word is the third level of this reality. This is not man on his own but as the one to whom God has said and given to understand what man cannot hear and understand, namely God himself at the primary level. The man of faith is thus this third level of reality.

Using the terms ontic and noetic *ratio*, we may describe the dialectical situation like this: God is the ontic *ratio* or corresponds to it. It is twofold in form; there is the ontic *ratio* of God as he is in himself and the ontic *ratio* of God as he is revealed in Jesus Christ. These represent the first and second levels of God's reality respectively. Man as addressed by revelation corresponds to the noetic *ratio*, the third level.[6]

This tripartite division imports a theoretical division for theology as much as for modern physics. But it shows that the object-subject dichotomy of cognition is overcome. Object and subject are rather complementary terms; man is seen to be drawn into the act of cognition, into revelation. He no longer stands outside of it looking in or on as a spectator.

The exclusion of the subject in the *one* scientific task, the pure cognition of the object, was the ideal for which Harnack strove as a theologian. The *one* scientific method corresponding to that task demanded that kind of objectivity. When Barth confronted Harnack with a dialectical method of theology in which object and subject have become complementary terms and the subject is said to be inseparably involved in the reality which the subject seeks to understand, the question to be put to Barth is certainly this: how is man part of this reality? Harnack found that Barth has put his case in such a way that it appeared as if man's understanding, hearing, speaking and grasping could be eliminated. This was the impression he had of Barth's dialectic. Indeed the answers Barth gave to questions 5–11 make one ask whether the relation of the phenomena of human life, of history, of culture and of the Church to God's Word is only negative. Is man's continuing existence in history, nature, culture and Church insignificant in view of the event of revelation which puts the truth of that existence into an either–or relation only to the truth of God's existence? How is one to understand the inclusion of man in the event of revelation, which in fact happens according to the dialectic of Barth, if the hermeneutics of that method speaks of *diastasis*, of a vacuum, of crisis only? How convincing is the refutation of the charge that the link between the human and faith is cut in a Marcionite fashion when the reply is 'I do not cut, but repudiate every continuity between hither and yonder; I speak of a dialectical relation which refers to an identity which we cannot accomplish and therefore cannot presume'? How is man part of the event

G

of God's Word when experience and faith only signify (*significat*) something or are only signs which are not identical (*est*) with the thing signified and when the attempt to identify them is refuted as the titanism of a *homo religiosus*? Is the remark 'this is totally incomprehensible to me' so unjustified?

Barth himself asked these questions and came to answer them clearly later. He was aware, however, even during the correspondence that his present position was disputable, and that it still demanded much more thought, while even if it were circumspect it might perhaps be unsatisfying.[7]

But then Barth was also aware that he was raising the ontological question of theology, the question about God in a different way from Harnack. The concepts of God's Word, faith and obedience indicate the difference from Harnack just as much as the actualism of revelation with which the position of Harnack is critically rejected. Even if man's participation in God is denied, the concepts of obedience, faith, and the Holy Spirit's inward testimony refer to the event of God's Word, through which alone man confronts the reality of God. When, therefore, Barth's dialectical or theological method repudiates the continuum of God and man, denies the identity of the ontic and noetic *ratio*, it does not mean that there is no relation between God and man. Direct participation in truth, in being, in life is certainly denied, but through faith and obedience man is drawn into the Word-event and thus becomes a part of the reality of God's revelation. In other words, God becomes real to man through the event of the Word into which by faith and obedience man is drawn.

How is this set out in the correspondence? Our answer is that Barth speaks of the Trinity as the tripartite area of the reality to which the dialectical method testifies. The hiddenness of God, the revelation of God in Christ as true God and true man and the revealedness of God in the Holy Spirit's testimony to man – this is how Barth speaks of God. Here we see the significance of the Harnack–Barth correspondence as a document of the new reformation of the Church. The dialectical method, as the scientific way of speaking about God, is appropriate for the pure teaching of the Gospel.

The primary level of reality is God in himself, the hidden God. This level man cannot know, and could not even speak of it if it had not been for God's self-unveiling to man.

In his replies to Harnack Barth continues his emphasis on the hiddenness of God. There is no way from man to God; God alone can be the goal and the way to the goal of our enquiries about him. God is not at all anything like the things said about him on the basis of humanity or history. We cannot say anything about him on our own and then have the assurance that we are in fact speaking about him. As he is in himself God is simply not knowable to man, he is not something we can express. Not only is he the wholly other, but also the wholly hidden. We cannot find God.

The expression 'hiddenness of God' does not appear in the letters, but throughout them Barth speaks of the superiority of God to our thought. It is exactly this reference to superiority which shows that God is hidden from us. Even God's revelation is incomprehensible to us. Why? Because God is the wholly other, and his reality not an object of human-historical cognition. Man's cognition of this reality occurs when this reality acts to unveil itself to man.

This act of unveiling is the revelation of God in his incarnation. It is Jesus Christ, the secondary level of God's reality. Barth describes it like this: God himself has said and done something new outside of the correlation of all human words and deeds, yet he has inserted it as this new thing into that correlation, a word and deed next to others, but this word and this deed. It is the possibility of God acting in the possibilities of man. The Word became flesh, God himself a human-historical reality in the person of Christ.

Without speaking of 'very God and very man', the meaning of the above is indeed identical with the meaning of the truth expressed in that concept. To this truth the Scriptures testify. But we have knowledge of the objective truth of the incarnation only when the content of the biblical testimony acts upon us and awakens our faith. Nothing other than the action of the 'content of the gospel' can give us reliable knowledge of God who is that content.

Barth speaks of the biblical witness as a witness to God's Word. The Word is 'the correlation of Scripture and Spirit'. Apart from this correlation the Bible is man's word only, but when this correlation becomes event, the testimony becomes transparent to the reality and rationality of God. To be sure, human words and deeds remain inadequate in relation to God's reality but through this testimony to God in inadequate concepts reliable knowledge of God is possible.

In the witness to revelation it is asserted that God became man in the person of Jesus Christ, very God and very man. What makes Jesus to be the Christ? The answer is in terms of the testimony to his resurrection, said Barth. There is no way for us on our own to this content of the gospel. The content must be not only God's way to us but also the way by which man is brought to God's reality. All other ways lead to other realities. But the point is that in witnessing to Christ, who is the possibility of God acting in the form of a human possibility, who is God's Word *in* the correlation of human words and deeds, man's words not only become transparent to but indeed capable of witnessing to the Word of God. Man's noetic *ratio* does not become identical with the ontic *ratio*, but by witnessing to the ontic *ratio* the noetic *ratio* mediates reliable knowledge of God. In Barth's words, the fact that eternity becomes time, the absolute relative and God becomes man, the fact that the reality signified and the sign pointing to it coincide, is true only as the Word and deed of God, as an act of the Trinity itself. This act can only be witnessed to and believed in.

Without at that time using the concept of *homoousion* Barth nevertheless asserts its truth that in man's witness to Christ as God's incarnate Word we do indeed – through God's grace – speak of God's reality, that through this witness we obtain real knowledge of God. Surely, this witness is dialectical, it speaks indirectly, it only points, but in that witness God may in fact reveal himself.

When he does reveal himself through such testimony it is an unprecedented event and one must speak of the Holy Spirit. God is working on us. The acceptance of this testimony is faith. When man hears the Word to which testimony is given in the Scriptures and believes it then it is the Holy Spirit's inward testimony which makes the Word to be addressed to and heard by man. Through the Holy Spirit man becomes the man of faith, the man who gives 'obedience to a human word which – as if it were in fact God's Word – proclaims to him that Word as a word addressed to him'. This man is the third level of God's reality. His understanding of the Word of God is not by this or that function of the soul or mind, but through the Spirit, which is identical with the Word of God, and thus through faith.

Through the Holy Spirit's testimony, therefore, God communicates himself to man, he establishes the relation between himself and man and founds man's knowledge of him. This means that when man speaks of God and this speaking moves within the sphere of the *homoousion*, the sphere of God's incarnation in Jesus Christ, then man is inextricably involved in that speaking since without God's revelation of himself to this man through the Spirit's testimony to Christ, man would not speak of God at all. Only the man of faith can really speak of God, but only through God does he become the man of faith. Thus our knowledge of God is moulded by God himself. Hence the necessity of obedience; man's knowledge is ac-knowledgment, his thought re-collection, *Erkenntnis* is *An-erkenntnis*, his *Denken* is *Nach-denken*. Man is required to yield his understanding to the object of inquiry and let it mould the method appropriate for its understanding. Theology is a bound science in the sense that it must let itself be assimilated to and be determined by the object. It cannot allow itself to have any prior understanding impinge on the reality to which it can no more than testify. For if it does not testify that its object is God the subject, if it does not begin by reminding itself that its object is one to which man can only testify since it is an otherwise totally incomprehensible object, it is not an objective science. Objectivity in theology is the courage to witness to God and the obedience to that witness, while it is through this obedience that theology attains persuasiveness and value. This is the obedience of faith through which man is enabled to speak of God.

At this point, however, a decision must be taken against all human preconceptions, prejudgments, or pre-understanding. Unless that is done the doors are flung open to all kinds of occult capabilities and anthroposophical chaos. The natural sciences and Harnack were right in demanding that such subjectivity be banned from our pursuit of knowledge, that specious sources of religious knowledge apart from reason be left untapped, because they only distort that knowledge. The surrender of all preconceptions is for theology an essential part of its complete obedience to its object, says Barth, and answers to the exclusive nature of God's revelation, and it is that revelation alone which makes theology possible. The epistemology of such a theology is determined however by an objectivity other than that to which Harnack adhered, for it has again understood Luther's insight that theology as a science is not based on questions posed by religion but rather on something which is given to it in faith prior to its enquiry. It begins with the Reformation conviction that 'I believe that I cannot believe in Jesus Christ my Lord nor come to him on the basis of my own reason or strength', as it is put in Luther's small catechism.[8] The categories of a theology which begins with the questions of religion are not only insufficient for the reality of theological enquiry, but they also distort and obscure it. They do not allow us to go beyond ourselves and the sphere of what is this-worldly.[9]

THE CORRESPONDENCE – WHAT IS ITS MEANING FOR CHURCH HISTORY?

What is the real significance of this dialectical way of speaking about God? What is the meaning of it as we see it developed or at least expressed by Barth in this exchange of letters of 1923? Why is the theology speaking in that way called 'a Copernican redirection of Protestant theology' (Berkhof), 'a new foundation of evangelical theology' (Moltmann), 'a revolutionary theology' (Smart)? 'What was the real concern of the school known as dialectical theology? It was anxious that theology should once again have the orientation in which alone it is justified, an orientation like that of the finger of John the Baptist in Mathias Grünewald's impressive painting. This was its concern, so that it was again a theology which points beyond man to the God revealed in the crucified, in other words a theology which lives completely in but not through that witness but rather through him to whom it witnesses.'[10]

But surely no theology wants anything other than to be appropriate speech and thought about God. Harnack specifically said that every statement of God must be *sub specie Christi* in order to be appropriate. Surely no theology wants to do anything other than to recall the Church constantly to its very origin and in this sense to be a reforming theology. Every theology is concerned with the 'pure teaching of the gospel'.

It was claimed above that the exchange of letters is indicative of a new reformation of the Church. Barth was as anxious as every theologian to speak adequately of God. He said clearly that a reformation of the Church was no less necessary today than it was in the early sixteenth century. The aims of a reformation, however, are not something obvious in or to man; they are alive only insofar as they are made alive in us. This occurs where there is a recollection of what confronts the Church as her object. 'If today you feel the longing for reformation more as a bitter anxiety than as anything else, remember that it may not be otherwise. According to the eighth chapter of *Romans*, there is more hope when one sighs *Veni Creator Spiritus,* than when he exalts as if the Spirit were already his. You have been introduced to "my theology" if you have heard this sigh.'[11] This desire to be part of the *ecclesia semper reformanda* is there, but more as well.

If we recall that for Barth the question regarding the appropriateness of theology and the proper orientation of it arose in the situation of the preacher, we shall see why this new way of speaking of God is the more appropriate. The question was not 'how do I speak of God?' but rather 'can I speak of God?'. 'This critical situation itself became to me an explanation of the character of all theology. What else can theology be but the truest possible expression of this quest and questioning on the part of the minister . . .?'[12] Theology cannot, must not neglect the need of the preacher who is to say what he cannot say. He is to say what God says to man and not what man thinks about God. It is not good to reverse the order and turn 'Thus says the Lord' into 'Thus hears man', Barth said to Harnack. And by persisting on this order the situation of the preacher is like that of the theologian; their task is identical, namely to receive and transmit the Word of God.

By having this Word at its theme theology is concerned with something which man does not and never can possess. It was this that gave rise to the criticism and the polemics so characteristic for the Barth of that period, as well as to his repudiation of every attempt to see God in a continuum with the human or history. And it was in this connection that he developed his criticism of the Church who sees her task in the salvation of souls and thus leaves the physical world void of the hope in God who will renew his kingdom and the world in it.

God cannot be possessed by man either in his conscience, in the supreme achievements of culture or for that matter in the critical protest against the world, the Church, the experience of God. Neither possesses God, for they do not go beyond the human and thus can only point to him. Therefore theology may look at the world in a radically secular fashion and thus come to see in it parables of the divine or sacred.

When man does in fact confront God then it is when God reveals himself. God's revelation is the precondition of theology but it is a precondition which depends on the freedom and good pleasure of God to give himself through the action of the Holy Spirit. This means that revelation is neither something for theology to prove or demonstrate nor something that is in need of such proof or demonstration. It is the event of God's confrontation with man. It is just because this event cannot be presumed that theology is freed from speaking of an imagined God and freed for speaking of the real, living God. 'When he reveals himself God becomes revealed as God – a statement which is a tautology only on the surface. It does in fact describe the freedom of God for and in the encounter with man as well as the freedom of theology from illusion and for objectivity.'[13]

And precisely here we seek the desire to reform fulfilled, in the freedom of dialectical theology to speak of God, the living, the real God, the free God who remains free in our speaking of him. The theology that speaks of this God must be free constantly to adapt itself to his freedom to reveal himself in ways that it cannot anticipate or presume. But this is to carry theology beyond the stage of being a descriptive and supporting science. The great merit of that science was its systematisation of the almost unlimited amount of knowledge gathered through its historical, philological and religio-historical studies. But this new theology goes on, using all these insights and the corresponding scientific apparatus, to come to grips with the claim that the Bible speaks of God's Word as addressed to us, and as such mediates to us a revelation of God which we could not discover or tell to ourselves.

The old discussion of Orthodoxy versus Liberalism was left behind here. An attack was made on cultural Protestantism and its theological positivism so that man, no matter in what situation he was, could be confronted and claimed by that Word. 'Dialectical theology did not try to separate men from science, as perhaps older apologetics had attempted (stuffing the joints and cracks developing in this effort with edificatory phrases). It rather insisted with annoying persistence that its science was an expression of the total situation of humanity, that it was able to raise questions which God's Word, spoken to man, had already asked and answered . . . This theology did not defend a partial bastion of faith, it opened the attack on man who was buried under the rubble of this world.'[14]

The beginnings of the 'New Reformation' are here, in the Harnack–Barth correspondence of 1923. Every reformation begins with correctives, with the 'pinch of spice'; but it cannot remain in that stage and be a reformation. It must begin a reconstruction. Two of Barth's addresses of 1922: *Not und Verheissung der christlichen Verkündigung*, delivered at Schulpforta in July, and *Das Wort Gottes als Aufgabe der Theologie*, delivered on the Elgersburg in October, along with these letters to Harnack, form the initial attempts to rebuild.

'What is revelation?' and 'How do we speak of God?', in other words, what ontology and what hermeneutics does an appropriate theology demand? were the questions Barth asked. The answers he gave may not have been entirely satisfactory. Certainly they were not final in the sense that what was said could not be said more effectively within the framework of that preliminary character which all our statements of God have because of their object. Nevertheless, the way had been opened up, the *differentia* determined, the reformation begun.[15]

But one may ask: is it an *ad hoc* reformation or one truly in the *semper reformanda* tradition?

One may speak of *ad hoc* reformation perhaps (but only perhaps) in the case of Barth's work in the Barmen Declaration of 1934 and its larger context, the Church struggle in the times of Hitler. That was distinctly a call to the Church to remember her foundation *vis-à-vis* a specific threat.

The same may perhaps (but only perhaps) be true in relation

H

to the vigorous ecumenical dialogue with Rome now. But then the now famous awareness and genuine understanding and appreciation of Barth's work by Catholic thinkers – von Balthasar, Küng, Söhngen, Petersen, Bouillard, Willems, Przywara, Rahner, to name a few – is not an appearance of recent years. In 1923 (!) the *Rhein-Mainzer Volkszeitung* called Barth and his friends 'serious partners for discussion' (Thurneysen in a letter to Barth, dated 2 January 1924). In February 1925 Barth makes reference to an article by a Catholic scholar who said that 'the Protestant theologian Karl Barth (was raising questions) which Catholic theology too would overlook at its peril'.[16] This ecumenical dialogue with Rome has gone on now for forty years, especially since Barth's famous attack on the *analogia entis*, an attack which Rome considered a real challenge to its very theological foundation. A common frontier between the two has developed, and centuries-old monological and narrow confessional polemic has given way to a common theological encounter, so that where there were once political, tactical or cultural considerations there is now genuine theological inquiry.

Again it may perhaps (and only perhaps) be *ad hoc* when the discussions today between theology and the sciences have entered a new and fruitful stage. Both have become aware of the categorical difference of their statements about nature. The norm for theology is the Bible, for science the controlled experiment. A theology which, unconcerned with relational points of contact, pursues its course and does not attempt discussions with non-theologians of their objects of inquiry on the standpoint of what is not theology, becomes a discipline which, on account of this single-mindedness, these non-theologians can respect for its objectivity. They confront here a theology which does not want to be theology *and* also a philosophy of nature. The captivity of theology in that apparent need to have a natural theology *vis-à-vis* science prevented the kind of dialogue among scientists and theologians which one now sees going on regularly in Göttingen (since 1949) and in Utrecht (since 1952).

Yet even in this area events have been taking place which make one realise that it was Barth's striving for an objective theological science which began, or certainly prefaced the way for, a new reformation of theology and Church.

Barth pleaded for a theology which studies its determinative object and understands it in accordance with its own interior logic or givenness and not in accordance with external authorities such as historical knowledge and critical reflection. These might be, and never should be more than, tools in the methodology of theology, but they must not be given the authority to undermine or indeed replace the centrality of the determinative object. In fact, when priority is given to methodology, when 'hermeneutics' becomes the predominant question in any science, the material gathered in the study of that science becomes systematised in terms of thought-forms and concepts not taken from that material or the special object studied but rather in terms of ideas and concepts of current patterns of thought. The danger of this, to say the least, is that the resulting system ceases to be scientific and becomes positivistic or ideological. The critical reference to the data obtained from the original studies is cut off here and what results is instead a 'dogmatism' in the deplorable meaning of that word. Thought then no longer follows the direction given in and indicated by the discovered data, in accordance with the uniqueness and dignity and the reality of the object studied. And such thinking is not objective, in the sense of being determined by the object, it is rather pre-judged thinking.

We maintained that Barth asked for a theology in which others in the *universitas litterarum* did not lay down rules or patterns of study for theology to adhere to. Rather he asked for a theological science – and his own theology shows that he followed his own advice – in which the determinative object, which was and is essentially subject and must become so again and again in our knowing of it, prescribes the method how it will be studied and become known. Barth said that our way of knowing this object and the object itself cannot be separated; we are addressed by God's Word and by thus being addressed we are ourselves drawn into the very event of God's self-revelation to us. The object of theological inquiry binds us, so to speak, to itself and takes us along a way on which we think of it in accordance with its own essence, its being and its act. Theology is a bound science, in the sense in which, incidentally, this is true for every *objective* science.

But in what sense is this plea for and this adherence to such an objectivity in theological science a reformation of Church and theology not merely in the *ad hoc* sense but indeed in the *semper reformanda* tradition? What would justify the application of the description 'a new reformation' to this emphasis of Barth's thought?

Barth warned that the theologians of the late nineteenth and early twentieth centuries had moved away too far from the proper object of theology, the one revelation of God. According to them, following Melanchthon, the benefits of Christ for man were said to be the basis of man's knowledge of God in Christ. The acts of God had, however, been unduly separated here from God's being in those acts. This was said to amount to the very loss of God at the hands of theologians (Moltmann). This loss of God, this loss of his Word, as the correlation of God's Spirit and the Scriptures, led to the interpretation of God's Spirit as man's self-awareness of being grasped by the beneficial action of Christ. Man was spoken of in a higher key, as Barth put it. Against this he recalled the Reformers' method in which God was spoken of in a correlation of his being and his act, in a togetherness of his being-in-the-act and his act-in-the-being (T. F. Torrance).

Their method followed the uniqueness and dignity of the determinative object of theology, the one revelation of God in the Incarnation. Barth also gave priority to revelation in terms of this affirmation of the Church, namely that God was in Christ. But he refused to accept this in a mythological or religio-anthropological sense. This truth has to declare itself in theology and the scientific character of theology would be its adherence to the recollection that its very object was and is subject. The meaning of this is that the concrete act of God in Christ is the basis of our interpretation of God's being, of God himself, an interpretation which prevents the creation of an 'imaginary Christ' who is simply the projection of man's ingenuity, a Christ 'according to the flesh'.

The re-forming aspect lies clearly in the emphasis Barth makes in the beautifully expressed sentence: 'the object of theology was originally subject and must ever become so again'. This recalls the theologian to the biblical witness to the Incarnation, to the 'very God and very man', to the *homoousion* of the Nicene confession to Christ. In the logic of this confession is given the logic which the mind of the objective theologian follows, inasmuch as here, in the 'totally incomprehensible, inaudible and unbelievable, the really scandalous testimony that God himself has said and done something, something *new* in fact, outside of the correlation of all human words and things, but which *as* this new thing he has injected into that correlation, a word and a thing next to others but as *this* word and *this* thing', the primacy of being is upheld against the primacy of thought. The centre of thought does not lie here with the scientist but rather in the object, which is the subject of Jesus Christ. In the emphasis of the *homoousion* conceptuality, theological knowledge is grounded in the revelation of God to man and theological language is the language about God's communication of himself to us and not the language, symbolic or analogical, about human states of self-awareness.

A reformation of theology and Church recreates the perspective of the determinative object of study and worship and focuses on Christ as himself the objective reality of God not as a mere reflection of him. It focuses on Christ as the God-given (that is to say revealed) form to which our thought must conform. A reformation, aiming at and striving to be grounded on 'the foundation which has been laid' by God in the witness of the prophets and apostles sees in Christ 'none other than . . . God communicating himself to us, the unconditional and sovereignly free self-giving of God . . .'[17]

Whether one may call the legacy of Karl Barth a reformation *ad hoc* or one in the *semper reformanda* tradition is something one cannot yet say with conclusiveness since we are still too close in time to the originating event. What is clear beyond a shadow of a doubt is that the consequences of his work, some of which we have indicated above, definitely point to a new and fruitful beginning in a situation which has too long been either stagnant or impossible.

The answer is made difficult also by the fact that the present period in the history of theology is – erroneously in my opinion – called post-Barthian. It is alleged that the era of dialectical theology is behind us, and it falls to us today to give more attention to what was problematical in that theology. Barth made too radical a break with the theology that preceded his own, so that the legitimate study of that aspect of the gospel

which is concerned with the human suffered a set-back. Barth
is said to have had no answer to the question as to the positive
significance of the gospel for culture. Also, his historical scepticism prevented him from considering the problem of the insepar-
ability of Christianity from history. Furthermore, his protest
against the Neo-Protestant affirmation of culture was condi-
tioned by the general cultural pessimism of the post-war years,
while his biblicism resulted from the hunger for authoritative
guidance.

To such criticisms, which in essence do not go beyond those
of Harnack, Troeltsch, Jülicher, Holl and others at that time,
there is added the charge that those who originally promulgated
that theology separated because they could not agree about the
kind of theology which was to grow out of the corrective they
had uttered. They were at one in the understanding that the
knowledge of the impossibility of possessing God had to be
proclaimed again. They also knew that this raised questions
which needed answers fairly quickly. While they were agreed
in their quarrel with the subjectivism of Neo-Protestantism,
they parted company when it came to answer the positive
questions arising out of their negative answers. Gogarten spoke
of the autonomy of the worldly and of a new secularism. Bultmann said that because the Word of God is not at our disposal
we must not speak of God as such but rather of the man who is
confronted by the ever new event of revelation. Barth maintained that although man cannot speak of God, God himself
speaks to us through himself in his Word which he gives to us
by assimilating it to man so that this Word is the real concern
of theology.

But the question now is this: if the meaning of theology is in
fact the *logos* of *theos*, have we, in this so-called 'post-Barthian'
period really proceeded beyond the preliminary inquiries necessary for theology in that sense? Is our concern with hermeneutics and the existential clarification of what it means to be
addressed by revelation and what human structures that elicits
and the search for structures in history through which again we
may discover a key to the mystery of revelation not an indication that we might perhaps be caught in a situation which has
not advanced at all beyond dialectical theology but has rather
fallen behind it? Is it really certain that our criticism of dia-

lectical theology is not an anaesthetisation of the critical questions which the early Barth posed? Is the suggestion that the finger of John the Baptist be given a rest not also an invitation to look in another, perhaps wrong direction, to the God-consciousness of man? Is it out of the question that the progress from the dialectics to the new hermeneutics and its weird by-products, such as the death of God 'theologies' (!), may be no more than the funeral cult of a theology without a determinative object? Is this perhaps an indication that we face the protest against the authoritativeness of methodology with an even greater lack of understanding than Harnack revealed? Perhaps the 'post-Barthian' generation is really post-Barthian because it has learned from him how one may really be immune against the quest of dialectical theology as to how theology could really be about the Word of God. It is not impossible that the discovery of a rigorous actualism in Barth, of that seriousness in the acceptance of God's becoming man and the consequent religionlessness of the gospel, has in fact turned our eyes once again away from the question of God to a renewed speaking of man in a higher key. Our 'post-Barthianism' with its critical going-beyond-Barth may well be the expression of the possibility that our theology will lead us to that point where dialectical theology thought it had to begin, lead us to another 'loss of God at the hands of theologians', to another loss of theology as an objective science. The contemporary criticism of the early Barth, coinciding as it does with the criticisms made in the twenties, would support these questions – and they are no more than questions – of what is done in the name of 'post-Barthian' theology.

For this reason it is quite in order to ask whether dialectical theology is in the *semper reformanda* tradition if our present theological endeavour is a continuation of the spirit of Neo-Protestantism. For if Barth with his renewed question for God does not really call us back to the Church's one foundation, then we cannot claim that he is a reformer. If he does not appear to move us by his call, he should not be regarded as a reformer. But there is another alternative. If we are not moved by him that may mean that we have not even perceived the danger of Neo-Protestantism. The ever-recurring call for a Barthian apologetics is an indication that the danger of such a venture is not at all clear. If we do not understand the 'need and promise' of theology, of which Barth spoke, could that not be because we ourselves, in our attempt to overcome the problematic of the early Barth, have not begun even where he began, namely with the daring question – which dialectical theology can well teach us – as to what is meant when we say *God?*

The very seriousness with which Barth asked this question is in itself reformatory. So also is the stimulation which Barth's work has exercised on subsequent theology. These alone entitle us to claim that if there is a new reformation of theology and Church going on in our century we must seriously consider Barth's 'reveille' as a contributing factor. Our contention, however, is that the systematic exchange of questions and answers, which we have observed between Barth and Harnack, is one of the very first documents in which that reformation becomes visible. It is not inappropriate to conclude that Karl Barth does indeed 'ring a bell' for us today.

NOTES

BIBLIOGRAPHY

INDEX

Notes to Introduction

1 Schneemelcher, 'Christliche Welt und Freunde der Christlichen Welt', in *Die Religion in Geschichte und Gegenwart*, 3rd ed., vol. 1, col. 1731.
2 Harnack's 'Fifteen Questions' appeared in vol. 37, no. 1/2, cols. 6–8, on 11 January; Barth's 'Fifteen Replies' in vol. 37, no. 5/6, cols. 89–91, on 8 February; Harnack's 'Open Letter' in vol. 37, no. 9/10, cols. 142–4, on 8 March; Barth's 'Answer' in vol. 37, no. 16/17, cols. 242–52 on 26 April; and Harnack's 'Postscript' in vol. 37, no. 20/21, cols. 305–6, on 24 May.
3 Agnes von Zahn-Harnack, *Adolf von Harnack*, pp. 414f. (hereafter cited as *AZH*).
4 Boniface A. Willems, *Karl Barth*, p. 16.
5 Quoted in Willems, *Karl Barth*, p. 18.
6 *Ibid.* p. 18. See Barth, *Theology and Church* (E.tr.), p. 7.
7 Barth, *Die Theologie und die Kirche*, p. 241 (E.tr., p. 239).
8 Quoted in Barth, *Die Theologie und die Kirche*, p. 247 (E.tr., p. 243).
9 Barth, *Theologische Fragen und Antworten*, p. 25.
10 Thurneysen, 'Karl Barths Theologie der Frühzeit', in Busch (ed.), *Karl Barth–Eduard Thurneysen: Ein Briefwechsel*, pp. 18ff. (E.tr., pp. 12f).
11 Translated as 'The Strange New World Within the Bible', in *The Word of God and the Word of Man*, pp. 28ff.
12 Barth, *Die christliche Dogmatik im Entwurf*, p. vi.
13 *Auf das Reich Gottes warten*, published in September 1916, now in the collection of sermons *Suchet Gott, so werdet ihr leben*. The other is *Vergangenheit und Zukunft*, published in August 1919, now in Moltmann (ed.), *Anfänge der dialektischen Theologie*, vol. 1, pp. 37ff. (E.tr., pp. 35f.).
14 *Vergangenheit und Zukunft*, in Moltmann, *Anfänge*, pp. 44f. (E.tr., p. 41).
15 *Ibid.* p. 45 (E.tr., pp. 41f.).
16 Barth, *Suchet Gott, so werdet ihr leben*, pp. 175f.
17 Quoted in Thurneysen, *Christoph Blumhardt*, p. 16.
18 *Ibid.* pp. 20f.
19 Cf. the chapter on Johann Christoph Blumhardt in Barth's *Die protestantische Theologie im 19. Jahrhundert*, pp. 588ff. *passim*.
20 Chr. Blumhardt, *Sterbet, so wird Jesus leben*, in the sermon on Luke 17: 20f., pp. 383ff.
21 Barth, *Theologische Fragen und Antworten*, p. 11.
22 Blumhardt, *Sterbet so wird Jesus leben*, pp. 255ff., in a sermon on Phil. 4:4f.
23 Quoted by Thurneysen, in *Christoph Blumhardt*, p. 38 (italics mine).
24 Blumhardt, *Sterbet, so wird Jesus leben*, pp. 288ff., in a sermon on Luke 17: 11f.
25 *Ibid.* pp. 112ff. and 349ff. in sermons on Psalm 34: 7 and Mark 16: 1f.
26 Even a hurried reading of the chapter 'Über den Heiligen Geist' in J. Chr. Blumhardt's *Schriftauslegung*, ed. by O. Bruder, pp. 1ff., will lead to this conclusion.
27 *Ibid.* pp. 30 and 37.
28 Thurneysen, *Christoph Blumhardt*, pp. 50f.
29 Chr. Blumhardt quoted in Thurneysen, *Christoph Blumhardt*, p. 52.
30 Compare Barth's answer no. 10 in his reply to Harnack's 'Fifteen Questions'.

That answer challenges the so-called 'scientific theology' on this very point. 'If the knowledge that "God is love" is the *highest* and *final knowledge about God*, how can one consistently pretend to be in possession of it? Is not the "transition point" just as long in duration as time? Is not *our* faith also always unfaith? Or should we believe in our *faith*? Does not faith live by being faith in God's *promise*? Are we saved in a way other than in hope?' Barth, *Theolgische Fragen und Antworten*, p. 12.

31 Blumhardt, *Sterbet, so wird Jesus leben*, pp. 91ff. in a sermon on Luke 17: 20f.
32 *Ibid.* pp. 227ff, in a sermon on Luke 18: 1f.
33 Quoted by Thurneysen in Busch, *Ein Briefwechsel*, p. 21 (E.tr., p. 15).
34 Barth, *Der Römerbrief*, 1st ed., p. vi.
35 Originally in *Erforschtes und Erlebtes*, now also in the anthology *Ausgewählte Reden und Aufsätze*, pp. 181ff.
36 Translated as 'Biblical Questions, Insights and Vistas' in Barth, *The Word of God and the Word of Man*, pp. 51ff.
37 *AZH*, pp. 412f.
38 *Ibid.* p. 415.
39 Barth, 'Biblische Fragen, Einsichten und Ausblicke', in *Das Wort Gottes und die Theologie*, p. 71 (E.tr., p. 53). (It has often become necessary for the sake of precision to adapt or even to retranslate passages from the German original. The references are, therefore, always to the German text with the English citation given in brackets.)
40 *Ibid.* p. 72 (p. 54).
41 *Loc. cit.*
42 *Ibid.* p. 72 (p. 55).
43 *Ibid.* p. 73 (p. 56).
44 Harnack in a letter to Barth. See Barth, *Theologische Fragen und Antworten*, p. 14.
45 Barth, *Biblische Fragen*, in *Das Wortes Gottes*, p. 74 (p. 58).
46 Harnack to Barth, in Barth, *Theologische Fragen*, p. 15.
47 Barth, *Biblische Fragen*, in *Das Wort Gottes*, pp. 78f. (pp. 64f.).
48 *Ibid.* p. 76 (p. 60).
49 *Ibid.* p. 79f (p. 66).
50 Quoted in Busch, *Ein Briefwechsel*, p. 112 (E.tr., p. 128).
51 Barth, *Theologische Fragen*, p. 14.
52 *AZH*, p. 416.
53 In Busch, *Ein Briefwechsel*, p. 112 (E.tr., p. 128).
54 An example which comes to mind here is the proclamation in support of the Emperor's war policy published in August 1914 by ninety-three German intellectuals, among whom were many of Barth's former teachers. The declaration reads as follows: 'We, the professors at German universities and academies, serve science and are engaged in a work of peace. But we are indignant to see that the enemies of Germany, England foremost among them, want to make a distinction – allegedly to our advantage – between the spirit of German science and what they label "Prussian militarism". There is no spirit in the German army that is different from that of the German nation, for both are one and we, too, are part of it. Our army also attends to science and owes no little of its achievements to it. Service in the army makes our youth diligent also for the work of peace as well as the work of science. This is because this service trains them in self-renouncing faithfulness to duty and gives them the self-consciousness and sense of honour of the truly free man, who readily submits himself to the whole. This spirit lives not only in Prussia but is the same all over the German Reich. It is the same in war and peace. Our army is now engaged in the struggle for Germany's freedom and,

therefore, for all the benefits of peace and morality not only in Germany. We
believe that for European culture on the whole salvation rests on the victory
which German "militarism", namely manly discipline, the faithfulness, the
courage to sacrifice, of the united and free German nation will achieve.'

55 In Busch, *Ein Briefwechsel*, p. 126f (E.tr., p. 144).
56 *Ibid.* p. 127 (E.tr., p. 144).
57 *AZH*, p. 417.
58 In Barth, *Theologische Fragen*, p. 10.
59 This was also the conclusion of Jülicher who accused Barth of 'Marcionism' in
    his review of the first edition of the *Römerbrief*. A reprint of it is in Moltmann,
    Anfänge, pp. 87ff. (E.tr., pp.72ff.).
60 It must be stressed here that this conclusion is no more than a conjecture of
    the writer. On 20 October 1966 Professor Barth wrote to me that in his
    opinion Harnack did not have an intimate knowledge of his writings, espe-
    cially not prior to the correspondence in *Christliche Welt*. That Harnack knew
    the article on Overbeck, 'Immer noch unerledigte Anfragen' (E.tr. 'Unsettled
    Questions' in *Theology and Church*) we know from his postcard to Barth of
    16 January 1923. But then Professor Barth believes that Harnack 'wird
    gewiss in den Römerbrief geschaut haben', which suggests that Barth does not
    think Harnack to have had adequate knowledge even of that work. In the
    postcard referred to Harnack says that he composed those fifteen questions
    on the spur of the moment without 'literary' preparation. It was rather on
    the basis of a complex of ideas and impressions gained during the previous
    year from books, essays and conversations that they arose. 'If I am not mis-
    taken,' Harnack writes there, 'I have read only one article by you during the
    last year.' Therefore, he was definitely *not* familiar with *Das Wort Gottes als
    Aufgabe der Theologie* and *Not und Verheissung der christlichen Verkündigung*. What
    Harnack had read of Barth is thus quite impossible to state with accuracy,
    but we must remember that he asked his fifteen questions on the basis of a
    general impression and that he addressed them to no one particular thinker.
61 In Barth, *Theologische Fragen*, p. 17.
62 Harnack, *Die Entstehung der christlichen Theologie und des kirchlichen Dogmas*, p. 1.
63 *Ibid.* p. 61.
64 Harnack in an editorial of *Theologische Literaturzeitung*, vol. 50, no. 1, col. 2.
65 In Barth, *Theologische Fragen*, p. 17.
66 *AZH*, p. 415.
67 Is it out of the question to interpret a statement as the following the way we
    suggest Harnack did? 'Jesus as the Christ is that *wholly unknown* plane which
    intersects vertically from above the plane we know. Within historical per-
    ceptibility Jesus as the Christ can be understood only as a myth. As the
    Christ, Jesus brings us to the world of the Father of which we *cannot* and *never*
    will know *anything* within this plane of historical perceptibility.' Barth,
    Römerbrief, 2nd ed., p. 6 (my italics). (As in the case with Barth's *Das Wort
    Gottes und die Theologie* it was necessary to use the German text of *The Epistle
    to the Romans* in order to have the meaning of the original as accurately as
    possible. The English citation will appear in brackets after the German one.
    In this particular instance it is pp. 29f.)
68 *Theologische Fragen*, p. 11. Elsewhere he said: 'The materialisation and
    humanisation of the divine in some specific religious or redemptive history
    are in *no* relation to God, because God is abandoned as *God* in them.' *Römer-
    brief*, 2nd ed., p. 53 (p. 79).
69 As an example of this we quote the following, again from the *Römerbrief*.
    'What God is and does is and remains different from man's being and action.

The "here" is unalterably separated from the "there" by the line drawn between them, the line of death which is also the line of life. It is the end which is the beginning, the *NO* which is the *YES*.' p. 86 (p. 111). It is to this kind of language that Harnack reacts: 'How many will be able ever to understand you, seeing that you are wholly submerged in highly sublime psychology and metaphysics?.' Barth, *Theologische Fragen*, p. 16.

70 *AZH*, p. 416.

71 Barth, *Theologische Fragen*, p. 31.

72 *AZH*, pp. 417f.

73 An example of this is Barth's letter to Harnack, dated 16 April 1924. It is cited and parts of it are quoted in *AZH*, pp. 416f. Harnack himself continued to send his publications to his former pupil. But the difference of outlook remained, their worlds never really met. In a letter Professor Barth wrote me (20 October 1966) he said that while he was at Münster Harnack visited him one day and was horrified to find him studying a commentary by Johannes Cocceius. In another letter, dated 1 November 1967 he wrote: 'The days in which I wrestled with my esteemed teacher Harnack, in which he found no delight with me and I with him, are now behind me. But I do hope that he and I will come to an understanding in heaven. But the way things stood in those "roaring twenties" this was practically impossible and I had to oppose him and had to remain "incomprehensible to him".'

Notes to Part I : An Analysis of the Text

1 A remark made by Harnack to Barth in April 1920, cited in Busch, *Ein Briefwechsel*, pp. 52f. (E.tr., p. 50).

2 *AZH*, p. 418.

3 Harnack in a letter to Barth, quoted in Busch, *Ein Briefwechsel*, p. 127 (E.tr., p. 144).

4 As early as April 1920 Harnack made this charge against Barth; cf. Busch, *Ein Briefwechsel*, p. 53 (E.tr., p. 50).

5 *Ibid.* p. 112 (E.tr., p. 128).

6 Overbeck, *Christentum und Kultur*, pp. 67 and 69.

7 *AZH*, p. 46.

8 *Das Wesen des Christentums*, p. 125. From now on this work will be cited as *Wesen*. (I have used the German edition of Harnack's *What is Christianity?* because at times it was apparent that Mr Saunder's translation did not render with the necessary precision what the German text actually said. On the whole that translation is admirable but for our purposes here it was essential that the exact meaning of the original be retained. The price to be paid for this is in the style of the phraseology.) (E.tr., p. 204.)

9 'Die Bedeutung der theologischen Fakultäten', in *Reden und Aufsätze*, p. 130, and *Wesen*, p. 125 (E.tr., p. 204).

10 *AZH*, p. 24.

11 *Ibid.* pp. 130f.

12 *Ibid.* p. 187.

13 *Die Entstehung der christlichen Theologie und des kirchlichen Dogmas*, p. 1.
14 Harnack, *Outlines of the History of Dogma*, pp. 7f.
15 *Ibid.* p. 2.
16 *Ibid.* p. 2.
17 *Ibid.* p. 1.
18 Ernst Wolf, 'Kerygma und Dogma?', in *Antwort, Festschrift* for Barth, p. 794.
19 *Wesen*, pp. 18 and 19f. (E.tr., pp. 6 and 10f.).
20 *Abhandlung von der freien Untersuchung des Kanons*, vol. 1, p. 161, quoted in Wolf, 'Kerygma und Dogma?', p. 785.
21 Harnack, *Wesen*, p. 20 (E.tr., p. 11).
22 *Ibid.* p. 20 (E.tr., p. 11).
23 *Ibid.* p. 22 (E.tr., p. 14).
24 In vol. 2 of *Aus Wissenschaft und Leben*, pp. 213ff.
25 *Ibid.* p. 215.
26 *Wesen*, pp. 42 and 52 (E.tr., pp. 51 and 68).
27 *Ibid.* p. 42 (E.tr., p. 51).
28 *Ibid.* pp. 43f. (E.tr., pp. 52f.).
29 *Ibid.* p. 81 (E.tr., p. 122).
30 *Ibid.* p. 9 (E.tr., p. x).
31 *Ibid.* p. 44 (E.tr., p. 54).
32 *Ibid.* p. 45 (E.tr., p. 56).
33 *Ibid.* p. 48 (E.tr., pp. 61f.).
34 *Ibid.* p. 45 (E.tr., p. 56).
35 *Ibid.* p. 76 (E.tr., p. 115).
36 *Ibid.* p. 42 (E.tr., p. 51).
37 *Ibid.* p. 49 (E.tr., p. 63).
38 *Ibid.* p. 51 (E.tr., pp. 67f.).
39 *Ibid.* p. 95 (E.tr., p. 149).
40 *Ibid.* p. 52 (E.tr., p. 69).
41 *Ibid.* p. 53 (E.tr., p. 70).
42 *Ibid.* p. 116 (E.tr., p. 187).
43 *Ibid.* p. 53 (E.tr., p. 71).
44 *Ibid.* p. 69 (E.tr., p. 100).
45 *Ibid.* pp. 53f. and 55 (E.tr., pp. 72 and 73f.).
46 *Ibid.* p. 55 (E.tr., pp. 75f.).
47 *Ibid.* p. 54 (E.tr., p. 73).
48 *Ibid.* p. 54 (italics mine) (E.tr., p. 73).
49 From Harnack's address to the world congress of science, meeting in St Louis in September 1904, 'The Relation between Ecclesiastical and General History'. In *Contemporary Review*, LXXXVI, pp. 846ff.
50 *Wesen*, pp. 95f. (E.tr., pp. 150f.).
51 *Ibid.* p. 96 (E.tr., p. 150).
52 *Ibid.* p. 82 (E.tr., p. 124).
53 Wayne Glick, *Adolf Harnack as Historian and Theologian*, p. 258.
54 Harnack, *Wesen*, p. 49 (E.tr., p. 63).
55 Harnack, *Das doppelte Evangelium im Neuen Testament*, pp. 223f.
56 *Wesen*, p. 109 (E.tr., p. 176).
57 *Ibid.* p. 112 (E.tr., p. 180).
58 *Ibid.* p. 112 (E.tr., p. 180).
59 *Ibid.* p. 112 (E.tr., p. 181).
60 *Ibid.* p. 113 (E.tr., pp. 181f.).
61 *Ibid.* p. 114 (E.tr., p. 184).
62 *Ibid.* p. 116 (E.tr., p. 187).

63 *Ibid.* p. 116 (E.tr., p. 188).
64 *Ibid.* pp. 122f. (E.tr., pp. 199f.).
65 *Ibid.* p. 123 (E.tr., p. 201).
66 Harnack, *Marcion*, p. 1.
67 *Ibid.* p. 199 (italics mine).
68 *Ibid.* pp. 199f.
69 *Ibid.* pp. 2f.
70 *Ibid.* p. 3.
71 *Ibid.* p. 4.
72 *Ibid.* p. 4.
73 *Ibid.* p. 5.
74 *Ibid.* p. 8.
75 *Ibid.* p. 16.
76 *Ibid.* p. 16.
77 *Ibid.* p. 196.
78 *Ibid.* p. 18.
79 *Ibid.* p. 256.
80 *Ibid.* pp. 94f.
81 *Ibid.* p. 94.
82 *Ibid.* p. 95.
83 *Ibid.* p. 94.
84 *Ibid.* p. 94.
85 *Ibid.* pp. 94f.
86 *Ibid.* pp. 96f.
87 *Ibid.* p. 201.
88 *Ibid.* pp. 224f.
89 *Ibid.* p. 225.
90 *Ibid.* p. 228.
91 *Ibid.* pp. 228f. The reference to Reformed Orthodoxy and *Kritizismus* is Harnack's way of saying Barth and Overbeck. That footnote, in other words shows the historic parallelism which Harnack maintains exists between Barth and Marcion.
92 *Ibid.* pp. 234f.
93 *Ibid.* p. 235.
94 *AZH*, p. 417.
95 *Ibid.* p. 413.
96 Busch, *Ein Briefwechsel*, p. 127 (E.tr., p. 144).
97 Harnack, *Marcion*, p. 231.
98 *Ibid.* p. 198.
99 *Ibid.* p. 217.
100 For the following see *ibid.* pp. 218ff.
101 *Ibid.* p. 220.
102 'Was hat die Historie an fester Erkenntnis zur Deutung des Weltgeschehens zu bieten?', in *Ausgewählte Reden und Aufsätze*, p. 183.
103 Harnack, 'Religiöser Glaube und freie Forschung', in *Aus Wissenschaft und Leben*, vol. 1, p. 270.
104 Bultmann in his Preface to *Wesen*, p. 11 (E.tr., p. xiii).
105 They are published in: (1) *Aus der Frieden- und Kriegsarbeit*, pp. 173ff.; (2) *Erforschtes und Erlebtes*, pp. 3ff.; (3) and (4) *Ausgewählte Reden und Aufsätze*, pp. 181ff. and pp. 177ff. respectively.
106 Cited in *AZH*, p. 427.
107 *Stufen wissenschaftlicher Erkenntnis, passim.*
108 'Was hat die Historie etc.', pp. 196f.

109 *Ibid.* p. 199.
110 *Ibid.* p. 201.
111 *Ibid.* pp. 201f.
112 *Wesen*, p. 18 (E.tr., p. 6).
113 'Was hat die Historie etc.', p. 197.
114 Harnack: *History of Dogma*, vol. 1, p. 77f.
115 Harnack quoted in *AZH*, p. 65.
116 Quoted in W. Glick, *Adolf Harnack as Historian and Theologian*, p. 58.
117 Harnack, 'Die Bedeutung der theologischen Fakultäten', in *Ausgewählte Reden und Aufsätze*, p. 129.
118 *Wesen*, p. 119 (E.tr., p. 194).
119 Harnack, *Das Christentum und die Geschichte*, pp. 9 and 18.
120 *Ibid.* p. 8.
121 We saw above (p. 104) that Harnack distinguishes between civilisation and culture. For him the latter is inseparable from the significance of the gospel. '[In the Christian communities throughout the Roman Empire] there were to be found a few only who were "mighty after the flesh" and of noble standing in society, and yet they were like "lights in the world" and *the progress of world-history rested on them* . . . The gospel speaks to us about the real work mankind has to accomplish; faced with this message we ought not to barricade ourselves behind our paltry "work of culture". "The image of Christ," in the words of a recent historian, "remains the sole foundation of all ethical culture and the degree by which this appearance [of that image] is able to influence men is indicative of the degree of morality of the nations themselves." ' *Wesen*, pp. 116 and 81f. (my italics) (E.tr., pp. 188f. and 120).
122 Harnack means by faith the *fides historica* and the *fiducia* in the revelation of God in Christ, cf. *Marcion*, pp. 224f.
123 This assertion is cited in *AZH*, pp. 56f. 'Whenever a higher religion develops a theology, it is usually a theology in a twofold form: a theology from within and one from without. The former presents the ideational content of religion from the point of view of the faithful and relies on the inner power of persuasion of the content to uphold its truth. A theologian of this kind knows that his is a charismatic theology . . . The latter considers religion to be a part of the circle comprising all objects of cognition and judges its veracity on the basis of generally valid historical, psychological and theoretical principles of knowledge . . . Christian theology began with Paul and was charismatic theology . . . But from the earliest times of the Church the theology which based itself on objective revelation and on contemporary idealistic philosophy, in which reason was apparent, has been victorious because it promised a generally valid exposition of the Christian religion. If it is granted that the particular idealistic philosophy is *die Vernunft* itself and if objective revelation has in fact been correctly determined, then this theology has a right to exist. If these two points are not granted then this theology breaks down and must be replaced, but not only by such however valuable complementary efforts as those of Irenaeus and Origen. This does not answer the question whether Christian theology must shun all ties with idealistic philosophy, but then the oldest development of Christian theology denies this anyway. Theologies which have not entered into a relationship with such a philosophy have never become a theology of the *Church*. Brittle charismatic theologies were never more than ferments of some effectiveness. A theology from within is never scientific theology . . . it is rather something else, something higher; it is confession. Only theology from without can create community. We may lament that the insufficiency of such a theology is so plainly

visible, but no one can change that. Should anyone attempt it, however, he will fail and create confusion for theology. Let him rather stick to his task – preaching.' Harnack, *Die Entstehung des christlichen Glaubens etc.*, pp. 54 and 87f.

124 These phrases are from Harnack's letter to Ritschl, dated 6 January 1882, quoted in Glick, *Adolf Harnack as Historian and Theologian*, p. 58.

125 *Wesen*, p. 125 (E.tr., p. 204).

126 Busch, *Ein Briefwechsel*, p. 53 (E.tr., p. 50).

127 'Die Aufgabe der theologischen Fakultäten und die allgemeine Religionsgeschichte, in *Reden und Aufsätze*, vol. 2, pp. 172f.

128 Barth, 'Der Christ in der Gesellschaft', in *Das Wort Gottes und die Theologie*, p. 39 (E.tr., p. 281). (This work is to be cited as *Wort* from now on.) See also another address of 1920, 'Biblische Fragen, Einsichten und Ausblicke', in *Wort*, pp. 70ff. (E.tr., pp. 54ff.). (As in the case with Harnack's *What is Christianity?* the author preferred to use the original German edition of this work instead of the translated version: *The Word of God and the Word of Man*, made by Dr. Horton. The reasons why this was done are the same as those given above in note 8.)

129 Barth, 'Not und Verheissung der christlichen Verkündigung', in *Wort*, p. 121 (E.tr., pp. 129f.).

130 *Ibid.* p. 121 (E.tr., p. 130).

131 Cf. J. M. Robinson (ed.), *The Beginnings of Dialectic Theology*, the chapter entitled 'A Modern Interpreter of Paul', pp. 72ff.

132 'Biblische Fragen, etc.', in *Wort*, pp. 83f. (E.tr., pp. 72f.).

133 The term 'historical pantheism' was taken from Bultmann's essay 'Die liberale Theologie' in his *Glauben und Verstehen*, vol. 1, pp. 1ff.

134 Barth, 'Der Christ in der Gesellschaft', in *Wort*, pp. 50f. (E.tr., pp. 298f.).

135 *Ibid.* p. 38 (E.tr., p. 281).

136 'Not und Verheissung etc.', in *Wort*, p. 99 (E.tr., p. 98).

137 'Der Christ in etc.', in *Wort*, p. 40 (E.tr., pp. 282f.).

138 *Ibid.* p. 40 (E.tr., p. 283).

139 *Ibid.* p. 41 (E.tr., p. 285).

140 *Ibid.* p. 42 (E.tr., pp. 285f.).

141 The review, written by A. Lasson, appeared in *Preussische Jahrbücher*, LVIII, and is cited together with Harnack's reply in *AZH*, p. 104.

142 Bultmann in his Preface to *Wesen*, pp. 9f. (E.tr., pp. xf.).

143 *Ibid.* p. 11 (E.tr., p. xiii).

144 *Ibid.* p. 13 (E.tr., p. xv).

145 *Die Bedeutung der Geschichtlichkeit Jesu für den Glauben*, pp. 34f.

146 Overbeck, *Christentum und Kultur*, pp. 9f.

147 *Ibid.* p. 7.

148 *Ibid.* p. 7.

149 *Ibid.* p. 28.

150 This is quoted by Ph. Vielhauer in his article 'Franz Overbeck und die neutestamentliche Wissenschaft' in *Evangelische Theologie*, x, no. 5, p. 205.

151 Overbeck, *Christentum und Kultur*, pp. 265f.

152 Vielhauer, 'Franz Overbeck etc.', p. 206.

153 Overbeck, *Christentum und Kultur*, p. 67.

154 *Ibid.* p. 279.

155 *Ibid.* p. 68.

156 *Ibid.* p. 8.

157 *Ibid.* p. 10.

158 *Ibid.* p. 70.

159 *Ibid.* p. 266.

160 Barth, 'Biblische Fragen, etc.', in *Wort*, p. 71 (E.tr., p. 53).
161 *Ibid.* p. 74 (E.tr., p. 58).
162 *Ibid.* p. 79 (E.tr., p. 66).
163 *Ibid.* pp. 79f. (E. tr., p. 66).
164 *Ibid.* pp. 81f. (E.tr., p. 69).
165 Harnack, *Die Entstehung der christlichen Theologie etc.*, p. 89.
166 Barth, 'Der Christ etc.', in *Wort*, pp. 41f. (E.tr., pp. 285f.).
167 Harnack, *Wesen*, p. 82 (E.tr., p. 124).
168 Barth, 'Biblische Fragen etc.', in *Wort*, p. 86 (E.tr., pp. 76f.).
169 Harnack, *Marcion*, p. 231 (his italics).
170 *Ibid.* pp. 228f.
171 Barth, 'Das Wort Gottes als Aufgabe der Theologie', in *Wort*, p. 158 (E.tr., p. 186).
172 Cf. 'Unerledigte Anfragen an die heutige Theologie' in *Die Theologie und die Kirche*, p. 25 (E.tr., *Theology and Church*, p. 73).
173 Barth, 'Das Wort Gottes etc.', in *Wort*, p. 158 (E.tr., p. 186).
174 Barth, 'Not und Verheissung etc.', in *Wort*, p. 108 (E.tr., p. 110).
175 *Ibid.* pp. 112f. (E.tr., pp. 117f.).
176 *Ibid.* p. 117 (E.tr., p. 124).
177 Barth, 'Das Wort Gottes etc.', in *Wort*, pp. 160f. (E.tr., pp. 189ff.).
178 *Ibid.* pp. 161f. (E.tr., pp. 191f.).
179 Barth, 'Not und Verheissung etc.', in *Wort*, p. 123 (E.tr., p. 134).
180 *Der Römerbrief*, 2nd ed., p. 5 (E.tr., *The Epistle to the Romans*, p. 29).
181 *Ibid.* p. xiii (E.tr., p. 10).
182 Harnack, *Marcion*, p. 228n.
183 Barth, *Römerbrief*, p. 163 (E.tr., p. 184).
184 *Ibid.* p. 5 (E.tr., p. 29).
185 *Ibid.* p. 6 (E.tr., p. 30).
186 *Ibid.* pp. 86f. (E.tr., p. 112).
187 This actualism in Barth's position eventually led to Bonhoeffer's charge of 'positivism of revelation', a charge which he made in 1944. Thirteen years earlier, much closer to the 'early' Barth, he pointed out what appeared to him to be an unresolved tension in Barth's theology, namely the problems created by this stress on *diastasis* or discontinuity. In his *Act and Being* he says that 'the whole situation impels one to ask whether a formalistic understanding of God's freedom in contingent revelation, conceived wholly in terms of the act, is really the proper groundwork for theology. In revelation it is a question less of God's freedom on the far side from us, i.e. his eternal isolation and aseity, than of his proceeding-forth, his given Word, his bond with which he has bound himself, of his freedom as it is most strongly attested in his having freely bound himself to historical man, having placed himself at man's disposal. God is not free *of* man but *for* man. Christ is the Word of his freedom. God *is there*, which is to say: not in eternal non-objectivity but (looking ahead for the moment) "haveable", graspable in his Word within the Church' (pp. 90f.). [Bonhoeffer is obviously right in emphasising God's election of man and God's grace in the statement that God has bound himself to man and that nonetheless in that election God's freedom is revealed. But how can such a statement be made? On what basis can it be said that 'God is not free from man', even if one takes it to be a sentence used to strengthen the affirmation which follows, namely that 'God is free for man'? Does revelation show us both these freedoms? Revelation asserts that God has given himself to man; does that say anything about God's freedom *from* man?]

'Yet if revelation is non-objective, the theological implication is that God always remains a subject and evades every human attempt to seize him cognitively. If, on the other hand, we are really speaking of *revelation*, it must somehow, by definition, become manifest to man and knowable to him; and in fact revelation has, as we know, become knowable in Christ. How are we to understand that? God can never become object of consciousness. Revelation can only be understood in such a way that God must be borne in mind as a subject; but this is possible only if God is also the subject of the knowing of revelation, since, if *man* knew, then it was not God that he knew. But this knowing of revelation is called "believing", what is revealed has the name of Christ, the subject of the understanding is God as the Holy Spirit. Thus in revelation God is in the act of understanding himself. That is his location, and he cannot be found in my consciousness for any reflection on this act. Essentially the representation of God which I have in my consciousness is not God himself. God is only in the act of belief. In "my" belief, the Holy Spirit is accrediting himself. That this is so is no demonstrable matter of fact but is merely "existentially" true, i.e. in the encounter with revelation, in the act of belief itself, which for the rest remains a spiritual act like the others. Accordingly my knowledge of God depends in the event on whether God has known me in Christ . . . whether he is effecting faith in Christ within me. There is therefore no prescriptive method for acquiring knowledge of God; man cannot transplant himself into the existential situation from where he could speak of God, for he is unable to insert himself into truth' (pp. 92f.).

So far Bonhoeffer's interpretation of Barth. But then he continues: 'God "is" only in belief, but the subject of the believing is God himself. Hence faith is essentially something different from religion. But (even in Barth) no light is shed on how we can envisage the human religious act in conjunction with the divine act of belief, unless we sever them in order to allot them essentially different spheres, or suppress the "subjectivity" of God if not, alternatively, the existential impact of revelation' (p. 94).

'It would therefore be impossible to speak of God or know about God in a science of theology unless it were incorrect to think of revelation as a pure act, unless there were such a thing as a being of revelation outside my existential knowledge of it – outside my faith – on which my faith, my thought, my knowledge could "rest" ' (p. 97).

Bonhoeffer asks: how is the existence of man before and after revelation related to the existence of the man 'born anew in revelation'? He interprets Barth as saying: 'as the negation of the old man, the new man can in fact be understood in the continuity of the I' (p. 102). Bonhoeffer himself suggests that the Church is to be seen as the 'unity of act and being', as the place where the act of revelation (as the subjectivity of God) and the being of revelation apart from man's faith (revelation as the *Existenzbetroffenheit* or existential impact on man) are one. Cf. pp. 117f.

Without this 'being' of revelation one makes this concept of revelation a positivism of revelation, as Bonhoeffer wrote on 30 April 1944 and once or twice again after that (*Letters and Papers*, pp. 90ff.).

Barth's rigorous actualism is behind this critique. *Actus purus*, either-or, either God's truth or our truth, discontinuity, contrast only – *all* these terms are evidence for a strong actualism. Bonhoeffer sees in them an abandonment of the world, a leaving it to itself, as he said in those letters (30 April 1944, 5 May 1944, 8 June 1944), which puts the 'content of revelation' into a 'take it or leave it' alternative.

Barth had maintained that revelation is something radically apart from the correlation of human words and deeds, yet something occurring in that correlation. It is not a human word, yet God speaks his Word in the language of men. Still, that correlation of human words and deeds cannot express revelation unless used by God for that purpose. One must ask indeed: how is one related to the other? Is our knowledge of the content of revelation like that vertical intersection of one plane by another, so that we merely accept it on a 'take it or leave it' basis? Harnack wanted to know this also and because he thought Barth to answer affirmatively, he called him unscientific and his thought charismatic theology.

But then does this actualism lead Barth to propose a concept of revelation which is to be labelled 'a positivism of revelation'? Does this concept make a science of theology impossible? When Barth speaks of the content of revelation, does he speak of individual truths to which he adheres as if they were *final* insights? In order to answer this, one would not only have to ascend to the source of revelation but also to descend on the 'trajectory' (to use a word which is in line with the remainder of Barth's image here) on which revelation, that 'vertical plane' intersects afresh each time (*je und je*), as Barth qualifies it. We would have to look at the Church and the life of the Christian.

God's sovereignty was the primary concern for Barth in the formulation of this concept of revelation. That was the reason for such expressions as: there is no human basis for revelation, which is an event based wholly on God; totally incomprehensible, believable only; it is no object at all of human knowledge, Christ is part of human history, but unlike anything else in history which is in need of fulfilment and which drives towards a goal. Christ is rather the *eschaton*, the fulfilment and therefore not open to historical analysis. Thus, when we ascend to the source of revelation, we find these rigorously actualistic statements which cut out anything on which our hands and feet might find a hold and thus once again establish a standpoint, a continuum between God and man.

At the same time Barth did not forget to speak of the place where God's self-revelation, where his Word affirms itself, the situation namely between sermon and text, the congregation, the Church where the existence of the Christian is touched by the self proclaiming Word of God. Does Barth do this as clearly now in his confrontation with 'liberalism' as he did later in his *Dogmatics*? No, but there is sufficient evidence to make the charge of 'positivism of revelation' at least questionable.

The Word of God makes history. Barth knew this from the Blumhardts. The response of the congregation, its humility in living obedience to that Word – the correlation of Scripture and Spirit – is the evidence of the impact, of the concretisation of revelation. The actualism remains, but this obedience of the Church – this penultimate matter – is done out of the ultimate, in the power of the ultimate, for the sake of the ultimate. The Church is the place where man is drawn by God's Word into the reality of that Word. (The classical definition of the Church is behind this: Wherever the Word of God is truly spoken and truly heard.) The Church is the place where man in his historical existence has an ear for God's Word, where he has faith and because of that also the capability of being genuinely attentive to and concerned with the world. 'In the course of history there have always been those peculiarities, those impressions of revelation, those opportunities and open doors which, from God's point of view, call us to our senses and lead us to an understanding. Wherever there are people who wait on God there remains a commission, a *character indelebilis*, even if it be shrouded in the darkest incomprehensibility for them and others . . . God has never and at no place revealed himself in vain' (*Römerbrief*, 2nd ed., p. 54, E.tr., p. 80). The indelible character of revelation stands, however, not in a direct but a dialectical relation to revelation when seen from the point of view of the way to the origin or source of revelation.

'In the Church man knows and has all manner of things of God which, consequently, he does not know or have. It is the place where somehow or other he is taken out of the unknown beginning and end into the well-known centre, where . . . he really possesses faith, hope and love, where he really is God's child and really waits and works for God's kingdom, as if they were things for him to possess, to be, to wait and to work for' (*ibid.* p. 316, E.tr., p. 332). Here Barth underscores the dialectical relation referred to. What man has is parable, testimony only but testimony to *that* reality. 'However questionable and ambiguous the position of righteous searching and waiting for God may be as a human position, it performs nevertheless a distinct and necessary function as a symptom of God's will and action . . . Compelled by their own and others' experiences to become still in the face of the unknown they demonstrate that this may as such become the object of cognition. By remembering the impossible, they show that the impossible – God – is in the realm of the possible, not of course as one possibility among others, but rather as the impossible possibility, which becomes apparent through them' (*ibid.* p. 53, E.tr., p. 79).

Through the congregation or the Church, revelation is in fact communicated to the world; here man, drawn by God into the reality of God, is able to witness and act appropriately in the world with an understanding of the world, with a concentration on the real, historical world to which he belongs.

If the Church is really the place where the Word of God communicates itself to the world, that is to say, if the Church is the medium of the communication of God's Word as it is accepted through faith by the community, if in the congregation there occurs the translation of the Word (and if the congregation is obedient to it) into a word addressed also to the world in its concrete existence – can one then really call this concept of revelation a 'positivism'? If positivism is an insistence on and an adherence to individual truths, their presentation for mere acceptance without showing how they are related to man, can this charge really be applied to Barth's views? Even if one upholds an actualism of Barth's kind, even if one says with him that the possibility of the Church speaking to the world and that the form and content of that speaking are something which is in the hand of God, the Lord of the Church, who lets the Church participate in his confrontation of the world, so that the measure for the concreteness and quality of that speech is not derived from the exigencies of the world – does that mean that one is involved in a positivism? Does it also mean that the witness of the congregation, its action, that the being of the Church under the promise of her and the world's Lord, that the preservation of the Church's substance for the sake of the Church's commission and that man's freedom given him in his obedience, are not a concretisation, a being of revelation apart from the event of the Word? Are all these factors of so little significance that one must conclude that God has revealed himself in vain? – I cannot agree that Bonhoeffer's charge is valid.

188 Barth, 'Das Wort Gottes etc.', in *Wort*, p. 166 (E.tr., pp. 198f.).
189 *Ibid.* p. 171 (E.tr., p. 205).
190 'Biblische Fragen, etc.', in *Wort*, p. 76 (E.tr., pp. 60f.).

191 I owe this term 'relationalism' to Dr H. W. Frei's *The Doctrine of Revelation in the Thought of Karl Barth 1909–1922*.
192 Barth, 'Biblische Fragen . . .', in *Wort*, p. 84 (E.tr., p. 72f.).
193 'Das Wort Gottes etc.', in *Wort*, pp. 171f. (E.tr., p. 206).
194 *Ibid.* p. 174 (E.tr., p. 210).
195 Barth, *Der Römerbrief*, 2nd ed., p. 342 (E.tr., p. 358).
196 'Not und Verheissung etc.', in *Wort*, pp. 114f. (E.tr., p. 120).
197 'Biblische Fragen, etc.', in *Wort*, pp. 71f. (E.tr., pp. 51f.).
198 'All that which is and occurs in man and on account of his actions is brought into relation to God in Jesus. God then judges its worth according to his pleasure. Everything must pass through this test, must be weighed on this scale; nothing can escape the action of this balance-wheel. This critical position signifies an understanding of the worldly, a comprehension of the human and an interpretation of the historical in their secular, relative and finally meaningless context as well as in their parabolic and witnessing aspect, through which they are a testimony to and a reminder of the wholly other world, the wholly other man and the wholly other history – of God . . . Jesus Christ is shown forth and accredited as God's Son, because in his Sonship man's flesh, being under the dominion of sin, becomes a parable. In his Sonship there is to be seen what the human, the worldly, the historical and the natural really are: only transparent things, only images, only signs, only relative things in relation to God, the Creator . . . Speaking in temporal language or expressing it in comprehensive terms we may say that we are "related" to Christ insofar as our existence, as existence under tribulation, is through no effort of our own a likeness or an analogue of his death. His death is, however, that by which men are led to apprehend themselves in God: namely in their decline lies their rise, in their weakness their strength, in their death their life. Christ's death is significant for us in that it is the threshold from judgment to the judge, from tribulation to him who is and makes free, from despair to hope. It is the event in which we apprehend ourselves in God.' Barth, *Der Römerbrief*, 2nd ed., pp. 82, 263 and 176 (E.tr., pp. 107, 280f. and 196).
199 'Die liberale Theologie etc.', in *Glauben und Verstehen*, vol. 1, p. 2.
200 Barth, 'Biblische Fragen, etc.', in *Wort*, pp. 86f. (E.tr., pp. 77f.).
201 *Ibid.* p. 91 (E.tr., p. 83).
202 Harnack in a letter to Barth, cited in Busch, *Ein Briefwechsel*, pp. 126f. (E.tr., p. 144).

Notes to Part II: An Evaluation of the Correspondence

1 Christoph Senft, *Wahrhaftigkeit und Wahrheit*, p. 129.
2 H.-W. Frei, 'The Doctrine of Revelation etc.', p. 512.
3 *Ibid.* p. 205.
4 Günther Howe, 'Parallelen zwischen der Theologie Karl Barths und der

heutigen Physik', in *Antwort, Festschrift* for Barth 1956, p. 413. This excerpt includes a quotation from Heisenberg.

5 Martin Heidegger, Holzwege, pp. 85f.

6 In Barth's discussion of Anselm's proof of the existence of God (*Fides Quaerens Intellectum*) these terms ontic and noetic *ratio* are used in the delineation of the *ratio* of revelation and faith. The problematic of the *diastasis* is overcome there by the use of this tripartite view of *ratio* in the concept of analogy which replaces the sheer either-or relation of God and man.

7 It is interesting to pursue this awareness on Barth's part in his correspondence with Thurneysen. These two ministers, sensing what was involved in their vocation as ministers of the Word of God, felt helpless in their work on account of their theological training. They began to ask questions about the meaning of the Bible, the answers to which led them away from their teachers. They were quite conscious of this and soon began to evaluate their own situation and preaching *vis-à-vis* contemporary thinking and preaching.

Barth knew that eventually there had to be a clear explanation of what he and Thurneysen wanted. 'A mighty blow against the theologians had to be dealt eventually,' he wrote on 1 January 1916. Later that year, on 27 July, he suggested that this blow might come in about ten years. In the meantime it would be good to 'lift our hats to the much greater knowledge of these *savants*, even if their knowledge looks like idols'. So he wrote on 14 July 1920. But even then the question raised itself whether they were saying what they believed had to be said adequately. On the one hand, one sees in those letters an ever recurring sense of frustration about the inadequacy of their own proclamation of the Bible's testimony. On the other hand, and more apropos to our discussion, there is the admission that all should be said more clearly and sharply. 'The Word of the cross must be said in such a way that it goes beyond the mere presentation of the absolute paradox, beyond the declaration of the general necessity of death, beyond the delineation of God and man, time and eternity and given a meaning which does not yet come to its rightful place in our utterances' (6 December 1920). Yet, this realisation, which we must firmly keep in mind, should not prevent us from 'drilling' (as these two country parsons called their questioning) some more, Barth maintained. 'In things necessary don't budge an inch, in things doubtful don't let on, and above all keep your pipe burning' (22 January 1922). Among themselves doubts were voiced openly. 'There is so much understanding and misunderstanding of Yes and No, of dialectics, of resurrection, of "God is God" and whatever else this stuff is called . . . Eduard, Eduard, oh! I invoked these ghosts' (7 July 1922). Or, three months later, even more dejectedly: 'I am more and more aware of the fact that I too am not able to do the great thing which three years ago Adolf Preiswerk told me he could not do' (7 October 1922). Therefore, 'would it not be better to leave our little boat for a while to itself and to the waves, for a few years at least, so that people could have a good rest from the hidden God, come to know that they are on earth and learn what that means?' (18 May 1923).

'In our theology, "subject" and "object", "the other" and "I", to know and be known, appear in what is not an altogether very clear fashion', Barth writes in that same letter and Thurneysen replies: 'Will we succeed? I am worried about the harvest which will grow from our work . . . So many simpletons who have subscribed to *Zwischen den Zeiten* just wait from one issue to the next to see what new, crashing strikes will be dealt this time against the barricaded doors . . . Really, if *Zwischen den Zeiten* does not soon become a wide field, worked by all kinds of serious workers, we will have to let it die

NOTES 215

in a short time . . . But then, you know, our own language is not without blame in this matter' (21 June 1923). It became increasingly obvious to both that a revision of what they had said so far was needed, even though neither thought that the criticisms of their position justified the discontinuation of their 'drilling'. 'We shall do well to work out the stance of obedience quite differently in order to stand up better to (certain critics)' (Thurneysen, 30 October 1923). 'Bultmann thinks that I do not have a "clean" system of concepts, about which something may indeed be said' (Barth, 15 February 1925).

But then a little more than half a year after the discussion with Harnack in *Christliche Welt*, Barth writes these remarkable words (remarkable only insofar as Barth said them in the early twenties!): 'There is a "natural theology", even the proofs of God's existence are not wholly to be despised; exactly on the basis of revelation a relative and naturally imperfect cognition of God must be postulated. But don't tell this to anyone; I must sleep on it for a while before it is ripe for promulgation' (20 December 1923). Then later, 'The problem of "natural" revelation causes me much more sorrow. The old reformed theologians relied on it a great deal. I do not yet know definitely where and how to fit it in. The Fatherhood of God comes in here and does so from several angles: *logos*, creation, providence. The Incarnation has to be dealt with carefully so that one does not fall into that exclusive Jesus Christ-"hole" of the Lutherans' (20 March 1924)!

Throughout his discussion with Harnack Barth knew well that the time would come when he had to say what he meant in better, different and more precise terms. But it was still the same matter he wanted to say. It was indeed said better later, but the beginnings of it are to be found here.

8 *Die Bekenntnisschriften der Evangelisch-Lutherischen Kirche*, pp. 511f.
9 Heidegger makes this point in *Sein und Zeit*, p. 11. See also T. F. Torrance, *Theology in Reconstruction*, p. 35.
10 Busch, *Ein Briefwechsel*, p. 10. Cf. Busch, 'Dialectical Theology: Karl Barth's Reveille', in *Canadian Journal of Theology* XVI, nos. 3 and 4, p. 168.
11 Barth, 'Not und Verheissung etc.', in *Wort*, p. 123 (E.tr., p. 134).
12 *Ibid.* p. 102 (E.tr., p. 101).
13 Busch, *Ein Briefwechsel*, p. 12. Cf. 'Dialectical Theology etc.', in *Can. Jour. Theol.*, p. 170.
14 M. Storch, *Exegesen und Meditationen zu Karl Barths Kirchlicher Dogmatik*, p. 187.
15 We cannot pursue in detail the course of that direction which was indicated here. But its highpoints should be mentioned. In 1927 Barth defined the significance and authority of the Scriptures, a 'principle' from which he never departed. In 1931 he outlined the *analogia fidei*, in which the nature of theological activity was depicted. Here, through conformity to the economic condescension of his Word and through following the incarnate Word in its advance to God we know God. The divine truth is apprehended in accordance with its own mode of activity and articulated with its own interior logic. This analogy is the Christological cornerstone of Barth's thought. Then in 1956 he defined the notion of the humanity of God, a notion which grew out of the implications of the *analogia fidei*. Between these two is the *Church Dogmatics*, that reconstruction of the affirmation made on behalf of the Truth to which the Bible witnesses, that reconstruction which must follow every corrective. It is that work which shows the continuing participation of Barth's own theology in the Church throughout the ages, for without that participation no theology is a theology of the Church of Christ.
16 Cited in Busch, *Ein Briefwechsel*, p. 182 (E.tr., p. 205).
17 T. F. Torrance, *Theology in Reconstruction*, pp. 265f.

BIBLIOGRAPHY

PRIMARY SOURCES

Karl Barth

Der Römerbrief, 1st ed. (reprint of the 1919 ed.), EVZ, Zürich, 1963.
Der Römerbrief, 2nd ed. (9th printing of the 1921 ed.), EVZ, Zürich, 1954.
   The Epistle to the Romans, E.tr. of the 2nd ed., translated by Edwyn C. Hoskyns, Oxford University Press, London, 1965.
Das Wort Gottes und die Theologie, Kaiser, Munich, 1924.
   The Word of God and the Word of Man, E.tr., translated by Douglas Horton, Harper, New York, 1957.
Die Theologie und die Kirche, Kaiser, Munich, 1928.
   Theology and Church, E.tr., translated by Louise Pettibone Smith, Harper, New York, 1962.
Theologische Fragen und Antworten, EVZ, Zürich, 1957.
Die christliche Dogmatik im Entwurf, Kaiser, Munich, 1927.
Die protestantische Theologie im 19. Jahrhundert, EVZ, Zürich, 1946.
   From Rousseau to Ritschl, E.tr., translated by Brian Cozens, SCM Press, London, 1959.

Karl Barth and Eduard Thurneysen

Suchet Gott, so werdet ihr leben, Kaiser, Munich, 1928.
Ein Briefwechsel, ed. Eberhard Busch, Siebenstern Taschenbuch Verlag, Munich, 1966.
   Revolutionary Theology in the Making, E.tr., translated by James D. Smart, John Knox Press, Richmond, 1964.

Adolf von Harnack

Das Wesen des Christentums, Siebenstern Taschenbuch Verlag, Munich, 1964.
   What is Christianity? E.tr., translated by T. Saunders, Harper, New York, 1957.
History of Dogma, translated by N. Buchanan, Dover, New York, 1961.
Outlines of the History of Dogma, translated by E. Mitchell, Beacon Press, Boston, 1959.
Das apostolische Glaubensbekenntnis, Haack, Berlin, 1892.
Das Christentum und die Geschichte, Hinrichse Buchhandlung, Leipzig, 1904.
Das doppelte Evangelium im Neuen Testament, Töpelmann, Giessen, 1906.
Marcion, J. C. Hinrichs Verlag, Leipzig, 1924.
Die Entstehung der christlichen Theologie und des kirchlichen Dogmas, Klotz, Gotha, 1927.
Reden und Aufsätze, 2 vols., Töpelmann, Giessen, 1906.
Aus der Frieden- und Kriegsarbeit, Töpelmann, Giessen, 1916.
Erforschtes und Erlebtes, Töpelmann, Giessen, 1923.
Aus der Werkstatt des Vollendeten, Töpelmann, Giessen, 1930.
Ausgewählte Reden und Aufsätze, deGruyter, Berlin, 1951.

SECONDARY SOURCES

Die Bekenntnisschriften der Evangelisch-Lutherischen Kirche, Vandenhoeck und Ruprecht, Göttingen, 1959.

Blumhardt, Chr., *Sterbet, so wird Jesus leben*, Rotapfel Verlag, Zürich, 1925.

Blumhardt, Johann Christoph, *Schriftauslegung*, ed. O. Bruder, Gotthelf Verlag, Zürich, 1947.

Bonhoeffer, Dietrich, *Act and Being*, Collins, London, 1961.

Bultmann, Rudolf, *Glauben und Verstehen*, vol. 1, Mohr (Siebeck), Tübingen, 1964.

Frei, Hans W., 'The Doctrine of Revelation in the Thought of Karl Barth, 1909–1922', unpublished thesis, New Haven, 1956.

Glick, Wayne, 'Adolf Harnack as Historian and Theologian', unpublished thesis, Chicago, 1957. In 1967 Professor Glick published a book, *The Reality of Christianity* (Harper, New York), into which the thesis was incorporated.

Heidegger, Martin, *Holzwege*, Klostermann, Frankfurt, 1957.

Sein und Zeit, Niemeyer, Tübingen, 1960.

Moltmann, Jürgen (ed.), *Die Anfänge der dialektischen Theologie* (2 vols.), Kaiser, Munich, 1962. The English translation was made by Keith R. Crim and Louis DeGrazia and was edited by James M. Robinson. *The Beginning of Dialectic Theology*, John Knox Press, Richmond, 1968.

Overbeck, Franz, *Christentum und Kultur*, Benno Schwabe, Basel, 1919.

Senft, Christoph, *Wahrhaftigkeit und Wahrheit*, Mohr (Siebeck), Tübingen, 1956.

Storch, Martin, *Exegesen und Meditationen zu Karl Barths Kirchlicher Dogmatik*, Kaiser, Munich, 1964.

Thurneysen, Eduard, *Blumhardt*, Zwingli Verlag, Zürich, 1962.

Torrance, Thomas F., *Theology in Reconstruction*, SCM Press, London, 1965.

Vielhauer, Philipp, 'Franz Overbeck und die neutestamentliche Wissenschaft', in *Aufsätze zum Neuen Testament*, Kaiser, Munich, 1965.

Willems, Boniface, *Karl Barth*, EVZ, Zürich, 1964.

Zahn-Harnack, Agnes von, *Adolf von Harnack*, deGruyter, Berlin, 1951.

INDEX